The Learning Societ from the Perspective of Governmentality

Edited by

**Jan Masschelein, Maarten Simons,
Ulrich Bröckling and Ludwig Pongratz**

Blackwell
Publishing

© 2007 by Philosophy of Education Society of Australasia

First published as a special issue of '*Educational Philosophy and Theory*' (Volume 38, issue 4).

BLACKWELL PUBLISHING
350 Main Street, Malden, MA 02148-5020, USA
9600 Garsington Road, Oxford OX4 2DQ, UK
550 Swanston Street, Carlton, Victoria 3053, Australia

First published 2006 by Blackwell Publishing Ltd

Library of Congress Cataloging-in-Publication Data

The learning society from the perspective of governmentality/edited by Jan Masschelein ... [et al.].
  p. cm.
Includes bibliographical references and index.
ISBN-13: 978-1-4051-5602-8 (alk. paper) 1. Education and state–Philosophy. 2. Continuing education–Philosophy. I. Masschelein, Jan.
  LC71.L337 2006
  379–dc22

                                                                                    2006035621

A catalogue record for this title is available from the British Library.

Set in 10pt Plantin
by Graphicraft Limited, Hong Kong
Printed and bound in the United Kingdom
by TJ International, Padstow, Cornwall

The publisher's policy is to use permanent paper from mills that operate a sustainable forestry policy, and which has been manufactured from pulp processed using acid-free and elementary chlorine-free practices. Furthermore, the publisher ensures that the text paper and cover board used have met acceptable environmental accreditation standards.

For further information on
Blackwell Publishing, visit our website:
www.blackwellpublishing.com

The Learning Society from the Perspective of Governmentality

Contents

Notes on Contributors

Ulrich Bröckling, Ph.D., is a sociologist. He is Coordinator of the Graduate Research Program 'Figures/Figurations of the Third' at the University of Konstanz, Germany. His research interests are: cultural theory, philosophical anthropology, sociology of self technologies and social technologies and governmentality studies.

Christoph Engemann studied psychology and is currently writing his PhD thesis on 'The Citizen of Electronic Government' at the Graduate School of Social Sciences, University of Bremen, Germany. He is Research Associate at the Faculty of Media, Bauhaus University of Weimar, and Non Residential Fellow at the Center for Internet and Society, Stanford Law School. His research interests are: media theory, political economy of the Internet and European unification and its media. Recent works are on Free Software, Smartcards and E-Government and Authentication Media.

Andrea Liesner is Assistant Professor for Philosophy of Education at the University of Hamburg, Germany. Her research focuses on historical and systematic studies and approaches of education, with an emphasis upon governmentality studies and the relation between education and economy.

Jan Masschelein is Professor for Philosophy of Education at the Catholic University of Leuven. His primary areas of scholarship are educational theory, political philosophy, critical theory, studies of governmentality and social philosophy. Currently his research concentrates on the 'public' character of education.

Ulf Olsson is Assistant Professor of Science of Education at Stockholm Institute of Education. He is currently working on a project 'The State, the Subject, and Pedagogical Technology: A genealogy of the present of political epistemologies and governmentalities at the beginning of the twenty-first century'. His main research interest concerns fabrication of subjects and governmentalities in the field of Public Health.

Kenneth Petersson is Associate Professor in Communication and Senior Lecturer at the Department of Social and Welfare Studies, Linköping University, Sweden. His research interests include the political government of the educational field and criminal justice in Sweden. At the moment he is studying Swedish mentalities that govern contemporary strategies of pedagogical thought and technologies in different discursive and institutional practices.

Thomas S. Popkewitz is Professor in the Department of Curriculum and Instruction, University of Wisconsin-Madison, USA. His research concerns the politics of present knowledge or systems of reason that govern policy, pedagogy and research, and teacher education, focusing on its production of difference and issues of social inclusion and exclusion. He is writing a book about 'reason of reason' that explores cosmopolitanism as a system of reason in modern schooling that produces distinctions and divisions about who the child is and should be.

Ludwig A. Pongratz is Professor of Educational Theory (Allgemeine Pädagogik) and Adult Education at the Darmstadt Technical University (Germany). His publications and research concentrate primarily on the history of educational theory and the methodology of pedagogy, critical theory and educational philosophy, school pedagogy and adult education. His research includes empirical studies alongside his historical and conceptual works.

Kerlijn Quaghebeur, studied educational sciences and is now researcher at the Centre for Philosophy of Education, Catholic University of Leuven, Belgium, where she is currently working on a PhD thesis on participation, more specifically in development cooperation. Her main research interests involve the later works of Michel Foucault and the related governmentality studies, participation, development, education.

Norbert Ricken is Professor for Educational Theory and History at the University of Bremen, Germany. His primary research interests are educational theory and methodology, especially pedagogical and philosophical theories of subjectivity and intersubjectivity, philosophy and anthropology of education. Currently he is interested in studies of educational governmentality and pedagogical readings of Foucault.

Maarten Simons is post-doctoral researcher at the Centre for Educational Policy and Innovation, Catholic University of Leuven, Belgium. His research interests are educational policy and political philosophy with special attention for governmentality and schooling, the past and future of the university and practices of e-ducation.

Anna Tuschling studied Psychology and Literature in Marburg, Trier and Bremen, Germany. Currently she is a doctoral candidate at the Institute for Media Studies, University of Basel, Switzerland, with a work on 'The Third in Gossip-Communication: A media- and cultural-analysis of online-chatting'.

Foreword

The Learning Society from the Perspective of Governmentality

This is a special volume in more ways than one. First, it is special for this journal by virtue of the fact that these editors and all but one of the contributors (Tom Popkewitz) are not from the English-speaking world of philosophy of education. They are European and as their biographies reveal come from Belgium, Germany and Sweden. Second, the volume is special because it combines work by educationalists, philosophers, historians and sociologists on the topic of the learning society from the perspective of governmentality, utilizing, developing and extending an approach by the late Michel Foucault. Thus the volume provides a novel perspective that demands an interdisciplinary approach to the core concept of the *learning society*.

I shall not document or comment on the theme of the volume or the approaches adopted by individual contributors as this has been done already by Maarten Simons and Jan Masschelein in their introduction where they detail Foucault's notion of governmentality, the rapidly growing secondary literature on studies of governmentality, its development in the field of education, and the scope of the volume including the individual contributions. The book thus brings together European perspectives with the Anglo-American literature focused precisely on the concept of the learning society, a concept that has loomed large in both national policy documents and conceptions promulgated by world policy agencies as a notion 'expressing principles of a universal humanity and a promise of progress that seem to transcend the nation', as Simons and Masschelein put it.

The learning society maps onto 'lifelong learning', informal education, cosmopolitan ideals, spaces of European higher education and, indeed, helps in refashioning the new Europe of the EU and, as the contributors to this volume ably demonstrate in novel ways, ultimately to questions of governance and governmentality. It is to be hoped that the volume will lead not only to further discussion and debate but also to greater international collaboration and understanding of the governmentality approach in all its possibilities and applications.

As is now well known and as the editors to this volume indicate, in his governmentality studies in the late 1970s Foucault held a course at the Collège de France on the major forms of neoliberalism, examining the three theoretical schools of German *ordoliberalism*, the Austrian school characterised by Hayek, and American neoliberalism in the form of the Chicago school. Among Foucault's great insights in his work on governmentality was the critical link he observed in liberalism between the governance of the self and government of the state–understood as the exercise of political sovereignty over a territory and its population. He focuses on government as a set of practices legitimated by specific rationalities and saw that these three schools of contemporary economic liberalism focused on the question of too much government–a permanent critique of the state that Foucault considers as a set of techniques for governing the self through the market.

Liberal modes of governing, Foucault tells us, are distinguished in general by the ways in which they utilise the capacities of free acting subjects and, consequently, modes of government differ according to the value and definition accorded the concept of freedom. These different mentalities of rule, as a number of commentators have observed, turn on whether freedom is seen as a natural attribute as with the philosophers of the Scottish Enlightenment, a product of rational choice making, or, as with Hayek, a civilizational artefact theorised as both negative and anti-naturalist. A foucaldian account of the market in relation to the concept of freedom lies at the center of questions of government and governmentality, of government by and through the market, a feature that we have experienced in a variety of different forms since the impact of globalization and the end political model of the welfare state.

Foucault's account of German *ordoliberalism*, a configuration based on the theoretical configuration of economics and law developed at the University of Freiberg by W. Eucken and F. Böhm, emphasizes the view that the market develops historically within a judicial-legal framework. The economy is thus based on a concept of the Rule of Law, anchored in a notion of individual rights, property rights and contractual freedom that constitutes, in effect, an economic constitution. German neoliberal economists (Müller-Armack, Röpke, Rüstow) invented the term 'social market economy' which shared certain features with the Freiburg model of law and economics but also differed from it in terms of the 'ethics' of the market (as did Hayek in *The Constitution of Liberty*). This formulation of the 'social market economy' proved significant not only in terms of the post-war reconstruction of the (West) German economy but through Erhard, as Minister and Chancellor, became important as the basis of the EEC's and, later, EU's 'social model'.

It is fitting that the volume should advance various understanding of the 'economization of human life' (Simons) and especially of education render as the ideal of a learning society from the perspective from and with a focus on Europe. I wish to thank the editors for a provocative, stimulating, and thoughtful analysis of the learning society that at once extends the compass of governmentality and demonstrates its clear implications for education.

MICHAEL A PETERS
University of Illinois at Urbana-Champaign

Introduction: The Learning Society from the Perspective of Governmentality

JAN MASSCHELEIN, MAARTEN SIMONS, ULRICH BRÖCKLING & LUDWIG PONGRATZ

In this book we present recent studies that investigate different educational ideas and programmes—ideas and programmes of enlightenment, creativity, participation, inclusion, learning, critique—from the perspective of 'governmentality'. This perspective was opened up by the later Foucault. Considering educational ideas and programmes from the perspective of governmentality implies their analysis and description as an element in the government of people. The studies which are presented here look at ideas and programmes (of education) as being part of the history of the ways in which human beings conduct and govern themselves and others in the light of specific truth games. They assume that there is an intrinsic relation between the intellectual and practical educational technologies on the one hand and the way in which political power is wielded in our societies as well as the way in which we govern ourselves on the other hand. In this way these studies also indicate how educational practice and educational theory (and science) have played and do play a constitutive role in practices of subjectivation which are crucial to our actual 'learning societies'—as societies which address us to become lifelong learning citizens. They thus want to contribute to a critique which is no longer referring to the practice of a legislating subject passing judgement on a deficient reality, but is rather a matter of 'making facile gestures difficult' (Foucault).

Educational research from the perspective of governmentality has been carried out in the Anglo Saxon world since the beginning of the 1990s. More recently a range of investigations have been set up in the continental context. Both lines of research are present in the list of authors who were invited to contribute to this volume, although the more recent continental research prevails. We believe that the volume allows us to appreciate the richness and fruitfulness of the perspective of governmentality for research in education and we thank especially Michael Peters for his support of the project.

1

The Learning Society and Governmentality: An introduction

MAARTEN SIMONS & JAN MASSCHELEIN

> This is because knowledge is not made for understanding; it is made for cutting.
>
> M. Foucault

We are (or should be) the inhabitants of a (future) learning society. At least, this is what is taken for granted in different contexts. For policy makers the learning society is the horizon to reflect upon their decisions and to frame governmental instruments. Also teachers, pedagogues and educational researchers focus on the learning society to select important issues, to reflect upon them and to rationalise what they and others are doing or what they or others have to do.

Furthermore, in all these contexts technologies and procedures are introduced to address us as lifelong learners and to create an infrastructure to operate in the learning society. The learning society thus not only seems to have become a necessary notion in the vocabulary to think and write about ourselves, others and the world, but is related to rather specific technologies and procedures to understand and guide ourselves as a particular kind of subjects i.e. subjects for whom learning is a natural force to live our life.

The main aim of the collection of articles in this book is to map the present by focusing on some of the heterogeneous components of the learning society.[1] The contributions do not only share a common interest in and attitude towards the present, but also focus on the present at a common level. They focus on the components of the actual governmental regime being installed in relation to the learning society. Michel Foucault could be named as the 'father' of this research attitude and approach. However, this goes without saying, the authors of this collection are not his well-educated children, if they are related at all. Maybe what Foucault claimed himself could be invoked here: 'I prefer to utilise the writers I like'. Nevertheless, a short overview of some work of Foucault and of the concept of governmentality could be helpful to explore this beloved use.

1. Foucault and Governmentality

During his courses at the *Collège de France* in the late seventies (*Sécurité, Territoire et Population (1977–1978)* and *Naissance de la biopolitique (1978–1979)*), Michel Foucault elaborated his analysis of power-relations (Foucault 2004a, 2004b; cf. 1978a/b, 1981). While previously he analysed disciplinarian forms of power (giving shape to modern institutions such as schools, hospitals and the prison), his interest shifted to broader governmental issues to address the exercise and development of power relations throughout the modern state. However, his point of departure was not to analyse the power of the state or the growing 'étatisation of society', and his aim was not to discuss the legitimacy of the state's power. Instead, his main interest was to analyse the exercise of power by focusing on the development of governmental rationalities and related governmental technologies. For this domain of analysis he introduced the neologism 'governmentality', combining 'government' and 'mentality'. In order to understand this particular domain of analysis and its importance, we should mention that Foucault was addressing also a specific development in the early modern period, i.e. the birth of the modern governmental state.

From a genealogical perspective the birth of the modern state is related to a crisis in the theological-cosmological order (of sovereign power) through which government became a problem, i.e. something that is not evident anymore and that opens up the question of 'how to govern?' and 'who and what should be addressed in government?'. The early modern reflections on the 'reason of state' and the focus on 'the population' are part of the early modern art of government or governmentality. In his lectures Foucault offered a detailed analysis of this art of government and its further development: mercantilism and Kameralism as governmental rationalities, the *polizey* (and related science) as a governmental technology (and as a secular pastoral technology), liberalism as a reaction against governing according to the 'reason of state', the incorporation of disciplinarian settings and apparatuses of security as governmental technologies, 'the social' as a governmental theme and domain of intervention, the crisis of the social state and the birth of neo-liberalism as both a reactivation and reformulation of the liberal attitude at the level of government. Referring to these rationalities and technologies, Foucault claims that the modern state—up to the twentieth century—is a governmental state, i.e. a complex of centralising governing relationships that aims at governing people. Or to put it otherwise: what characterizes the modern state is a '*governmentalisation* of the state'.

In order to have a clear understanding of what is at stake in this governmentalisation it is important to focus on how Foucault understands government. Foucault describes government as 'conduire des conduites' or 'the conduct of conduct' (Foucault, 1982, p. 237). This formula expresses that the object of government is not a passive pole (outside) but people who are governing themselves in a specific way. Government thus is acting upon the self-government or 'conduct' of people. This self-government is not something natural, but is being shaped. In the eighties Foucault focused explicitly on (the history of) technologies of the self which allow human beings to relate in a particular way to themselves and to constitute themselves as subjects (cf. Foucault, 1984a, 1984b, 2001). Although in his lectures on governmentality Foucault does not (yet) address this level of self-government and the formation of subjectivity throughout (ethical) technologies of the self, it allows us to clarify what is at stake in the 'government of self-government' and the 'governmentalisation of the state'.

Modern governmental rationalities and technologies seek to promote a kind of self-government or subjectivity that is of strategic importance for its operations. Modern liberal governmentality for example correlates with a rather specific individual freedom. Individual freedom is thus not a natural state of human beings but implies a kind of self-government. And within liberal governmentality bringing about this self-government or these subjects (e.g. people who understand themselves in terms of freedom, having interests and a guiding reason and who understand their environment as a civil society) is of strategic importance. Therefore, liberal governmentality is recoding settings of disciplinarian power (such as schools and factories) in order to secure the existence of freedom upon which it can act. In short, in a regime of liberal governmentality individual freedom is both an effect and instrument. This illustration clarifies that the 'governmentalisation of the state' is closely related to the 'governmentalisation of freedom'. It is not through brute force that people are being incorporated within the modern state. Instead, throughout a rather particular form of self-government and at the level of our very subjectivity, people are being included in the governmental state. Within the modern state freedom, as a particular practice of self-government, is being governmentalised.

Although Foucault focused mainly on past forms of governmentality, he also analysed more recent developments. He noticed that after the Second World War a new crisis of government occurred and he focused on what could be the beginning of a new rationalisation of government, new governmental technologies and finally new forms of self-government (Foucault, 1980, p. 94). Neoliberalism is the central concept here. Within neoliberal governmentality people are not addressed (anymore) as social citizens (whose freedom or autonomy is guaranteed through social normality or who have a normalised relation to the self) but as entrepreneurial selves and entrepreneurs of the self. Entrepreneurial self-government implies looking at oneself as inhabiting an environment, having needs and producing goods (or investing in human capital) in order to meet or satisfy these needs. For government addressing the self-government of the entrepreneurial citizen the main task of 'the state' is creating and controlling a market environment to enable entrepreneurial freedom. Confronted with the early crisis of the social welfare state Foucault thus described a new phase in the 'governmentalisation of freedom'. It is a regime of government and self-government in which 'the economic' (redefined as entrepreneurship or the 'permanent economic tribunal') plays a central, strategic role. And this analysis of actual governmentality has been an important background of the so-called 'studies of governmentality'.

2. Studies of Governmentality

As Foucault's lectures on governmentality have not been published (until recently), the access to this domain of analysis has been relatively difficult. Only some courses, interviews and short summaries have been published. Important for the introduction to the idea of governmentality has been the book by Burchell, Gordon & Miller, published in 1991 and titled *The Foucault Effect. Studies in governmentality (with two lectures by and an interview with Michel Foucault)*. Besides the rather detailed introduction of Colin Gordon, two of Foucault's lectures and an interview, this book includes original work of researchers examining themes inspired by Foucault and governmentality: the reason of state, the police-state, civil society, government and poverty, work, insurance, risk, statistics. During the 1990s the 'Foucault effect'— at least with regard to governmentality—has grown and meanwhile scholars all over the world have been engaged in studying issues related to governmentality. It is not unimportant to mention that this interest in governmentality and especially in Foucault's analysis of neoliberalism was first developed in the Anglo-Saxon world. Recalling the influence of Thatcher and Reagan could help to explain this interest. Meanwhile, the group of researchers dealing with governmentality or 'studies of governmentality' is still growing. Let us point to a few more important publications that could help to give an impression of the focus of these studies and their topics.

In 1996 *Foucault and Political Reason: Liberalism, neo-liberalism and rationalities of government* was published (Barry, Osborne & Rose, 1996).[2] As the subtitle of the book suggests, the essays focus on liberalism and neoliberalism as rationalities or mentalities of government, i.e. strategies aiming at governing people. The main interest is neoliberalism, or to use the formulation of Rose, 'advanced liberalism' (Rose, 1996, p. 50). What the essays have in common is that they use analogous 'analytical tools' to map actual forms of governmentality. One could refer to these studies as 'studies of governmentality' and as a kind of new subdiscipline within the humanities (Dean, 1999, p. 2). However, the term 'discipline' may not be adequate since these studies are very diverse, both at the level of research domain and at the level of method (Rose, 1999, p. 9). What they share (beside some general 'analytical tools') is an interest in actual forms of governmentality, understood in a minimal way as the strategies of governing people and governing ourselves. This interest is also underlying the German collection entitled *Gouvernementalität der Gegenwart. Studien zur Ökonomisierung des Sozialen* (Bröckling, Krasmann & Lemke, 2000). What the essays in this collection, which received a lot of attention in Germany, have in common is '[...] die (Selbst-)Zurichtungs- und Herrschaftseffekte neoliberaler Gouvernementalität präziser in den Blick zu bekommen.' ('... to try to have a better view on the effects of self-discipline and domination of neoliberal governmentality') (ibid., p. 32).[3] Both collections illustrate that from the 1990s onwards a relatively autonomous line of research has been developed that focuses on actual forms of government and self-government.[4] The following list could give an idea the variety of topics being studied: the constitution of the consumer (Miller & Rose, 1997); the government of the unemployed (Dean, 1995); the government of love in a therapeutic setting (Kendall & Crossley, 1996); risk and responsibility (O'Malley, 1996); self-esteem and 'empowerment' as correlates of government (Cruikshank, 1996); quality-management (Bröckling, 2000); the neoliberal command 'be-yourself' (Greco, 2000); government and mathematical justice (Schmidt-Semisch, 2000); contractualism (Yeatman, 1998); performance appraisal (Findlay & Newton, 1998).

3. Foucault, Education, Governmentality

Foucault is of course not a new name in educational research and theory.[5] As it is not possible to mention here all studies in education inspired by or based upon Foucault, we limit ourselves to some main directions in educational research. Foucault's genealogy and related concepts such as normalization have played a major role in the history of education, and more specifically the history of the school and the classroom and the history of educational science (cf. Depaepe, 1998; Hunter, 1994). At a more analytical level *Surveiller et Punir* (Foucault, 1975), a book that dealt with the birth of the prison and related settings of disciplinarian power, influenced researchers to focus on power relations within education as well as the power effects of educational research (e.g. Pongratz, 1989; Ball, 1990). During the 1990s, the meaning of Foucault for educational research could be situated at a continuum with two poles going from theoretical to analytical.

At a theoretical level Foucault has been used to reflect upon and redirect central concepts (autonomy, liberal education) within philosophy of education (Marshall, 1996). More generally, he has been seen as representing postmodernism and poststructuralism and his work played a role in discussions on (epistemological and ethical) relativism and the (modern) conception of the subject underlying educational theory (e.g. Smeyers, 1996; Wain, 1996; Blake *et al.*, 1998; Biesta, 1998). Within poststructuralism Foucault has been used to argue for the value of a historical materialistic approach (Olssen, 1999) and for a reformulation of the concept of the self (Marshall, 2001). Furthermore, he has influenced reflections on methodology for educational research, sociology of education and underlying epistemologies (Ball, 1994; Popkewitz, 1996; Popkewitz & Brennan, 1997). Although this list is not exhaustive, it allows us to have an idea of the influence of Foucault at a theoretical (philosophy, epistemology, ethics, sociology, methodology) level.

Also at an analytical level there are many studies based upon a Foucauldian approach. Examining specific practices and developments, these studies are inspired by Foucault's (genealogical) research attitude. They make use of his analytical tools (analysis of discourses and power relations) or adopt parts of his genealogical analysis. It is at this level that during the 1990s 'studies of governmentality' (combing both a specific theoretical framework or attitude and a domain of analysis), have inspired educational research or have been adapted to and reformed for educational topics. The following examples could give an idea of these studies: governmentality, busnopower and liberal education (Marshall, 1995a, 1995b); pastoral power at the university (Howley & Hartnett, 1992); classroom management (Tavares, 1996); entrepreneurship and education (Peters, 2000); the soul of the teacher, teacher reflection and teacher identity (Popkewitz, 1998; Ball, 2003; Fendler, 2003; Zembylas, 2003); mobilization and lifelong learning (Edwards, 2002); the permanent quality tribunal in education (Simons, 2002; Wain, 2004); neoliberalism, globalization and democracy (Olssen *et al.*, 2004); Europe, governmentality, immunization (Masschelein & Simons, 2003); the care of the self in a knowledge economy (Drummond, 2003); see also the collection in Baker & Heyning, 2004; Pongratz *et al.*, 2004 and Ricken & Rieger-Ladich, 2004.

Parallel to the general reception and use of 'governmentality', these studies in education were developed mainly in an Anglo-American context. The postponed reception of Foucault and governmentality in some countries of the continent is difficult to explain. With regard to the German reception of Foucault, Peters states: '[...] the question of why was it postponed has much to do with the lack of interpenetration of philosophical traditions, intellectual antipathies and defensiveness on both sides, and Habermas' early polemic intervention when he accepted the Adorno prize from the City of Frankfurt in 1980 with a piece that drew sides in the debate between modernity and postmodernity, indicating that he held that modernity was an "incomplete project" and calling the French poststructuralists "neo-conservatives" likening them to the conservatives of the Weimar Republic' (Peters, 2004, p. 197). However, meanwhile the situation has changed. At least some indirect observations point in the direction of a growing interest in Foucault and governmentality. In Germany the book mentioned earlier *Gouvernementalität der Gegenwart. Studien zur Ökonomisierung des Sozialen* is a rare academic bestseller (Bröckling, Krasmann & Lemke, 2000/2004). And with regard to (philosophy of) education in 2004 two edited books have been published: *Nach Foucault. Diskurs- und machtanalytische Perspectiven der Pädagogik* (Pongratz *et al.*, 2004) and *Michel Foucault: Pädagogische Lektüren* (Ricken & Rieger-Ladich, 2004).

The growing interest in Foucault's ideas on governmentality (and in its elaboration in 'studies of governmentality') could also be linked to social developments and more specifically changes in government (and the welfare state) and educational policy. During the 1990s and in the beginning of the twenty-first century one could notice a general tendency towards de-centralisation in educational policy and towards an autonomisation and responsabilisation of schools. Furthermore, there is a growing impact of 'Europe' on (higher) education—a kind of re-centralisation. The European project of the knowledge society and knowledge economy has been (and still is) the background for (national) regulations and redirections of education. These changes at the level of educational policy stimulated and still stimulate looking for adequate tools and frameworks for critical analysis (see Wain, 2004). The growing importance of 'studies of governmentality' and to a certain extent also its introduction within or translation to many different intellectual traditions could be understood against this background.

This brings us finally to the scope of the volume. The collection of articles that is presented here articulates a common interest in the present, i.e. for our present society that is addressed in many different contexts as a (future) learning society. Furthermore, the articles focus on how the learning society is related to specific governmental rationalities, governmental technologies and forms of self-government. They look at educational ideas and programmes as being part of the history of the ways in which human beings conduct and govern themselves and others. They assume that there is an intrinsic relation between the intellectual and practical educational technologies on the one hand and the way in which political power is wielded in our societies as well as the way in which we govern ourselves on the other side. In this way these studies also indicate how educational practice and educational theory (and science) have played and do play a constitutive role in practices of subjectivation which are crucial to our 'learning societies'—as societies which interpellate us to become lifelong learners.

Almost all authors are related to universities on the continent. Therefore, this volume could also be regarded as an introduction to the Continental reception of governmentality and perhaps also as an illustration of the force of intellectual traditions. Although some authors take as a point of departure present developments in their home country, we think their analysis is exemplary for developments in other countries as well. Moreover, and this could be a question for future research, it is interesting to notice how developments at the level of governmentality are similar within different countries. Could it be explained by the use of similar research methods (too much focus on method instead of a kind of critical attitude towards one's present)? Or is there something underlying or outside regimes of governmentality that is directing these regimes all into the same direction?

4. Mapping the 'Learning Society' and its Limits

The 'learning society' expresses principles of a universal humanity and a promise of progress that seem to transcend the nation. *Thomas Popkewitz, Ulf Olsson* and *Kenneth Peterson* let us see how this society is governed in the name of a cosmopolitan ideal which despite its universal pretensions embodies particular inclusions and exclusions. These occur through inscribing distinctions and differentiations that distinguish between the characteristics of those who embody a cosmopolitan reason that brings social progress and personal fulfilment and those who do not embody the cosmopolitan principles of civility and normalcy. Mapping the circulation of the notion of the 'learning society' in actual arenas of Swedish health and criminal justice, and Swedish and US school reforms permits the appearance of the mode of life of the citizen of this society, the learner, as an 'unfinished cosmopolitanism' and also directs attention to its 'other(s)'—those that are outside.

The commitment to cosmopolitanism as commitment to reason, science and principles of human rights is embodied in a particular way in Europe and placed in a landscape of lifelong learning. *Anna Tuschling* and *Christoph Engemann* describe how the discourse on and the administration of lifelong learning in the European Union is generating a European population of self-organizing learners. They trace the origins of lifelong learning to the discussions on alternative education in the 1960s and 1970s and demonstrate, along the lines of the distinction between formal and informal learning, how the field of learning is transformed from enclosed environments into a totality of learning events, while simultaneously, as a strategy of subjectivation, individuals are provided with the necessary skill-sets to become inhabitants of Europe as a learning society. We can see from this how 'Europe' is not to be considered so much as a kind of super-state, but rather as an assemblage of discourses and governmental techniques and strategies.

In their contributions both Pongratz and Liessner sketch how some of these 'European' strategies and techniques are operating. Taking the turmoil caused in Germany by the results of the PISA-study (Programme for International Student Assessment) as a starting point *Ludwig Pongratz* indicates how this turmoil points to a self understanding and self-government which is generated through the disciplining effect of educational reform measures as governmental strategies, of which the PISA study is itself an element. This linkage of 'technologies of the self' with new governmental strategies of control—the 'voluntary self-control' of individuals—manifests itself at all levels of the education system: at the level of individual learning processes (through which the participants in educational processes are to be transformed into 'I-Ltd.' firms), at the level of methodological-didactic arrangements (increasingly using post-Fordist, 'soft' forms of regulation), and finally at the institutional level (through the reconstruction of educational institutions as market-oriented, profitable agencies, trading with knowledge as a commodity).

Taking up these different levels and concentrating on the German university landscape, *Andrea Liesner* analyses the transformations that are at work in the so-called 'harmonisation of the architecture of the European higher education system' which finds its origin in the 'Sorbonne Declaration' (1998) and in the 'Bologna Conference' (1999). She sketches how teaching and learning appear in the 'new' higher education area and indicates how in the reorganisation of the curriculum the university appears as an environment that fosters students and teachers to conceive of themselves as entrepreneurial customers and service providers. As such the political 'Europeanization' program of the universities puts a new mode of government and self-government at work. This actual government of the learning society involves a claim to freedom.

Quaghebeur and Bröckling explore this freedom as it takes shape in the invocations for participation and creativity that are very popular today. As *Kerlijn Quaghebeur* states, 'participation' has become a buzzword and has been linked up with personal promises of self-fulfilment and with democratic ideals. Through the analysis of a concrete training programme for participation she shows how the possibilities and opportunities that are offered in participation are actually governing the subject in a particular way—they have as an effect a specific practice of freedom as obedience to particular norms. And she asks whether practices of freedom have to imply subjection to a norm.

Ulrich Bröckling's 'brainstorming session' indicates how the appeal ('be creative') and self-understanding ('I'm myself to the extent I'm creative') come together and how creativity appears simultaneously as an anthropological capacity, a binding norm, a *telos* without closure and a learnable competence. Moreover, he shows that the imperative to be creative entails many paradoxes, contradictions and ambiguities and that the response to it cannot be another imperative—'don't be creative'—but a turning away from speaking in the imperative and stopping wanting to be creative.

Being an inhabitant of the learning society means not only to want to be creative and to want to participate, but implies in a more general way the will to invest with regard to a future return, i.e. to subjugate under a permanent economic tribunal. Taking the 'European Space of Higher Education' as a starting point *Maarten Simons* indicates how the regime of learning implies that the distinction between the social and the economic becomes obsolete. His investigation is focusing (following the perspective of Bröckling) on the intersection between a politisation and economisation of human life. Using Foucault's understanding of biopolitics and discussing the analyses of Agamben and Negri/Hardt he argues that the actual governmental configuration, i.e. the economisation of the social, has a biopolitical dimension and that what is at stake is a 'bio-economisation' which could turn into a regime of terror. Or to put it differently: fostering the (lifelong) learning (to learn) i.e. fostering life (as learning process) could turn into 'let die' and even into 'make die'.

But, one could ask, what makes us governable and enables us to govern? *Norbert Ricken* addresses this issue by rephrasing the question 'what is power?' into the question: 'to what power can be seen as a response?'. This allows us to keep the 'power of power' in sight. He then elucidates the 'how' of power through some conceptual explorations and theoretical clarifications as well as through an explicitly anthropological problematisation of power, as the way in which power is understood depends always also on the way in which people understand themselves. Reassessing Foucault's rejection of anthropological reflections Ricken sketches a structural matrix of human self conceptions through which power and also critique can be reconstructed systematically.

This brings us to issue of the (possibility of) critique of the actual regime. Following Foucault, critique could be regarded as being the art not to be governed in this way or as a project of desubjectivation. *Jan Masschelein* tries to show how such a project could be described as an 'e-ducative' practice and explores this idea through an example which Foucault himself gave of such a critical practice: the writing (and reading) of 'experience books'. Thus it appears that such an e-ducative practice is a 'dangerous', public and uncomfortable practice that is not in need of pastoral care but requires generosity, presence and attention. As such it demands a pedagogy of experience which is to be invented in order to 'make' oneself into a question, to transgress the limits of a governmental regime.

Premature Epilogue: E-ducational Maps

What could be the meaning of mapping our society, i.e. a society referred to in educational and political discourse as a learning society? Are these maps drawn and presented with a specific reader in mind? Are the cartographers addressing someone who is in need of orientation and guidance, someone who could not find her way without a carefully designed map in her hands? Are we putting ourselves as cartographers into a critical Kantian position, claiming that what is needed in our society are guidelines or orientations for our thinking? (Kant, 1786/1981) Do we want to provide an orientation? (Elden, 2001) Do we want to help to find a place in the world? (Crampton, 2004) And do we ask the reader to judge whether we succeed? No, or at least, we had something else in mind. We believe—and this is a confession-without-address—that what is and should be at stake are gestures of disorientation and maps that are helping us to get lost, maps that are not simplifying but making everything more complex, maps that are not offering an overview or a liberating view but that liberate our view.

And let us be straightforward about this by using a positive formulation of what we believe. Being orientated, to have an orientation, to have a direction (be it a utopia) is the state of mind of a subject, of whatever kind of subjectivity and implies (taking) a position (be this, as Kant would have it, a subjective feeling). In contrast, being disorientated, being without direction is about having an experience, it is the state of mind of a being that is exposed, of a being out-of-position. Or to put it otherwise: while reason, knowledge, and learning could be regarded as giving orientations, experience is what is happening to us, and that something is happening to us. Experience thus, is not to be understood as what is blind without an orientating reason and reason is not what is empty without real-life experience. What we would like to do is to resist the blackmail of Enlightenment, to go beyond the distinction between the transcendental and the empirical and to point to another idea of experience (Foucault, 1984c, 1984d).

Our belief is that the meaning of mapping or cartography is neither to offer a representation nor to be a construction or to reveal a unity behind the complex diversity in order to find our place. Instead, its meaning is to generate places and moments for experience and this experience has an e-ducational value. Therefore, we believe that a map is not an (edifying) story or a narrative (about ourselves, about education) that is transmitting a personal experience and that has a learning potential. Mapping the learning society or our actual being is a gesture of e-ducation, of leading out. Or, if one would like: it is an act of enlightenment, not through reason and learning but through experience. It is an act of critique, but not in the sense of defining the limits of reason and claiming the blindness of experience. Critique is about transgression. But going beyond is not entering that space of emptiness and darkness (without reason) as the blackmail of Enlightenment would let us have it. Transgressing our actuality or present, transgressing who we are and what we should be like is entering the world of experience and e-ducation. And in order to do so, we believe that it is necessary to leave behind our intellectual, pedagogical and academic comfort.

This comfort is about having a 'position', a particular position. It is the position of someone who is speaking in the name of a court (of reason, truth, science, humanity, history …) and regards people, including oneself, as in need of permanent (spiritual) guidance and orientation (to find their place in society, to survive in this society, to enter the kingdom of reason, to become truly human, to become a learning citizen, to be a scientist …). We believe that mapping the present starts by resisting precisely the comfort of a 'position' and by refusing to bring that present before a court. The point of departure is being ex-posed or out of position. What is at stake then can be indicated in terms of the kind of questions this being exposed allows, and in a certain way also forces us, to ask. The initial questions are not: 'what is the learning society?', 'what is lifelong learning?', 'what is participation?', 'what is creativity?', 'how does all this affect education and people involved in education?', 'how do we have to judge this learning society?'. Instead, the initial question is: who are we, we for whom the learning society is important (to organize, to reflect upon …), we who regard ourselves as inhabitants of a society in which learning is a fundamental process or we for whom learning is a notion to refer to when we think on what life is about?

And the question is: what is there to say when we leave the comfort of the position and the court? Is there still anything to say? To whom?

Notes

1. For the notion 'map' and 'mapping' see Flynn, 1994, 2005.
2. This collection of studies came out of a conference at Goldsmiths College (University of London) in 1992, and was supported by the journal 'Economy and Society'. Topics related to governmentality are often discussed in this journal, including also the presuppositions and critical dimensions of studies of governmentality (O'Malley, Weir & Shearing, 1997; Stenson, 1998).
3. *Eine Kritik der politischen Vernunft. Foucaults Analyse der modernen Gouvernementalität* (Lemke, 1997) has been important with regard to the introduction of governmentality in Germany. The author offers a detailed overview of Foucault's two courses on governmentality as well as links with his later work.
4. Examples of other collections include Hänninen, 1998 (Finland); Dean & Hindess, 1998 (Australia).
5. For an overview of Foucault in Anglo-American research see Peters, 2004. With regard to the Foucault reception in educational theory in Germany see Balzer, 2004. For a recent collection see Baker & Heyning, 2004.

References

Baker, B. & Heyning, K. (2004) *Dangerous Coagulations? The uses of Foucault in the study of education* (New York, Peter Lang).

Ball, S. J. (ed.) (1990) *Foucault and Education. Disciplines and knowledge* (London, Routledge).

Ball, S. J. (1994) *Educational Reform: A critical and post-structural approach* (Buckingham, Open University Press).

Ball, S. J. (2003) The Teacher's Soul and the Terrors of Performativity, *Journal of Education Policy*, 18:2, pp. 215–228.

Balzer, N. (2004) Von den Schwierigkeiten, nicht oppositional zu denken. Linien der Foucault-Rezeption in der deutschsprachigen Erziehungswissenschaft, in: N. Ricken & M. Rieger-Ladich (eds) *Michel Foucault: Pädagogische Lektüren* (Wiesbaden, VS Verlag Für Sozialwissenschaften).

Barry, A., Osborne, T. & Rose, N. (eds) (1996) *Foucault and Political Reason: Liberalism, neo-liberalism and rationalities of government* (London, UCL Press).

Biesta, G. J. J. (1998) Pedagogy Without Humanism: Foucault and the subject of education, *Interchange*, 29:1, pp. 1–16.

Blake, N., Smeyers, P., Smith, R. & Standish, P. (1998) *Thinking Again: Education after postmodernism* (New York, Bergin & Garvey).

Bröckling, U., Krasmann, S. & Lemke, T. (eds) (2000) *Gouvernementalité der Gegenwart. Studien zur Ökonomisierung des Sozialen* (Frankfurt am Main, Suhrkamp).

Bröckling, U. (2000) Totale Mobilmachung. Menschenführung im Qualitäts- und Selbstmanagement, in: U. Bröckling, S. Krasmann & T. Lemke (eds), *Gouvernementalité der Gegenwart. Studien zur Ökonomisierung des Sozialen* (Frankfurt am Main, Suhrkamp) pp. 131–167.

Burchell, G., Gordon, C. & Miller, P. (eds) (1991) *The Foucault Effect: Studies in governmentality* (Chicago, University of Chicago Press).

Crampton, J. W. (2004) *The Political Mapping of Cyberspace* (Edinburgh, Edinburgh University Press).

Cruikshank, B. (1996) Revolutions Within: Self-government and self-esteem, in: A. Barry, T. Osborne & N. Rose (eds), *Foucault and the Political Reason: Liberalism, neo-liberalism and rationalities of government* (London, UCL Press) pp. 231–251.

Dean, M. (1995) Governing the Unemployed Self in an Active Society, *Economy and Society*, 9:3, pp. 47–68.

Dean, M. (1999) *Governmentality. Power and Rule in Modern Society* (New Delhi, Sage).

Dean, M. & Hindess, B. (eds) (1998) *Governing Australia. Studies in contemporary rationalities of government* (Cambridge, Cambridge University Press).

Depaepe, M. (1998) *De pedagogisering achterna: aanzet tot een genealogie van de pedagogische mentaliteit in de voorbije 250 jaar* (Leuven, Acco).

Drummond, J. (2003) Care of the Self in a Knowledge Economy: Higher education, vocation and the ethics of Michel Foucault, *Educational Philosophy and Theory*, 35:1, pp. 57–69.

Edwards, R. (2002) Mobilizing the Lifelong Learner: Governmentality in educational practices, *Journal of Education Policy*, 17:3, pp. 353–365.

Elden, S. (2001) *Mapping the Present. Heidegger. Foucault and the project of a spatial history* (London/New York, Continuum).

Fendler, L. (2003) Teacher Reflection in a Hall of Mirrors: Historical Influences and Political Reverberations, *Educational Researcher*, 32:3, pp. 16–25.

Findlay, P. & Newton, T. (1998) Re-framing Foucault: The case of performance appraisal, in: A. McKinlay & K. Starkey (eds) *Foucault, Management and Organization Theory* (London, Sage Publications) pp. 211–229.

Flynn, T. (1994) Foucault's Mapping of History, in: G. Gutting (ed.), *The Cambridge Companion to Foucault* (New York, Cambridge University Press).

Flynn, T. R. (2005) *Sartre, Foucault and Historical Reason* (Chicago & London, University of Chicago Press).

Foucault, M. (1971a) Nietzsche, la généalogie, l'histoire, in: D. Defert, F. Ewald & J. Lagrange (eds), *Dits et écrits II 1970–1975* (Paris, Gallimard) pp. 136–156.

Foucault, M. (1975) *Surveiller et punir: naissance de la prison* (Paris, Gallimard).

Foucault, M. (1978a) La philosophie analytique de la politique, in: D. Defert, F. Ewald & J. Lagrange (eds), *Dits et écrits III 1976–1979* (Paris, Gallimard) pp. 534–551.

Foucault, M. (1978b) La 'gouvernementalité', in: D. Defert, F. Ewald & J. Lagrange (eds), *Dits et écrits III 1976–1979* (Paris, Gallimard) pp. 635–657.

Foucault, M. (1980) Entretien avec Michel Foucault, in: D. Defert, F. Ewald & J. Lagrange (eds), *Dits et écrits IV 1980–1988* (Paris, Gallimard) pp. 41–95.

Foucault, M. (1981) 'Omnes et singulatim': vers une critique de la raison politique, in: D. Defert, F. Ewald & J. Lagrange (eds), *Dits et écrits IV 1980–1988* (Paris, Gallimard) pp. 134–161.

Foucault, M. (1982) Le sujet et le pouvoir, in: D. Defert, F. Ewald & J. Lagrange (eds), *Dits et écrits IV 1980–1988* (Paris, Gallimard) pp. 222–243.

Foucault, M. (1984a) *Histoire de la sexualité 2. L'usage des plaisirs* (Paris, Gallimard).

Foucault, M. (1984b) *Histoire de la sexualité 3. Le souci de soi* (Paris, Gallimard).

Foucault, M. (1984c) Qu'est-ce que les Lumières?, in: D. Defert, F. Ewald & J. Lagrange (eds), *Dits et écrits IV 1980–1988* (Paris, Gallimard) pp. 562–578.

Foucault, M. (1984d) Qu'est-ce que les Lumières?, in: D. Defert, F. Ewald & J. Lagrange (eds), *Dits et écrits IV 1980–1988* (Paris, Gallimard) pp. 679–688.

Foucault, M. (2001) *L'Herméneutique du sujet. Cours au Collège de France (1981–1983)* (Paris, Gallimard/Le seuil).

Foucault, M. (2004b) *Sécurité, territoire, population. Cours au Collège de France (1977–1978)* (Paris, Gallimard/Le seuil).

Foucault, M. (2004a) *Naissance de la biopolitique. Cours au Collège de France (1978–1979)* (Paris, Gallimard/Le seuil).

Gordon, C. (1991) Governmental rationality: an introduction, in: G. Burchell, C. Gordon & P. Miller (eds), *The Foucault Effect: Studies in governmentality* (London, Harvester Wheatsheaf) pp. 1–51.

Greco, M. (2000) Homo Vacuus. Alexithymie und das neoliberale Gebot des Selbstseins, in: U. Bröckling, S. Krasmann & T. Lemke (eds), *Gouvernementalité der Gegenwart. Studien zur Ökonomisierung des Sozialen* (Frankfurt am Main: Suhrkamp) pp. 265–285.

Hänninen S. (ed.) (1998) *The Displacement of Social Policies* (SoPhi, University of Jyväskylä).

Howley, A. & Hartnett, R. (1992) Pastoral Power and the Contemporary University: A Foucauldian analysis, *Educational Theory*, 42:3, pp. 271–283.

Hunter, I. (1994) *Rethinking the School. Subjectivity, bureaucracy, criticism* (St. Leonards, Allen and Unwin).

Kant, I. (1786/1981) Was Heisst: Sich im Denken orienteren?, in: W. Weischedel (ed.), *Schriften zur Metaphysik und Logik* (Band 5) (Darmstadt, Wissenschaftliche Buchgesellschaft).

Kendall, T. & Crossley, N. (1996) Governing Love: On the tactical control of counter-transference in the psycho-analytic community, *Economy & Society*, 25:2, pp. 178–194.

Lemke, T. (1997) *Eine Kritik der politischen Vernunft. Foucault's Analyse der modernen Gouvernementalität* (Berlin/Hamburg, Argument).

Marshall, J. D. (1995a) Foucault and Neo-Liberalism: Bio-power and busno-power, in: A. Neiman (ed.), *Proceedings of The Philosophy of Education Society* (Normal, IL, Philosophy of Education Society).

Marshall, J. D. (1995b) Governmentality and Liberal Education, *Studies in the Philosophy of Education*, 14:1, pp. 23–24.

Marshall, J. D. (1996) *Michel Foucault: Personal Autonomy and Education* (Dordrecht, Kluwer).

Marshall, J. D. (2001) A Critical Theory of the Self: Wittgenstein, Nietzsche, Foucault, *Studies in Philosophy and Education*, 20:1, pp. 75–91.

Masschelein, J. & Simons, M. (2002) An Adequate Education for a Globalized World? A note on the immunization of being-together, *Journal of Philosophy of Education*, 36:4, pp. 565–584.

Masschelein, J. & Simons, M. (2003) *Globale immuniteit. Een kleine cartografie van de Europese ruimte voor onderwijs* (Leuven, Acco).

Miller, P. & Rose, N. (1997) Mobilizing the Consumer: Assembling the subject of consumption, *Theory, Culture & Society*, 14:1, pp. 1–36.

Olssen, M. (1999) *Michel Foucault. Materialism and education* (Bergin & Garvey, Westport).

Olssen, M., Codd, J. & O'Neill, A-M. (2004) *Education Policy: Globalization, citizenship, democracy* (London, Sage).

O'Malley, P. (1996) Risk and Responsibility, in: A. Barry, T. Osborne & N. Rose (eds), *Foucault and the Political Reason: Liberalism, neo-liberalism and rationalities of government* (London, UCL Press) pp. 189–207.

O'Malley, P., Weir, L. & Shearing, C. (1997) Governmentality, Criticism, Politics, *Economy and Society*, 26:4, pp. 501–517.

Peters, M. A. (2000) Neoliberalism and the Constitution of the Entrepreneurial Self: Education and enterprise culture in New Zealand, in: C. Lankshear, M. Peters, A. Alba & E. Gonzales (eds), *Curriculum in the Postmodern Condition* (New York, Peter Lang).

Peters, M. (2004) Why Foucault? New Directions in Anglo-American Educational Research, in: L. Pongratz *et al.* (eds), *Nach Foucault. Diskurs- und machtanalytische Perspectiven der Pädagogik* (Wiesbaden, VS Verlag Für Sozialwissenschaften).

Pongratz, L. A. (1989) *Pädagogik im Prozess der Moderne. Studien zur Sozial- und Theoriegeschichte der Schule* (Weinheim, Deutscher Studien Verlag).

Pongratz L. *et al.* (eds) (2004) *Nach Foucault. Diskurs- und machtanalytische Perspectiven der Pädagogik* (Wiesbaden, VS Verlag Für Sozialwissenschaften).

Popkewitz, T. S. (1996) Rethinking Decentralization and State/civil Society Distinctions: The state as a problematic of governing, *Journal of Education Policy*, 11:1, pp. 27–51.

Popkewitz, T. S. & Brennan, M. (eds) (1997) *Foucault's Challenge: Discourse, knowledge, and political projects of schooling* (New York, Teachers College Press).

Popkewitz, T. S. (1998) *Struggling for the Soul. The Politics of Schooling and the Construction of the Teacher* (New York, Teachers College Press).

Ricken, N. & Rieger-Ladich, M. (eds) (2004) *Michel Foucault: Pädagogische Lektüren* (Wiesbaden, VS Verlag Für Sozialwissenschaften).

Rose, N. (1996) Governing 'Advanced' Liberal Democracies, in: A. Barry, T. Osborne & N. Rose (eds), *Foucault and the Political Reason: Liberalism, neo-liberalism and rationalities of government* (London, UCL Press) pp. 37–64.

Rose, N. (1999) *The Powers of Freedom. Reframing political thought* (Cambridge, Cambridge University Press).

Schmidt-Semisch, H. (2000) Selber Schuld. Skizzen versicherungsmathematischer Gerechtigkeit, in: U. Bröckling, S. Krasmann & T. Lemke (eds), *Gouvernementalität der Gegenwart. Studien zur Ökonomisierung des Sozialen* (Frankfurt am Main, Suhrkamp) pp. 168–193.

Simons, M. (2002) Governmentality, Education and Quality Management: Toward a critique of the permanent quality tribunal, *Zeitschrift für Erziehungswissenschaft*, 5:4, pp. 617–633.

Smeyers, P. (1995a) Education and the Educational Project I: The atmosphere of post-Modernism, *Journal of Philosophy of Education*, 29:1, pp. 109–119.

Stenson, K. (1998) Beyond Histories of the Present, *Economy and Society*, 27:4, pp. 333–352.

Tavares, H. (1996) Classroom Management and Subjectivity: A genealogy of educational identities, *Educational Theory*, 46:2, pp. 189–201.

Wain, K. (1996) Foucault, Education, the Self and Modernity, *Journal of Philosophy of Education*, 30:3, pp. 355–360.

Wain, K. (2004) *The Learning Society in a Postmodern World. The education crisis* (New York, Peter Lang).

Yeatman, A. (1998) Interpreting Contemporary Contractualism, in: M. Dean & B. Hindess (eds), *Governing Australia. Studies in contemporary rationalities of government* (Cambridge, Cambridge University Press) pp. 227–241.

Zembylas, M. (2003) Interrogating Teacher Identity: Emotion, resistance, and self-formation, *Educational Theory*, 53:1, pp. 107–127.

2

The Learning Society, the Unfinished Cosmopolitan, and Governing Education, Public Health and Crime Prevention at the Beginning of the Twenty-First Century

Thomas S. Popkewitz, Ulf Olsson, Kenneth Petersson

Introduction

While there are probably earlier references to the learning society, but browsing educational journals from 1982 there appeared an article, entitled 'Japan: The learning society' (Schiller & Walberg, 1982). It was written at a time when the US feared that the Japanese society was moving economically ahead and that fear gave expression to the need to reform its educational systems. The American educators argued that schooling permeates the whole of Japanese society and that it was a prime instrument in the country's miracle of the 1970s and 1980s. The Learning Society that Japan typified was, according to the authors, related to 'post-industrial, global society in which information is more than ever the primary source of economic development and cultural influence'. And as a prophecy of the benefits of the Learning Society and the need for American educational reforms, the authors forecast the future that Tokyo will become the world's central city.

As such prophecies go, Japan had its cultural and economic difficulties since then. But the idea of a learning society is a persistent cultural theme that is not merely instrumental in relation to economic growth and national exceptionalism. It embodies a cultural thesis about a cosmopolitan mode of life that mutates through modern schooling. An idea of a learning society is embedded in Dewey's pragmatism. Pragmatism embodies a mode of living through the use of reason as a continual process of problem solving in which the individual is linked to the collective good of the society (the community). That optimistic future is mutated in the new millennium talk about the learning society and other phrases such as the global society and the information society, used to mobilize school reforms in the making of a new world order. A European Union planner in a recent speech reiterated this optimism in a range of policies from the 1980s that emphasized the future of European spaces as occupied by lifelong learners and the learning society.[1]

Our interest in cosmopolitanism is not one that traces a philosophical discourse from Diogenes or Kant to the present. Cosmopolitanism is an historical 'tool' to consider the transmogrifications of European Enlightenment images of a universal reason, rationality and progress as a mode of living inscribed in the Learning Society.[2] The learner of this new society is a cosmopolitan guided by compassion for continual change and innovation. It is a consuming project of life that regulates the present in the name of the future action. For some, the learning society is composed of a continual process of individual choice that promises the Philosopher's Stone. Maeroff (2003), for example, offers online learning as enabling a learning society where all children and adults are cosmopolitan in outlook through a continual process of learning made possible through the computer and Internet. The new technologies, he argues, provide a new era that relates the free-market Neoliberalism approaches and equity in schooling through online learning. It interjects 'more choice into the system, advocates reason, the richer the offerings and the greater the benefits to consumers (students and their families)' (Maeroff, 2003, p. 4).

From a different ideological perspective, Hargreaves (2003) speaks against the overly stressed materialism and marketization of Neoliberal reforms. In its place is a knowledge society that 'is really a learning society ... [that] process(es) information and knowledge in ways that maximize learning, stimulate ingenuity and invention and develop the capacity to initiate and cope with change' (Hargreaves, 2003, p. xviii). Schooling, he continues, is an institution that prepares the child for the future. Also concerned with equity and justice, the child of the Learning Society has 'a cosmopolitan identity which shows tolerance of race and gender differences, genuine curiosity toward and willingness to learn from other cultures, and responsibility toward excluded groups within and beyond one's society' (Hargreaves, 2003, p. xix).

What can we make of these prophecies of the Learning Society as a moral life organized through continuous innovation with no finishing point? In the following, the prophecy of the Learning Society is treated as a technology that orders, interns and encloses the possibilities of one's life. Our framing of the problem, discussed in the first section, is through the notion of cosmopolitanism. Cosmopolitanism is a cultural thesis about modes of living. The Enlightenment's cosmopolitan was an urbane individual who possesses agency. That agency entails the use of reason and rationality to promote universal values of progress and humanity. Cosmopolitanism, we argue, is a continual theme of pedagogy inscribed in the Learning Society. That inscription entails principles about who 'we' are, should be, and who is not that 'we'—the anthropological 'Other' who stands outside reason and its civilizing manners of conduct.

Cosmopolitanism functions as an interpretive lens to explore the political objects of social administration of the child and family. We are interested in the rules and standards of conduct in producing the self-governing actors who are simultaneously responsible for the social progress and for the personal fulfilment of one's life. Today's cosmopolitan, as in the turn of the 20th century, is spoken about as the global citizen freed from provincialism and tradition, and ruled by universal principles of human rights rather than social or theological certainties. The contemporary form of this mode of living is expressed as the *topoi* of 'the knowledge' and 'communication society' and the child who is a lifelong learner who continually re-creates one's self through being a problem solver. Cosmopolitanism, then, provides a way to examine the systems of reason that regulates, differentiates and divides the acts and participation of the child in the name of universal human principles such as the Learning Society.

Working through Foucault's (1991) notion of governmentality[3] the first section explores cosmopolitanism as an intellectual tool. It considers the changing pedagogical practices to enact a change in the conditions of people as enacting changes in who those people are and should be. The second section focuses on the Learning Society, with Swedish and US schooling, and Swedish health promotion, and crime prevention as our sites of investigation. We discuss the learner of the Learning Society as fabricating[4] the unfinished cosmopolitanism. That individuality is talked about as a lifelong learner. It is an individuality that plans one's biography as continuously solving problems, making choices and collaborating in 'communities of learners' in a process of continuous innovation. The only thing about the future that is not open to choice is choice itself. We talk about the unfinished cosmopolitan rather than use the contemporary phrase of lifelong learner to historicize the present and its cultural thesis about a mode of living. The third section concerns the problem of the notion of design in making the unfinished cosmopolitan: design is what one does with problem solving to order one's mode of living, and design is what research does to calculate and administer the future of who is to design one's life. These first two sections explore the cosmopolitanism in policy and research as the characteristics and capabilities of the unfinished cosmopolitanism cultural practices assembled and connected to form the principles governing who the child and citizen are and should be.

The fourth section links the universal claims of inclusion with exclusions. Embodied in the design of the unfinished cosmopolitan is a duality. The unfinished cosmopolitan inscribes fear of what is not cosmopolitan and 'civilized'—the disadvantaged and at-risk child, the sickly individual, and the criminal. Our analysis moves across different sites with broad strokes and we realize that nuances and differences are left unexamined, limitations we believe are warranted at this point in the diagnosis of the present.

Governmentality and Cosmopolitanism

If we examine the two above references about online learning and the knowledge society, cosmopolitanism is a theme within the Learning Society that moves along different ideological positions. It also travels in a range of literatures about transcendental values of a global citizen, reason, and action untangled from provincialism, tradition, and social or theological certainties (also see, e.g. Beck, 2000; Castells, 2000).[5] But the narratives and images of the individuality that brings forth the future of progress are not merely there by the grace of contemporary wisdom. It is a mutation that moves in uneven flows and different configurations from the European Enlightenment and the Reformation to the present.[6] The investigation of the learner of the Learning Society requires historicizing the mutations as narratives of cosmopolitanism and its production of the 'Others' travels to the present.

The images and narratives of the Enlightenment's cosmopolite are neither as straightforward nor as universal in values as they might seem. The ideal(s) of the cosmopolitan was not only an altruistic quality or about pure thought that was superimposed on the historical individual. The seeming universalism of cosmopolitanism embodies a particular historical scaffolding of rules and standards about who the citizen is or should be, and who does not embody that reason and 'reasonableness'.

The values and norms of the Enlightenment's cosmopolitan have a mixed history. European cosmopolitan values have been used in battles against European colonialists. It has also been used to commit the violence of colonialism in justifying the superiority of the West. The ironies, internments, and enclosures are evident as the northern European Reformation and the Enlightenment that were to rise above the nation in securing progress. Its universalism was in fact inscribed in the construction of the nation, for example, in the American and French Revolutions. Further and central to this study, cosmopolitanism was and is about exclusions, in its inclusions that disqualified some as not embodying the capabilities of the 'reason' of the cosmopolitan.

At this point, we can summarize briefly our use of cosmopolitanism as an intellectual tool to diagnose the mode of life embodied in the Learning Society in US schooling, and Swedish health and the social policing of crime.

First, the notion of Learning Society makes it possible 'to think' and act through a range of historical inscriptions that travel in the present about a cosmopolitan way of living. That is, cosmopolitanism is not one thing or a constant that moves untouched within the vagaries of history. Whether one approaches cosmopolitanism from the social or individual side of the Learning Society, there is an Enlightenment attitude toward 'reason' and rationality, to use Foucault's (1984) discussion. Cosmopolitanism is formed through an assemblage in which reason is related to notions of agency and progress, stability and consensus as governing principles of action and reflection. Today's cosmopolitan is the agential individual who is talked about as empowered, having a voice, and self-responsible in producing innovation in the processes of change.

Second, there is a sacredness to agency inscribed in cosmopolitanism theories of pedagogy and the social and educational sciences; yet it is rarely explored that this agency is a particular register that intersects with the formation of the modern state and the art of governing. Meyer (1986) argues, for example, that there was a progressive discovery of human personality in the eighteenth and nineteenth centuries; that each person carries a whole system of motives and perceptions that reflect different biological and social forces through which the individual self is integrated. Theories of the agential individual constituted persons as moral subjects of their own actions. Theories of action and actors/agency were central to the international spread of mass education in the construction of the modern nation in the late nineteenth and early nineteenth centuries (Meyer, Boli, Thomas & Ramirez, 1997).

Third, cosmopolitan reason is the cornerstone of agency, but also the limit and object of government.[7] From Kant through Dewey and into current notions of emancipation and empowerment, the calculation of cosmopolitan reason and the 'reasonable person' is a *sine qua non* of the joining of individual enablement and public capabilities. Cosmopolitanism recovered Stoic ideas in French intellectual circles of the Enlightenment to join the natural (nature) and human realms of reason (Toulmin, 1990, pp. 68–69). The reason of the Enlightenment was to correct visual perceptions and the errors of the senses. Kant's (1784/1970) 'What is the Enlightenment?' offers the enlightened leader as a guardian, who teaches the duty of all citizens to think for themselves. But the guardian in Kant's text embodies the dual attempt to order the world through reason and to administer through reason. Augustus Comte's positivism epitomized the double time of reason as bringing order and harmony as well as change, captured in his famous phrase about the new secular religion of positivism, 'Order and Progress'. The cosmopolitanism of Comte embodied science as 'the Religion of Humanity, and all true Positivists sought to unite science and religion' (Nisbet, 1979, pp. 172–173).

Reason, then, is not something that is merely there to recuperate in decision making or problem solving; rather reason comprises historically produced systems of rules and standards that order reflection and participation. The notion of cosmopolitan reason is something calculated and administrable, for governing reflection and action in the name of social progress and personal fulfilment.

Fourth, while the Enlightenment philosophers talked about reason and rationality (science) as values that enable the individual to transcend the local and the provincial, the rules and standards of cosmopolitan reason assume a particular type of expertise in ordering daily life. Science becomes experimental and empirical and thus no longer merely the provenance of philosophers. And science is not merely a professional activity to gain knowledge and control of the external physical world. The human sciences emerge as particular technologies that give attention to the internal qualities of the mind and social interaction.

The expertise of human sciences were to constitute cosmopolitan freedom and liberty. John Dewey, an American philosopher and progressive educator, is one icon in bringing notions of a cosmopolitan individual into a populist form related to everyday activities. Dewey thought of the scientific method as the most potent force shaping the modern world in images related to Enlightenment ideals of cosmopolitanism. He wanted to humanize the creative power of science in the name of universal values and 'thereby to gain control of the future' (Rockefeller, 1991, p. 3). The cosmopolitanism of the new sciences of pedagogy and childhood organized life through values that were thought of as universal, and which promised progress through individual and community actions.

This brief discussion about the scaffolding of different cultural practices that give focus to cosmopolitanism, is a strategy to think historically about the Learning Society and its learners. Current reforms about the lifelong learner and the Learning Society make 'sense' in this historical context of narratives and images of cosmopolitanism. They function as technologies of administering the principles of self-reflection, action, and participation. Agency, progress, and reason are part of this grid, as is the taming of change in the name of progress and self-fulfilment. The inscriptions of the Learning Society, as Wagner (1994) writes more generally about modernity, 'cannot simply be written in terms of increasing autonomy and democracy, but rather in terms of changing notions of the substantive foundations of a self-realization and of shifting emphasis between individualized enablements and public/collective capabilities' (Wagner, 1994, p. xiv).

'The Learning Society as the Future Here and Now—What Are We Waiting For!'[8]

This and the next section focus on three overlapping cultural practices in policy and research that connect in the cosmopolitanism of the Learning Society—the inscription of the future as a regulating principle of the present, design as a practice of planning biography, and community as a space to link collective norms and values to individuality. Whereas one can think of the child and adult of the late 19th century as a subject who embodied the collective social narratives of the nation, today's individuality is a 'lifelong learner' who is flexible, continuously active, and works collaboratively for the future in a decentralized world.

The future functions as a governing practice. This future is not something decreed by Fate and out of sight of our own activities. Nor is this a future of strange, unexpected spaces that must be defended against. It is a future mobilized to design people in the present. As one Swedish politician recently said, 'We have to mobilize people to be citizens of the new Society'.[9] This future of a new society is of the here and now. The US educational policy reform document *No Child Left Behind* (Bush, 2001),[10] as well, makes the future in the governing of the present. The goal is a future inclusive society through school reform that is 'to build the mind and character of every child, from every background' (Bush, 2001).

In different contexts and with different logics, the same story seems to be told. The story is that we are now, more or less, obliged to live with constant change in society. Modern schooling, for example, continually links the individual to narratives of social or economic progress and the revitalization of democracy that will bring personal betterment. In a statement resonating across American school subject reforms, the National Council of Teachers of Mathematics (2000) model for curriculum reform argues that the student needs to be prepared for a future where change is 'a ubiquitous feature of contemporary life, so learning with under-standing is essential to enable students to use what they learn to solve the new kinds of problems they will inevitably face in the future' (pp. 20–21). The 'ubiquitous' uncertainty of the future that mathematics education tames has less to do with learning the norms of inquiry in mathematics than with the inscription of particular norms for planning one's future of continuous innovation and choice through, as we argue in the next section, a self-improvement process of problem solving.[11]

In a similar way, the Swedish Public Health policy is not simply about health. First and foremost the narrative about health is about Society, the Citizen, and the Future. The Swedish Governmental Commission, Health on Equivalent Conditions—National Targets for Health (SOU, 2000: 91) proposes national targets for public health in Sweden that seems to carry the same language. State health reforms are concerned with present changes in society in order to secure the future. According to the Commission, the Swedish model of the welfare state and public health development is 'exposed to huge outer and inner tensions' and 'different kinds of threats' (p. 55). Increasing differences in health and social conditions threatens the basic trust in society and the possibility of founding a society on solidarity between different population groups.

A pedagogical paradigm of a Learning Society is inscribed as a public health strategy and the public health paradigm. According to the Commission, it is 'important for a society that the citizens look upon learning and personal development as a life-long process' (SOU, 2000: 91, p. 423). Being a lifelong learner is significant for the health of the population and the future conduct of the individual subjects not only within formal educational settings, but also in people's everyday life and in society as a whole. Schooling is seen 'as a fundamental and gigantic public health investment' and a key element to bring about changes needed to make health a possibility for all (p. 385). The State Committee strives to make visible, problematize and reorganize the activities in schools with this view of pedagogy as an organizing principle for the future health of the public.

Present Swedish crime prevention, as well, is ordered as a pedagogical problem of the future of a Learning Society rather than being about the punishment of wrong-doing. Crime prevention is about learning to be law-abiding, problem solving, communicative and responsible than about punishment for wrongdoing. The offender must be instructed and educated to gain a better insight into the consequences of crime. And the victim is invited to listen, to understand, and to learn the whole story of the offender's crime activity. The Public Health Committee emphasizes that the mentalities and the knowledge of health issues needed are something that the subject has to capture over and over again; it's a life-long project (SOU, 2000: 91).

The narratives of the unfinished cosmopolitan in the Learning Society embody new relations between individuality (the lifelong learner) and the social. The fabrication of the child as a problem solver no longer bases responsibility in the range of social practices directed toward a single public sphere. The new individuality traverses diverse and plural communities to constitute the common good. The struggle is now in the autonomous learners who are continuously involved in self-improvement and ready for the uncertainties through working actively in communities of learning (see, e.g. The National Council for Teachers of Mathematics, 2000). Reason is no longer for the perfection of the nation as the collective embodiment of the social good. Change, contingency and uncertainty in daily life are tamed through the rules and standards that place the problem-solving child in diverse communities where the common good is formed.

Education is once again a project for national mobilization, but with a hugely different meaning than in earlier times. Education as once before, forms the ethical substance of the individual in all social activities. But the pedagogical principles of learning are spread now to the entire social body. 'Working with education' is not limited to learning and training of pupils in the classroom or to a specific place or time; rather school and education expands and connects to all aspects of society in an everlasting way. The subject must be prepared to learn during the whole life and be connected to learning in a wider sense (see Dalin, 1994, p. 11).

The notions of life-long learning and a Learning Society operate in different political and institutional areas that are no longer enclosed in the previously conceived spaces of the educational. The life-long learning destroys the boundaries between political sectors. Education policy, employment policy, the policy of industry and commerce, regional development policy and social policy have a common responsibility for life-long and life-wide learning (The Swedish National Agency for Education, 2000, p. 10f).

The governmental reason of the 21st century takes the pedagogical task of learning as a boundary-crossing route to unite the increasing and unforeseeable multiplicity, fragmentation and diversity within subject-oriented democratic education. Pedagogical reason is expected to both widen and strengthen the solidarity of society (see Petersson, Olsson, Hultqvist & Popkewitz, 2004). The governmentality orders and controls the future in the present by qualifying and preparing the individual citizen with dispositions for new cosmopolitan commitments. This is evident in the writing of a prominent Scandinavian educator in an authoritative professional journal. The Learning Society is viewed as a sign of the future and part of a visionary world.

> We are entering a knowledge society since the speed of the changing process is increasing and since the new society demands new, increasing and greater qualifications of each of us. Education will no longer be something linked to a certain range but will be a necessity and a self-evident part of everyday life to all ranges, social classes and occupational groups. We are already there. We know that 'life-long education' has become a reality. (Dalin, 1994, p. 143)

The citizens' work toward a never-ending future as an educational subject. It does not seem farfetched to argue that society has turned into a school (see Hultqvist & Petersson, 2000). Thus, Dewey's notion of 'School as Society' has been reshaped into 'Society as School'.

The Unfinished Cosmopolitan: Designing the Problem Solving Lifelong Learner and Community

One might say that most of the above is only policy about The Learning Society of the future, so let's get to what is happening on the ground. The divisions of text/context and the ideal/real create binaries that misrecognize how knowledge fabricates, that is, both construes and constructs, and thus functions 'materially.' The unfinished cosmopolitan inhabitants of the Learning Society are an assemblage of practices that order a cultural thesis about a mode of life. The taming of change is one part of the assemblage. In this section, we discuss (a) the notion of designed spaces and the designed individuality, (b) the making of the characteristics of the problem solver in search of a life of choice and innovation, and (c) 'community' as a place of belonging and home in the problem solving of the future. We call these 'cultural practices' as they overlap in ordering a mode of living of the unfinished cosmopolitan inscribed as an unfinished lifelong learner.

The Learning Society as a Design Problem

Today's pedagogical reforms and research talk about children and teachers designing their own learning, and research as a particular design problem to produce the agency of the individual who lives a life of continual innovation. The notion of design embodies a turn in 21ˢᵗ century narratives of democracy, empowerment and human agency for teachers, children and researchers.

The design for the future is a word that previously spoke in terms of what God gave to human affairs. The social and pedagogical interventions of 19ᵗʰ century America and Sweden were to complete the latent design of God within each child, the family and the citizen in their ways of living.[12] The Swedish educator Rudenschöld placed the notion of design in the Ståndscirkulation, the outer technological side of an evolutionary process that would inaugurate Christian values and life forms on earth (Hultqvist, 2004). The evolutionary process embodied Sweden as an exception from other nations through its heritage of the virtues of modesty or freedom from vanity and the Lutheran ethic of individualism and self-improvement.

The idea of design in making the citizen was also a part of an American Exceptionalism. The Exceptionalism was an epic of the nation told as a unique human experiment of a society that provides an exemplar of the highest ideals of human values and progress. The early founders of American sociology sought to guarantee the future of the republic's exceptionalism through deliberately designing the social order and the individual. The notion of design embodied elements of a social gospel that contained secularized elements of Puritan notions of salvation. Urban design and the design of the inner characteristics and capabilities of the child were to produce the 'reason' and 'reasonable' citizen of the future. The new psychologies, for example, envisioned the empirical building blocks of selfhood as of deliberate design rather than of something related to a static, metaphysical soul (Sklansky, 2002, pp. 148–9). William James' notion of a pragmatic psychology placed a premium on habit formation as the main means of acting in accord with one's designs (p. 146). Design's reach into the interior of the individual was spoken of as bringing the great panacea of equality.

Today design is to fabricate the individuality of life in the Learning Society. At one level, it is spoken about as part of democracy and its cosmopolitanism. Design in the online learning spoken about earlier is to make an individual whose life is of infinite choices. Design is also a research project of the learning sciences directed at the continuous intervention in the classroom. Design Research treats the classroom as a continuous open system for continuously inventing feedback loops. Feedback loops are to bring together reform goals, the ongoing development of the system, dispositions of participants, and professional expertise. Biography is the project of design. That biography is of an unfinished cosmopolitan in which deliberate, intentional acts lead an individual from one sphere of life to another as if life were a planning workshop that had a value in and of itself. Action is a continual flow toward a future that occurs through designing not only what will be done but also planning who that person will be.

The learning, problem-solving design of pedagogies is morphologically related to new principles of restorative criminal justice. The tools of this reasoning are communication and interaction between parties involved in crime and it focuses on what should be done (the future), not on what has been done.

> Restorative justice places both victim and offender in active problem-solving roles that focus upon the restoration of material and psychological losses to individuals and the community following the damage that results from criminal behaviour. Whenever possible, dialogue and negotiation serve as central elements of restorative justice. (This is true primarily of property crimes, although also of a growing number of more violent offences.) Problem solving for the future is seen as more important than establishing blame for past behaviour. Public safety is a primary concern, yet severe punishment of the offender is less important than providing opportunities to: empower victims in their search for closure and healing; impress upon the offender the human impact of their behaviour; and promote restitution of the victim. (Umbreit, 1994, p. 2)

The unfinished cosmopolitan in these different social spheres is oriented to the future through unfinished processes that are viewed as expressing universal human attributes of reason, science and progress. The unfinished cosmopolitan problem-solves to chase desire and works in a global world in which there is no finishing line. The child, for example, is someone who can choose to refuse allegiance to any one of the infinite choices on display, except the choice of choosing. The ordering, designing, and taming of the undefined future is a technology that connects the scope and aspirations of public powers with the personal and subjective capacities of individuals through mediating the 'interactions between intervention and setting' (The Design-Based Research Collective, 2003, p. 5).

Community as 'the Home' of the Unfinished Cosmopolitan

The autonomy of the problem solver is given a home and sense of belonging by connecting learning psychologies with communication and interactional practices embodied in the notion of 'community'. The problem solver learns by participating in a classroom community, 'a community of discourse', 'a community of learners', and 'a community of mathematicians'. Earlier 20th century notions of the classroom spoke of it as a place for socialization in which the child was to internalize universal, collective norms of identity that are pre-established. Today's reforms involve the continual forming of identity mediated through the communication systems of the classroom community (see, e.g. Cobb, 1994). The classroom community is thought of as a 'participation structure' in which communication theories are concerned with the ongoing processes that create fluid identities. Community inscribes cultural spaces in which problem solving and the Learning Society function as a performative quality of 'community'.

The evocation of community is intended to revive the ideals of a democracy by producing greater representation of those directly involved in schooling, public health and victim-offender mediation. Community evokes a concept of restorative justice and the reformation of democracy through the governing patterns of community. Community embodies a salvation theme about involvement and empower-ment, in which problem solving produces responsible citizenship. The communication networks are a way of providing harmony; that is, we make peace by speaking to each other and we become reconciled with each other by telling the 'truth' about ourselves. This new way of doing justice is very much about interaction, at the same moment as it is an ambition to personalize and humanize the judicial process in order to facilitate 'the empowerment of both parties to resolve the conflict at a community level' (Umbreit, 1994, p. 17).

Community is a discursive site to connect the intimate relations and inner capabilities of the child and family with cosmopolitan images and narratives of collective belonging and 'home'. The 'Community Sociology', developed at the University of Chicago during the early decades of the 20ᵗʰ century, sought to reshape the urban culture of immigrant families through social psychologies of the child and family in the work of, for example, Charles Horton Cooley, George Herbert Mead and John Dewey. Cooley saw the family and the neighbourhood as providing the proper socialization through which the child could lose the innate greed, lust and pride of power that was innate to the infant, and thus become fit for civilization. The communication systems of the family would, according to Cooley, establish the family on Christian principles that stressed a moral imperative in life and self-sacrifice for the good of the group. These Christian principles were viewed as the embodiment of a cosmopolitan citizen in a democratic society. Theories of the family and social interactions were a social education in which school and local communities related to a cosmopolitan image in which the indi-vidual submitted to a 'wider outlook, a higher and clearer idealism, and so be prepared to create that free, righteous and joyful system of life to which they aspire' (Cooley cited in Reuben, 1996, p. 156).

Contemporary crime prevention, misconduct and wrong behaviour re-inscribe notions of community as governing practices but in a different assembly of practices than at the turn of the 20ᵗʰ century. Crime is corrected and prevented informally at the local level (The National Council for Crime Prevention, 1999: 12, p. 11). In this context 'The State' is no longer imagined as the victim, rather 'restorative justice theory postulates that criminal behaviour is first a conflict between individuals' (Umbreit, 1994, p. 2). One of the aims of the restorative mediation is to have the offender confess shame and ask the victim's forgiveness. The victim is invited to listen, and to understand, the whole story of the offender's crime activity, and the story has to be told in front of the mediator/confessor. But crime prevention as a project of restorative justice is also part of the curriculum of the Swedish high school. State curriculum projects function to link the student with the broader purpose 'to provide a basis for pupils to continue in community involvement both as citizens and professionals (…) to nurture pupils in democratic participation' and 'to provide knowledge and therewith the power to realize positive changes both on the individual and social level' (p. 4). This course in crime prevention is a course to improve the feeling of agency or empowerment, a course that is well suited to The High School's 'obligation to nurture civic awareness' (The National Council, 2002, p. 1).

There is a paradox involved here. On the one hand, it seems that educational thought is spreading and tends to take charge of even more spaces in the name of the future and the enlightened cosmopolitan. The prevention of criminality, the bodily and mental health of a person, and the citizen of the future are all in the hands of pedagogy. But the learning society of this unfinished cosmopolitan has enclosures and internments. 'The theory of restorative justice contributes to the will of empowering the local community and the local influence of the individual by moving the legal system to a lower level—one is of the opinion that misconduct and wrong behaviour should be corrected in a more informal way by social control on the local level' (The National Council for Crime Prevention, 1999: 12, p. 11).

Paradox involved in the Learning Society occurs between broader tendencies of a society as a school and the tendencies to narrow the same to a question of individual commission (often expressed, for example, in terms as life-long and life-wide learning, self-regulation, and empowerment) seems to be the governmental condition in the early 21st century. But there is more to the paradox. The future citizens are both more and less active participants. Problem solving and collaboration give flexibility in learning how to appreciate the majesty of that already-given reality. Science curricula across different nations followed a similar pattern (McEneaney, 2003). The curriculum provides students with greater opportunities for participation. But this participation occurs with more and more of the world represented by the iconic images of the expertise of science. Thus, while there is greater participation of the student in the curriculum, that participation occurs in narrower areas as the expertise of science is given increasing authority.

Turn of the 20th and 21st century reforms no longer seem guided by externally validated social morals and obligations as earlier. The freedom of the empowered who lives in multiple communities is to secure change, contingency and uncertainty in daily life. The contingency is tamed through the rules and standards of 'reason' that place the problem-solving child and participation in spaces increasingly classified through the iconic expertise of science and its consecrated knowledge of the world.

The Lifelong Learners and Those Who Are Not Learning

The redemptive hopes and desires of the unfinished cosmopolitan are a double narrative that expresses the fears of the individual who will prevent and destroy that future and its notions of the civilized. The affirmations about an inclusive society are simultaneously narratives of moral disintegration and apprehension about those who will bring down the walls of civilization. The dangers are, for example, of the child not adequately prepared to live in the global world while still maintaining a collective national identity. The fears, however, do not appear as such. They are often expressed in terms of inclusion and questions of equity, to reach out to those at risk of falling behind or not catching up—immigrants, ethnic, and racial groups who have not succeeded and who are marginalized. Fears about the psychological decay and social psychological conditions that produced the decay are part of the policy and research about the 'sanctity' of the traditional family and its norms of the home and childhood. These fears are rarely talked explicitly through categories of race, gender or class but are established through categories of difference in policy and research such as the single parent, and the teenage mother, or the at-risk child.

In the Swedish context, the fear of the crime prevention is the prisoner who does not become a member of the Learning Society. The redemption of the criminal is to embrace the cosmopolitan mode of living as 'a lifelong learner'. The fear of the criminal seems less in what crime was committed, than in reclaiming one's self through the redemptive treks of lifelong learning. This requires a correctional system that deals with the intimate social and psychological relations of the criminal being reclaimed. Programs are composed of 'offering the prisoners possibilities to life-long learning as close as possible to their own settings and with the possibilities of online learning support wherever it is possible' (Sjöberg & Roitto, 2001, p. 10).

Most crime prevention investments do not target the criminal but young prospective offenders. The logic is clear: the child and the youth have to be rescued before they enter the gateways to the prison, since the prison does not provide the rescuing 'skills' in the same effective way as it provides skills for a further criminal career. The potential criminal limits the possibility of learning to become a proper citizen. The potential criminal, the criminals, and the recidivists share common psychological and social family backgrounds in terms of low education, drug abuse, unemployment and so forth. The same characteristics appear when it comes to the question of identifying those who are able to learn or not in the context of restorative justice. The offender and the at-risk offenders are offered a chance to be rescued and included and integrated into the community, and to be educated into a civic manner, but if he/she does not accept the offer, the other side of the coin is obvious: that is exclusion.

The anxiety of Public Health is about citizens only grasping a partial understanding of what life-long learning is and refusing to learn that health is not only about health. The anxiety is not directed to the sick but towards where the autonomous subject egotistically does not take responsibility for his community by quitting smoking or drinking. Each are seen as unhealthy moral dispositions that overlap with a physical degeneration that has an impact on others as well as one's self. The healthy citizen feels and acts with responsibility for their immediate and broader community as a personal obligation for the future and the society as a whole.

On a more general level we can say that the anxieties of both crime prevention and the health field are twofold. On the one hand, to paraphrase Rose (1993), it is about the fear of governing too much, which is not, in the name of liberal way of ruling, the proper way of designing, empowering and ordering the autonomous cosmopolitan modes of living. On the other hand it is also about the fear of governing too little, which is the fear of not making a success of preparing and ordering all individuals and groups (not yet included) into the society in the name of learning, agency and community-participating. These double-edged styles of governing do not always operate in opposition to each other, but rather in a cross-fertilizing manner.

The fears of social disintegration, the loss of civilization, and moral degeneration are not only about the probability of rescue and redemption. The individual who is not the unfinished cosmopolitan is distinct human kinds that demand programs to govern the processes of exclusion in the move to create an inclusive society. This is one way to read educational research and reform proposals that speak of redressing the inequities of education as the need for *all* children to learn, for all children to be lifelong learners with No Child (is) Left Behind, the title of US legislation in 2001. The phrases 'that all children learn' and 'that no child is left behind' express concerns and general commitments for redressing situations of poverty and discrimination. But the general hope and commitments also embody the fears of the society. Special theories and programs are constructed to make the excluded into unfinished cosmopolitans (see Popkewitz, 1998). The social practices about exclusion embody recognition of cultural and social distinctions about deviance and difference. The clarion call for reform is not only a call to meet future economic progress but is also a call about the threats of moral and cultural disorganization.

A continuum of values is evoked through phrases about programs to ensure that all children learn. The phrase 'all children' provides determinate categories and distinctions about a particular 'child' who does not fit into the maps of 'all children'. It is the child, but also the future adult, who does not choose, chases desire, and becomes a lifelong learner. The children who are included in the distinctions given to the category of 'all children' have particular characteristics. The characteristics of children who are not included in the distinctions given to the category of the child is one 'who live[s] in poverty, students who are not native speakers of English, students with disabilities, females, and many nonwhite students [who] have traditionally been far more likely than their counterparts in other demographic groups to be victims of low expectations' (National Council of Teachers of Mathematics, 2000, p. 13).

This Other child is to be rescued through finer and finer distinctions that order and classify the wayward child; the child is one who has not yet the 'problem-solving skills' and is not a flexible learner. The child who does not 'fit' in the map of the 'all children' is the child who lacks self-esteem, who has a poor self-concept, and scarcity of skills, and does not embrace 'problem solving', collaboration, and a life of continuous innovation and choice that mark the autonomous, unfinished cosmopolitan.

The fears of moral disintegration and social instability projected into psychological qualities of learning, problem solving and self-esteem overlapped with social narratives about the moral disintegration of the community, family and environment. The latter are single parents and teenage mothers, and 'recidivists'. The determinate categories of this human kind relate to other distinctions that function as both symbols of deviance and targets of rescue, such as low income, lack of books in the home, unemployment, drug abuse (see, e.g. Popkewitz, 1998; Lindblad & Popkewitz, 2004).

The inscriptions come together as an assemblage of characteristics to produce a determinate classification that performs in criminal prevention, schooling, and health education, with some variation on a theme of the categories in the two countries about who is left behind. This latter human kind, in comparison to the lifelong learner, has qualities and characteristics of the child who needs remediation. Difference is discursively made into characteristics of deviance! While programs are to rescue that particular human kind through better management and self-management, the human kind is one that is in perpetual preparation but never achieves the norms of 'the average'.

The Art of Governance in the Name of Cosmopolitan Learning Society

Knowledge, we have argued, is not epiphenomenal but is itself part of the productive qualities of the world. This concern with the making of 'reason' and 'the reasonable person' in the Learning Society today stands as an embodiment of the cosmopolitan who is civilized and progressive. We have sought to diagnose cosmopolitanism as a cultural thesis in generating principles governing who the individual is and should be in the Learning Society. Our focus on cosmopolitanism is to historicize its present as a phenomenon transmogrified from the northern European Enlightenment. Its narratives are about individuals whose lives are ordered through principles of rationality, progress and of a universal reason.

What is 'new' in the present is the particular amalgamation of cultural practices that fabricate 'the social' and individuality. Our relating 'society' and 'learner' in the Learning Society focuses on the cultural practices that generate principles about who 'we' are, should be, and who is not that 'we'. This context of governing we spoke about in the designing of the unfinished cosmopolitanism as embodying an individuality of never-ending changes where choice and lifelong learning are the only things that are certain. This autonomous cosmopolitan subject has a double responsibility. There is responsibility for one's own life-style and for creating an environment, supportive for learning and for the security and health of everybody, including one's self. But those images and narratives of the social and the individual are also divisions that place some as outside its cultural mapping: uncivilized, barbaric and outside the pale of humanness.

The qualities of the unfinished cosmopolitan circulating in Sweden and the US produce a pedagogical world where the governing principles of the child are morphologically related to multiple arenas of social life. Dispositions for a personal commitment to the unfinished cosmopolitan in family life and participation in volunteer organizations are significant parts of the new ordering of hope and fear in Public Health policy, new pedagogies of the school, and crime prevention. While Swedish reformations of Criminal Justice and Public Health and US schooling are bearers of their own specific traditions and terms of opportunity, they have morphological relations in the ordering of the objects of reflection and action.

One might say, as do many of the authors of the texts examined here who embrace the idea of a Learning Society, that this new individuality brings to fruition the realization of the goals of the Enlightenment. Our discussion should put this normative and utopian claim about this unfinished cosmopolitanism to rest. It is not only about empowerment and the future. There are internments and enclosures that continually need diagnoses that historicize the 'commonsense.' The Learning Society is a governing practice and an effect of power. Its pedagogical individuality circulates to order, differentiate and divide who is and who is not the 'reasonable' cosmopolitan.

Our focusing on the Learning Society and the lifelong learner within a broader historical context of cosmopolitanism is to focus on the changing enablements, enclosures, and internments of the present. This historicity in contemporary analyses of policy and the problem of changes provides an alternative to policy studies that view the changes in individuality as part of a global example of neo-liberalism. The difficulty of such Neoliberal arguments is that they take a contemporaneous framework of national and international policy about privatization and marketization as the categories of analysis, thus reinserting and conserving the existing framework of reasoning as its foundation of critiques. It is as though the lifelong learning or the unfinished cosmopolitan miraculously appears with the Chicago economists in the 1950s, and brought into the political projects of Reagan, Thatcher and world agencies such as the World Bank. By focusing on the broader concept of the unfinished cosmopolitan, our intent is to historically explore how it is possible that the Learning Society, the individual as a lifelong learner, and more broadly the policy sciences 'think' about change and choice, and human interests. The notion of governmentality provides a strategy to historicize this present.

Notes

1. These different policies are interesting in themselves, as education is an official prerogative of the nation and not of the European Union, but concerns about European identity are placed within labour policy. See the discussion in Nóvoa and Lawn, 2002.
2. Recent scholarship has pointed to the different notions of the Enlightenment, differentiating it in the fields of cultural and political practices in Britain, France, and the United States, for example. It is this historical differentiation that Foucault (1984) made indirectly when he talks about the *attitude* of the Enlightenment versus the doctrine of modernity.
3. Foucault and political reason is discussed in, for example, Barry, Osborne & Rose, 1996; Hultqvist & Dahlberg, 2001; Popkewitz, 1991, 1998; Popkewitz & Brennan, 1998; and Popkewitz, Franklin & Pereyra, 2001.
4. We use 'fabricate' to focus on a double quality of 'thought' that construes and constructs.
5. The power of the normative images of the cosmopolitan can be seen in the Soviets' incorporation of the slogans of the French Revolution of equality, liberty, and fraternity as a step towards the fulfilment of a communist society.
6. It is embodied in the work of Adam Smith, Karl Marx, the Fabians, Durkheim, among others. This is not to say that an image of the individual as a cosmopolitan miraculously appears in the Enlightenment or that there were not multiple cosmopolitanisms (see, e.g. Breckenridge *et al.*, 2002). Rather, the long 19th century is a point of entrance. The national projects, the secularization, individualization, and imposition of science in the ordering of reason make this a convenient starting point in our discussion.

7. Our argument about agency here and later is its inscription in social and educational practices as a governing mechanism. Our discussion is historical and not normative about its goodness or badness.

8. The title is borrowed from Lena Fejan Ljunghill's article in *Pedagogiska Magasinet* (The Journal of Education), published by the Union of Teachers, no. 1, 1996, p. 6.

9. Ibid., p. 7.

10. The same trend is evident in the reforms of Swedish teacher education.

11. Mathematics education as a governing practice is more fully discussed in Popkewitz, 2004.

12. There are differences in this notion of design in the Counter-Reformation, Counter-Enlightenment, although one can also point to a particular globalization occurring in relation to discourses of Learning Societies and the lifelong learner. We can only point here to some general diagnostics while recognizing there are different patterns and assemblies as well as counter discourses. In a different context, we have talked about this through exploring the multiple modernities constructed in the 20ᵗʰ century (Popkewitz, 2005). Also see Simola, Johannesson & Lindblad, 2002; Nóvoa & Lawn, 2002 and Tuschling & Engemann (in this issue) for discussions of lifelong learning in Europe. Thus, while our documentation is related to Sweden and the US, we do not think that we are examining only local phenomenon.

References

Barry, A., Osborne, T. & Rose, N. (1996) *Foucault and Political Reason. Liberalism, neo-liberalism and rationalities of government* (Chicago, IL, The University of Chicago Press).

Beck, U. (2000) The Cosmopolitan Perspective: Sociology of the second age of modernity, *British Journal of Sociology*, 51:1, pp. 79–105.

Breckenridge, C., Pollock, S., Bhabha, H. & Chakrabarty, D. (eds) (2002) *Cosmopolitanism* (Durham, NC, Duke University Press).

Bush, G. W. (2001) *No Child Left Behind* (Washington, DC, Department of Education, US Government Printing Office).

Castells, M. (2000) Materials for an Exploratory Theory of the Network Society, *British Journal of Sociology*, 51:1, pp. 5–24.

Cobb, P. (1994) Where is the Mind? Constructivist and sociocultural perspectives on mathematical development, *Educational Researcher*, 23:7, pp. 13–20.

Dalin, P. (1994) *Utbildning för ett nytt århundrade. Bok 1.* (Stockholm, Liber).

Foucault, M. (1991) Governmentality, in: G. Burchell, C. Gordon and P. Miller (eds), *The Foucault Effect: Studies in governmentality* (Chicago, IL, University of Chicago Press).

Foucault, M. (1984) What is Enlightenment? in: Paul Rabinow (ed.). *The Foucault Reader* (New York, Pantheon Books) pp. 32–50.

Hargreaves, A. (2003) *Teaching in the Knowledge Society, Education in the age of insecurity* (Maidenhead, Open University Press).

Hultqvist, K. & Dahlberg, G. (eds) (2001) *The Changing Child in a Changing World: Current ways of thinking and practicing childhood* (New York, Routledge Falmer).

Hultqvist, K. & Petersson, K. (2000) Iscensättningen av samhället som skola. I Pedagogik en: Jens Bjerg (ed.), *Grundbok*, (Stockholm, Liber).

Hultqvist, K. (2004) The Travelling State, the Nation and the Subject of Education, in: B. Baker & K. Heyning (eds), *The Uses of Foucault in the Study of Education*, (New York, Peter Lang).

Kant, E. (1784/1970) Idea for a Universal History with a Cosmopolitan Purpose, in: *Kant's Political Writing*, H. Reiss (ed.) H. B. Nisbet (trans.) (Cambridge, Cambridge University Press).

Ljunghill, L. F. (1996) The Future is Here and Now—What Are We Waiting For! *Pedagogiska magasinet*, 1:1, pp. 6–7 (Stockholm, Lärarförbundet).

Lindblad, S. & Popkewitz, T. (eds) (2004) *Educational Restructuring (International Perspectives on Traveling Policies)* (Greenwich, CT, Information Age Publishing).

Maeroff, G. (2003) *A Classroom of One: How online learning is changing our schools and colleges* (New York, Palgrave Macmillan).

McEneaney, E. (2003). Elements of a Contemporary Primary School Science, in: G. S. Drori, J. W. Meyer, F. O. Ramirez & E. Schofer (eds), *Science in the Modern World Polity: Institutionalization and globalization* (Stanford, CA, Stanford University Press) pp. 136–154.

Meyer, J. W. (1986). Myths of Socialization and of Personality, in: M. S. Thomas, C. Heller and David E. Wellbery (eds), *Reconstructing Individualism: Autonomy, individuality, and the self in Western thought* (Stanford, CA, Stanford University Press) pp. 208–221.

Meyer, J., J. Boli, G. Thomas, and F. Ramirez (1997) World Society and the Nation-State, *American Journal of Sociology*, 103: 1, pp. 144–181.

Nóvoa, A. & Lawn, M. (2002) *Fabricating Europe: The formation of an education space* (Dordrecht, Kluwer Academic Publishers).

Petersson, K., Olsson, U. Hultqvist, K. & Popkewitz, T. (2004) *Reframing Educational Thought, Subjects and Technologies of the Future in the Early 2000's*. Paper given at The European Conference on Educational Research, Crete.

Popkewitz, T. (1991) *A Political Sociology of Educational Reform: Power/knowledge in teaching, teacher education, and research* (New York, Teachers College Press).

Popkewitz, T. (1998) *Struggling for the Soul: The politics of education and the construction of the teacher*, (New York, Teachers College Press).

Popkewitz, T. (2004) The Alchemy of the Mathematics Curriculum: Inscriptions and the fabrication of the child, *American Educational Research Journal*, 41:4, pp. 3–34.

Popkewitz, T. (2005). *Inventing the Modern Self and John Dewey: Modernities and the traveling of pragmatism in education* (New York, PalgraveMacmillan).

Popkewitz, T. & Brennan, M. (eds) (1998) *Foucault's Challenge: Discourse, knowledge, and power in education* (New York, Teachers College Press).

Popkewitz, T., Franklin, B. & Pereyra, M. (eds) (2001) *Cultural History and Critical Studies of Education: Critical essays on knowledge and schooling* (New York, Routledge).

Reuben, J. (1996) *The Making of the Modern University: Intellectual transformations and the marginalization of morality* (Chicago, IL, The University of Chicago Press).

Rockefeller, S. (1991) *John Dewey: Religious faith and democratic humanism* (New York, Columbia University Press).

Rose, N. (1993) Government, Authority and Expertise in Advanced Liberalism, *Economy and Society*, 22:3, pp. 283–99.

Schiller, D. P. & Walberg, H. (1982) Japan: The learning society, *Educational Leadership*, 39:6, pp. 411–414.

Simola, H., Johannesson, I. A. & Lindblad, S. (eds) (2002) Changing Education Governance in Nordic Welfare States: Finland, Iceland and Sweden as cases of an international restructuring movement, *Special Issue of Scandinavian Journal of Educational Research*, 46:3.

Sjöberg, H. & Roitto, M. (2001) *Kriminalvårdens klientutbildning—kartläggning, problembeskrivning och förslag till åtgärder*, (Norrköping, Sweden, Kriminalvården, Kriminalvårdsstyrelsens Förlag).

Sklansky, J. (2002) *The Soul's Economy: Market society and selfhood in American thought, 1820–1920*, (Chapel Hill, NC, University of North Carolina Press).

SOU 2000:91. *Health on Equivalent Conditions—National Targets for Health*, (Stockholm, Socialdepartementet).

The Design-Based Research Collective (2003) Designed-Based Research: An emerging paradigm for educational inquiry, *Educational Researcher*, 32:2, pp. 5–8.

The National Council of Crime Prevention (1999) '*The Hjällbo Estate Security Group*', (The local Council of Crime Prevention in Hjällbo): http://www.bra.se/extra/publication/.

The National Council of Crime Prevention (2002) '*Via Wargen—a course in crime prevention in a High School*', (The Local Council of Crime Prevention in Östersund): http://www.bra.se/extra/publication/.

The National Council of Teachers of Mathematics (2000) *Principles and Standards for School Mathematics* (Reston, VA, NCTM).

The Swedish National Agency for Education (2000) *The Life-Long and Life-Wide Learning* (Stockholm).

Umbreit, M. S. (1994) *Victim Meets Offender. The impact of restorative justice and mediation* (New York, Willow Tree Press).

Wagner, P. (1994) *The Sociology of Modernity* (New York, Routledge).

3

From Education to Lifelong Learning: The emerging regime of learning in the European Union

ANNA TUSCHLING & CHRISTOPH ENGEMANN

Introduction

During the last fifteen years governmentality literature has extensively analyzed how current political programs interrelate with regimes of government and its subjects. Building upon the reassessment[1] that Michel Foucault undertook of his theory of power in the lectures given at the Collège de France in the late 1970s,[2] governmentality theory focuses on the techniques that allow the alignment of governmental interventions with self-regulative capacities of individuals, simultaneously spawning and utilizing them.

Among the authors in this field, including the late Foucault himself, it is the general consensus that the framework of relations between individuals and governments is currently undergoing a profound transition. The beginnings of this transition are located in the 1970s, with a phase of buildup in the 1980s and a general visibility in the late 1990s, especially in the social-democratic regimes of the so called 'Third Way' in Great Britain and Germany. The administrative initiatives brought forward by these ruling parties made rich use of a political rhetoric asserting a profound change in the distribution of responsibilities between state and individuals, calling for a stronger utilization of individual 'resources' for the good of the society. Especially in the realm of social welfare, new arrangements were sought where individual action is increasingly invoked to ideally foster both individual chances and collective good. The new modes of organization—frequently labeled as neoliberal—seek to relate the conduct of one's own life to the performance of the state.[3] Reflecting the notion of 'No rights without responsibilities' social rights are increasingly implemented in a reciprocal fashion. The paradox that governmentality studies highlight within these 'novel links between the *personal* and the *political*' (Rose, 2000, p. 1398), where the individual and 'its' society become ever more interwoven, is that individual freedom in handling life situations effectively grows. People are set free from the comparably rigid frameworks of the classical social welfare states, and are rather confronted with a field of incentives suggesting ways of utilizing individual skills and circumstances maximizing their own 'life-chances' while minimizing their cost to the state. This arrangement pluralizes self conduct, while simultaneously teaching hindsight to the community. In the govern-mentality literature these developments have been labeled as individualization and totalization (Gordon, 1991, p. 36).

In this paper, we argue that lifelong learning (LLL) plays a special role in implementing the outlined models of governing individuals. Lifelong learning aims at a revision of education, which in modern societies is assigned a central role among the techniques of subjectivation, currently shaping almost one third of an individual's life in a given population. In *Discipline and Punish* Foucault (1977) used the invention of schooling and education to illustrate the advent of 'discipline'. Although we agree with the critique on discipline given by Gilles Deleuze in his 'Postscript on the Societies of Control' (1990), we want to emphasize the actuality of Foucault's assertion that the analytical instruments developed in schooling institutions are important contributors in generating knowledge within and about the individual. We assume and intend to show that lifelong learning has a very similar role in the current transformation of subjectivation techniques. It is a prime venue where individuals are confronted with and have to learn to act upon new principles of conducting oneself. It is furthermore a prime venue of generating knowledge within and about individuals. We will illustrate this with the educational programs of the European Union. The focus on the EU results from two elements: (1) the EU has declared LLL as one of its most important projects, and (2) the process of Euro-pean unification is necessarily accompanied by the emergence of a refined govern-mentality, since the EU has to integrate 25 populations into one 'new' population. With the further unification of the EU it is possible to witness an emerging and evolving statehood, trying to develop intellectual technologies that allow it to con-nect with *its* people. In the Lisbon European Council Presidency Conclusion it is clearly stated: 'People are Europe's main asset and should be the focal point of the Union's Policies' (European Council, 2000).[4] Instruments of knowledge con-ceived within the context of Europe's lifelong learning are an important part of this process. We will concentrate our investigation on the reconfiguration of the individual's role in this context, but still discuss parts of extensive institutional premises involved.

Lifelong Learning in the EU

The unification of Europe is a gradual process. Political and monetary union are already achieved, but other aspects of statehood, like military and social-welfare still remain under the primary rule of the member states. Building a 'social Europe' may be one of the most complicated tasks, since the social welfare frameworks in Europe differ fundamentally and are a main source of national identity.[5] None-theless the influence of the EU in these fields is steadily growing. From 1995 on the European Union pushed for means of integrating the vastly different educa-tional frameworks of its member states. While the currently most advanced part of this development, the 1999 initiated Bologna Process, led to factual uniformization of parts of the tertiary education sector, the picture is much more heterogeneous considering schools, vocational training and learning in later life.

The outcomes of the numerous initiatives launched during the past 10 years by the European Commission are uncertain, but one can conclude that a profound unification of education among the European member states is the most unlikely result. To this date national frameworks have proven to be extremely rigid,[6] as the social partners, especially the Trade Unions, actively obstruct fundamental changes to local educational standards, because these are deeply interwoven with the definition of professions, which in turn are the bases of wage agreements. Currently a true European comparability of skills and competencies within professions threatens the Tariff-autonomy and therefore the power of Trade Unions and business alliances alike. Consequently most of the European Union's initiatives in the field of education either directly fail or are brought down to the lowest common denominator.

In the realm of social policy the European Commission shifted recently to an approach that tries to establish uniformity within diversity. The prime instrument in achieving this is the so called 'Open Method of Coordination' (OMC) formally initiated by the EU during the Lisbon Summit 2000. OMC is an implementation of a 'participative management by objectives' approach on the European level. Without going into detail—which remains to be done in a future article—the OMC basically is a process whereby the European Commission develops certain objectives and a corresponding timeframe in a specific area of (social) policy, which then become the basis for contracts with the member states.[7] By signing the contract, the particular member state agrees on achieving the contracted goals within the specified timeframe—for example reducing youth joblessness by 5% in two years. The means by which this goal is achieved usually remain free to the member state. In the second step the EU can evaluate and benchmark the performance of the member states. OMC ideally should lead to a competition for the most efficient framework of social policy between the member states, although the factual impact and importance of the systems remains contended.

Lifelong Learning is a particular prominent discourse within the attempts to change and connect the educational frameworks in Europe. Although not yet part of an OMC process, lifelong learning plays a very similar role in the educational reforms:

> Lifelong learning is an overarching strategy of European co-operation in education and training policies and for the individual. The lifelong learning approach is an essential policy strategy for the development of citizenship, social cohesion, employment and for individual fulfillment. (European Commission, 2002, p. 4)

The aim is not to directly change the national approaches to education, as in the Bologna process, but to find ways to compare and evaluate the different systems on the European metalevel. It was also the Lisbon Summit where the European Commission published its outlines on the future of education in Europe in the 'Lisbon Memorandum on Lifelong Learning' (European Commission, 2000; see also Bretschneider, 2004). Three years later the European Commission declared lifelong learning as a major strategic asset in making the European Union 'the most competitive and dynamic knowledge-based economic market of the world'

(Commission of the European Union, 2003, p. 3) by 2010. In the same year the Education and Culture Directorate-General of the EU Committee established the Regional Networks for Lifelong Learning Initiative (R3L) stating that:

> ... LLL is not seen in a holistic and strategic way, and there is not a fundamental understanding of how LLL is important for the overall regional development. The main objective of this project is therefore through inter regional co-operation and exchange of experiences, to develop policy recommendations, which will be supported by a number of good practice examples, showing examples of working methods and tools. (Commission of the European Union, 2003, p. 2)

It can be concluded that the European Union, faced with the problem of finding means of modernization and integration for the vastly different educational systems of its member states, the rapidly changing market demands on the skill sets of human-capital and concurrently the problem of maintaining the employability of its ageing populations over their whole lifespan, expresses the political will to utilize lifelong learning in order to overcome these challenges.

The New Learning Field: Informal Learning

Humanistic ideas of a free and holistic human development stemming partly from educational discourses of the 1960s and 1970s are an important contributor to the lifelong learning debate. Not solely acquiring and extending theoretical knowledge was here believed to be the primary purpose of learning and education but 'to develop one's own character, a character, that becomes reality as a result of growing experience' (Lengrand, 1972, p. 59). The scientific and technical revolution—so Edgar Faure in the first official document on modern lifelong learning, the UNESCO-report *Learning to Be—The World of Education Today and Tomorrow* has revealed the deficiency of some common training methods and made clear the strength of others: 'they have enhanced the functions of autodidactic practice and education and raised the value of active and attentive learning attitudes (Faure *et al.*, 1973, p. 41). Active learning focuses on everyday life—the work place as well as sports, home or hobbies—viewing it as an at least equally, if not more important educational setting than organized, institutionalized contexts. Respectively Faure *et al.* criticized the habit of equalizing school and education (see Faure *et al.*, 1972, pp. 140–141). And accordingly Paul Lengrand demands in his influential work on permanent education that special attention should be paid to experiential learning, or learning from experience, outside of schools (Lengrand, 1972).

In an attempt to differentiate the various contexts of learning, UNESCO invented during the early 1970s a triad of terms that is widely used until today: formal, non-formal[8] and informal education (see Gerlach, 2000, p. 53; Cropley, 1978, p. 13). Originally coined to signify knowledge acquirement in adult education, these terms eventually became applied to the whole lifespan and all educational phases, while likewise encompassing learning and not only referring to the narrower concept of education.

Generally non- and informal learning are declared as pristine modes of learning. Implicitly almost all authors share the assumption that the wish to obtain knowledge is basically inherent to (wo)man,[9] but either is being ignored or ruined by current education (see as an example of such a critique Garrick, 1998): there are the 'provinces' of informal learning that need to be colonized (see Kirchhöfer, 2003, p. 220), while the Lisbon Memorandum on Lifelong Learning states: 'Informal contexts offer a vast reservoir of learning possibilities and could be an important source of innovations in the field of teaching and learning methods' (Commission of the European Union, 2000, p. 10), the German Federal Ministry of Education speaks of a 'neglected basic form of human learning' (Dohmen, 2001) and UNESCO discovered: 'Learning: The Treasure Within' (Delors, 1996).

Nonetheless it has to be noted that there is no homogeneous use of the terms formal, non-formal, informal. Currently common usages encompass the differentiation of degrees of the formalization and institutionalization of training—this point will be discussed below—and the question to which extent learning occurs incidentally or even unintentionally. Within the institutional context of the EU informal learning has been defined in the CEDEFOP[10]-Glossary as follows:

> Informal learning is defined as learning resulting from daily life activities related to work, family or leisure. It is often referred to as experiential learning and can to a certain degree be understood as accidental learning. It is not structured in terms of learning objectives, learning time and/or learning support. Typically it does not lead to certification. Informal learning may be intentional but in most cases, it is non-intentional. (or 'incidental'/random)[11]

This disengagement of learning from organized contexts is a major factor of the so-called maximalistic view of lifelong learning. Minimalistic and maximalistic approaches have been distinguished in the discussion since early on (see Hager, 2001, p. 79; Cropely, 1979, p. 105). The minimalistic view concentrates on voluntary accessible adult education facilities and mainly demands sufficient funding for it. This is the focus of the early OECD's concept on 'recurrent education' that frequently is cited as a precursor of lifelong learning (OECD, 1973). The maximalistic view on the other hand stresses the importance of learning outside of classical educational contexts and premises, consequently concluding that learning not only has to become lifelong but also lifewide (e.g. Cropley, 1980, p. 4, see also National Agency for Education, 2000). The two dimensions—expansion over the lifespan and extension to leisure and private spare time activities—combine to form a principal boundlessness of learning in time and space. In the maximalistic approach a process of outsourcing of learning from the educational system, into the lives of the individuals takes place. Learning expands over the adult life course and across all life spheres, demanding it as a way of life.

The activities of the European Union rank among the maximalistic views, as for example expressed in the Commission Paper on lifelong learning dating to the year 2000: 'The continuum of lifelong learning puts the non-formal and informal learning in perspective' (Commission of the European Union, 2000, p. 10), moreover the Commission stresses, that the importance of non-formal learning is generally being underrated (ibid.).

The maximalistic view with its encouragement of non-formal and in-formal learning conjures a universality of learning opportunities and defines the new field in which learning takes place. The formation of this field, literally a totalization of learning, is the first important change that the politics of lifelong learning desire to achieve.

It is necessary to stress that this is not a perversion of the humanistic roots of lifelong learning by Eurocrats, but a development that is consistent with the original demands. Paul Lengrand's early and influential book, which played a major role in the creation of the debate, bears the name *Permanent Education* (1972), and six years later Arthur Cropley postulates in his book *Lifelong Education and the Training of Teachers* a 'totality of learning' (Cropley, 1978, p. 13).

Within this totality, individuals and not institutions seemingly become the centerpiece of learning, but totalization means also that every actor is potentially a learner regardless of being an individual, a group, an organization or an institution.[12] Moreover everything, including the actors in the field, becomes simultaneously potential learning content. Individuals become entities of the educational systems, multiplying it a thousand fold, each unit becoming a representative of education as a whole. The term 'System competency of the individual' (Kriz, 2000; in Höhne, 2003, p. 258) hints at this context. System competency means that the individual can translate its condition according to external demand, taking responsibility for the performance of the organizational context in which the individual acts. Conflicts should ideally reside within the individual and not become a disadvantage for the organizations (see ibid.). The relationship between the 'modernized' learners can be understood along the notion of 'distributed expertise' (Reinmann-Rothmeier & Mandl, 2000, p. 35) as a complementary one. Education as an increasingly coherent structure, where each participant is dependent on the other and only gains significance within the relation to others, was already the dream of Paul Lengrand (see Lengrand, 1972, p. 71). The structure sought here is integrative, a self-reflective technique of self-performance ideally centered in the individual. It seeks to make learning independent from setting, from personal and financial effort. Informal learning can take place regardless of circumstances: 'Every spot can be a learning spot' (Erpenbeck, 2003, p. 28). Especially media are increasingly becoming not only an instrument of transferring knowledge but becoming a space for learning itself (ibid. p. 31).

Some authors called the changes that '*éducation permanente*' and 'lifelong learning' intends, a Copernican revolution of the educational system (see Hausmann in Lengrand, 1972, p. 14). Considering that it pretends a reversal in the relation of the learner and educational institution this may be all too true. The promise expressed in the omnipresent lifelong learning slogan 'learner in the center' is to make the institutions subordinate to the learner and let them act merely as supporting units, while teaching transforms to counseling, mediating and mentoring (see Commission of the European Union, 2000, p. 17).

The diffusion of the labor market and education is one prominent example of such a totalization. It is no surprise that research on non-formal and informal learning predominantly was and still is conducted in human labor relations (see

Hager, 2001, p. 80); the pioneering studies by Victoria Marsick and Karen Watkins were conducted on training-seminars for managers in Sweden (Marsick & Watkins, 1990). Some authors speak euphorically of a 'renaissance of learning at work' (Dehnbostel, 2002, p. 37) and that work itself would be finally accredited as a medium of teaching and education (see ibid.). The borders of (vocational) training and professional life are vanishing alongside the borders between work and recreation. A boundlessness of learning that is an integral part to the flexibilization of work in post-Fordist organizations (see Kirchhöfer, 2000 and Voß, 1998), where lifelong learning takes the place of lifelong employment. Equally learning becomes mandatory in periods of unemployment, in the sense of using all opportunities for finding out how to manage oneself in changing living and working conditions. The management of the formation of one's own self, and one's performance in the labor-market are concurrent processes that are labeled as learning.

To our understanding non-formal and informal learning essentially disembogues in a rearrangement of the learning field. While the classical field of learning was formed by closed institutions, that were to be attended in the first quarter or third of the lifespan, lifelong learning declares any place and any time as suitable for learning. A development exactly fitting the predictions that Gilles Deleuze made in his 'Postscript on the Societies of Control' (1990). With the advent of what Deleuze called 'Control Societies' institutional frameworks of enclosures and molds that Foucault had described as the fundamentals of discipline would come to an end. Schools were one prominent example of the enclosing institutions of 'disciplinary societies', whose importance would vanish in favor of 'perpetual training' (Deleuze, 1990). Non-formal and informal learning are the stratagems that set this breaking of molds into place.

The New Learner: Techniques of Self-Performance

The rearrangement of the field of learning is at the same time a rearrangement of the conception of the learners. It is a reorganization of the role of the subject in the field of education, shifting from conceptualizing the learner as a passive container that is exposed to education to promoting an active individual that seeks to augment its attributes. At the center of attention is no longer the curriculum that learners have to master but their abilities to organize themselves and to perceive and use their circumstances as learning opportunities. It is within the individual that the newfound diversity of learning contexts unites: in its subjective learning ability, which simultaneously is its unique personality. A personality that now is faced with the task to become both staging area and director of acquiring knowledge—an arrangement, where learner and educator merge into the same person.

Mandate and authority for education shall no longer be exclusively bound to institutions and their agents, but partly shift to the learning individual. 'Responsibilisation' (Peters, 2001, p. 59) of the self for educational careers and outcomes ought to take place. Becoming educated is more at the disposal of the individual, a development that is two edged, providing simultaneously more freedom and more risks. More freedom since more control on learning circumstances are in the hands of the individual; more risk since the responsibility for failures in learning shifts from the institutions to the learners. Lifelong learning means self-determination and self-responsibility in educational tasks, including the financial aspects, since the learner has to 'co-finance his own learning' (Commission of the European Union, 2000, p. 15).

But such an individual is currently an idealistic conception, strikingly similar to the modes of subjectivation described in the governmentality literature. The life-long learning discourse identifies a broad need to teach individuals to become autonomous learners: 'The most important change, that should be reached by this integrative educational policy approach of lifelong learning is a change of the human attitude towards learning', writes Gunther Dohmen (Dohmen, 1996; in Gerlach, 2000, p. 179). And Christiane Gerlach reassures us that lifelong learning policies face the crucial task of their 'internalization into the individual human being' (Gerlach, 2000, p. 181). A rich draft of this 'internalized educational aspir-ation' (ibid., p. 189) is given by Kirchhöfer: 'In the context of the new learning concepts the individual is not only responsible for the content, the level and the structures of his education, ... but also has to take possession of the process of acquir-ing and reproducing education via self-organization. It appoints the times, the measures, the media, the duration and is constructing its own learning arrangement. It becomes the "entrepreneur" of its education, managing its own self and herewith also the formation of itself' (Kirchhöfer, 2003, p. 222). It is the recognition and subsequent fostering of these 'subjective' factors of learning that lifelong learning marks as its center and that is praised as progressive in opposition to older educational strategies. These are accused of oppressing the wealth of the individual strategies, now merely perceived as critical resources of individuals (see Tuschling, 2004).

Individuals are neither born with such self-technologies, nor are the existing populations already equipped with them. Lifelong learning seeks to provide tools to individuals that make them able to act in the cited manner. While knowledge remains important to individuals, 'learning to learn', to reorient and even to forget, when new circumstances demand it, are the challenges that a lifelong learner has to master. Again Deleuze has very early outlined the *gestalt* of this arrangement, 'limitless postponements' (Deleuze, 1990) where not levels of acquired knowledge are the obtainable goal, but 'perpetual training' (ibid.) takes place. The frequent use of the future tense in lifelong learning concepts reveals the ideal of a technique of permanent self-performance: Self-responsible individuals learn to generate ever suitable self-concepts on the basis of what they judge as an existing demand. The ability to orientate oneself in such a manner is condensed in the second core concept of lifelong learning, the so-called 'social competencies' and 'key qualifications' (Wellhöfer, 2004; Beck, 2001): terms that point to 'basic self-organizational dis-positions' (Erpenbeck & Heyse, 1999) of being able to interpret one's own circumstances, self-directed in a way that leads to learning.

Institutional Premises of Lifelong Learning

Although lifelong learning requires a re-evaluation of educational institutions, where a need for institutional measures to foster the 'key-competencies' is generally expressed, existing educational settings are criticized as having neither enough awareness nor as providing suitable instruments for a systematic approach to generate key-competencies among individuals. Some authors seek to demonstrate the historical roots of applicable concepts. Ancestors are identified in both Ancient Greek and medieval times, respectively in the works of Plato and Augustinus (see Aspin *et al.*, 2001, p. 17). Their forgotten insights on learning are finally reasserted in lifelong learning, is the tenor here. Lengrand declares the necessity to create environments that allow the learning individual to easily relate 'concrete' and 'abstract', to fuse theoretical knowledge and individual action (see Lengrand, 1972, p. 66). Education should be conducted as closely as possible to everyday situations, to labor practices and the like, in order to let people develop their own modes of action. The currently favored models are complex, multidimensional problem-solving situations experienced in the IT-Sector. These non-formal and informal learning settings are perceived as the primary environments in which people currently acquire and use their key-competencies—work life in general is thought to be the most important contributor; a fact that is reflected in recent EU's programs that seek to assist the obtainment of key-competencies in informal learning contexts (see Overwien, 2002, p. 13).[13]

Such a reliance on settings distant from educational establishments could be understood as a campaign for the de-institutionalization and de-bureaucratization of education. Kirchhöfer argues along this notion, claiming that the concept of informal learning implicitly provides a critique of institutions since it is 'turning against over-directed and not self-organized learning through teaching in institutions' (Kirchhöfer, 2003, p. 220). A promise that was already prevalent thirty years earlier in the beginnings of the debate on lifelong learning: 'Softening the institutions' was a statement made by Faure (Faure *et al.*, 1972, p. 251). Rigidity and dominance of educational institutions were also the central points of critique brought forward by Ivan Illich in his famous book 'De-schooling Society—The concept of a democratic educational system' (Illich, 1970). But while current lifelong learning is partly rooted in the radical reform movements of the 1960s and 1970s, there is an important difference to note. The protagonists at that time didn't just expect a modernization but a revolution through the learning society. Students' leader Rudi Dutschke demanded in 1967 in an 'Interview about the Future' that a revolutionary and free society had to transform itself to a 'learning society' (see Dutschke *et al.*, 1968, p. 169).

Lifelong learning, if successful, will not mean a decomposition of schools, which will remain important contributors for primary education, e.g. basic literacy, numeracy and fact-based knowledge, but merely intends to invent new techniques of generating and using knowledge for the individual. Lifelong Learning intends no disorganization or a dismantling of national educational systems; instead a flexibilization of the given frameworks of education is sought after, not least in order to minimize the 'time-lag' between education and socio-economic developments (see Kraus, 2001, p. 117). The purpose is not to deinstitutionalize but rather to inter-institutionalize learning. Two of the three components of inter-institutionalization were already described: 1. changing the field of learning in order to totalize learning to all imaginable situations; 2. initiating a change in the self-performance of individuals so that they act as learners in all imaginable situations. With these two components the learning individual is configured as an inter-institutional entity traversing situations and institutions, obliged to strategically show knowledge and skills. Especially non-formal and informal learning have to be presented as accessible and manageable. This is the task of the third component of inter-institutionalization: the techniques that allow both individuals and institutions to inscribe, store, process and transfer actions as learning. The main activities of the European Union in this field are centered on these techniques. It is within them that lifelong learning is getting a density and becomes most palpable.

Administering Lifelong Learning

The inherent desire of lifelong learning to organize non-formal and informal learning raises an important paradox. As the term itself expresses, informal learning can only be defined in difference to organized, institutionalized schooling. The elements that lifelong learning aims to integrate, are differentiated along the 'Intensity of their Institutionalization' (Gerlach, 2000, p. 53; see also Erpenbeck, 2003, p. 29 and Overwien, 2002, p. 17). They are not characterized by their distinct qualities but mainly by their degree of formalization. If the elements of knowledge acquisition that are labeled as informal are to become commonly acknowledgeable, even certified, as intended by the EU (see Commission of the European Union, 2000, p. 9), a formalization of the alleged informal has to take place. The whole development of lifelong learning can be in fact described as a 'formalization of non-formal education and non formalization of formal education' (Straka, in press). With the latter being a result of the increased value of unconventional learning techniques in institutionalized education, where individual approaches are fostered in order to build self-assurance and key-competencies. Either formalization of the informal or informalization of the formal, both have in common that they need new modes of inscribing the state of individuals—modes of inscription that change for both individuals and institutions alike. A twofold process emerges, individuals are destined to find new ways to represent their knowledge and skills, ever uncertain whether they are or will be recognized as such, while institutions seek to build a strategic bureaucracy able to foster, interface and process ever changing demands on individual skills.

The development in the European Union is complex partly due to reliance on competition in concept creation between member states and other actors. No common solution has yet been established; instead research on statistical tools, assessment methods and qualification schemes is underway in numerous pilot projects, as well as in the analysis of the educational frameworks of the different member states. The consolidation of the efforts into a European framework for transparency of qualifications and competences is currently projected for the year 2010 (ENSR, 2003, p. 17). Formally acquired education increasingly is recognizable among all EU member states, whereas the development of measures that may lead to the recognition of informal and non-formally acquired knowledge are a main focus of the EU since the year 2000: 'Gradually, validation of non-formal and informal learning is becoming a key aspect of lifelong learning policies' (Colardyn & Bjornavold, 2004, p. 69). Here the creation of indicators that allow statistical assessment of non-formal and informal learning is one of the most controversial topics (see Straka, in press; Eurostat, 2001; and Hoerner, 2002, p. 67f.). Since the EU follows the maximalistic approach to lifelong learning, methods that reach well beyond the limits of the educational system are a necessity. Besides attempts to mine available statistics[14] for fitting data, a broad consensus exists that the individual level needs to be assessed more profoundly. The Statistical Office of European Communities 'Eurostat' has established a 'Task Force on Measuring Lifelong Learning' (TFMLLL) which stated in its recommendations issued in 2001:

> The best source of information on LLL seems to be the individual (rather than education/training providers). ... (European Commission, 2002, p. 15).

As a first measure the quarterly conducted European Labor Force Survey[15] was extended with accordant 'ad hoc modules' for lifelong learning in 2003 and 2004.[16] The same holds true for the forthcoming European Survey on Income and Living Conditions (EU-SILC), which will include indicators tailored specially to assess lifelong learning, asking participants to identify themselves their abilities. For a more comprehensive and in-depth investigation on lifelong learning a multiyear and pan-European European Adult Learning Survey' (EU-AES) is to be conducted by Eurostat and national statistical offices from 2005 on. The EU-AES will have a crucial role in building the dataset and formulation of future recommendations for lifelong learning policy in Europe and will ask participants to self-report skills and knowledge. A 2001 proposal for the EU-AES issued by Eurostat clearly expresses the necessity for a totalizing approach in data collection for lifelong learning:

> This notion of (lifelong) learning also encompasses *the entire population* independent of age and independent of their labor market status. It includes in principle all kinds of activities ranging from early childhood education to leisure education for retired persons. The terms 'knowledge, skills and competence' are not limited to work related outcomes of education and learning but also to societal and personal outcomes (...). There is a general agreement that system based information is not enough in a knowledge economy and society. The data we get from educational institutions refer only to participants and focus on formal (or else 'regular') learning. Today we need information also on *non participants*, that is potential learners. Also for those who learn we want to know to what extent they are involved in *non-formal education and informal learning*. If people do not participate we need to know why, so as to increase their participation in learning and thus their potential to improve their condition in the knowledge society. The learning environment is constantly changing. As it was mentioned above we need to focus on the learner. System-based data should be complemented/enriched by learner-centered data (...). (Eurostat, 2001, pp. 8–9, emphasis in original)

Besides the outspoken intention to use the knowledge generated here in order to 'increase' the 'participation' of potential learners for supposedly their own good, we want to stress that the statistical assessment of lifelong learning: 1. calls for a inclusion of the individual level in an unprecedented amount, 2. relies highly on the active input by self-reporting of the individuals.

This also holds true for a parallel development of new accreditation-regimes that allow the reorganization of skills acquired outside of educational settings. Several member states already have working programs that are frequently referred to as viable examples. In France individuals can obtain the 'Bilan de Competences' and the 'Certificat d'aptitude professionnelle', state recognized documents showing skills and achievements of individuals. Great Britain, lacking a comprehensive vocational training system, has established a highly successful program called 'Accreditation of Prior Learning' (APL) since the early 1990s. Switzerland, although not a member of the EU, has the 'Schweizer Qualifikationshandbuch' (CH-Q[17]), that alongside the French example is discussed as an outstanding solution. All three systems combine an assessment-center-like exam of acquired knowledge with tools for the self-reporting of skills. The Swiss CH-Q provides the most comprehensive instruments in this respect, allowing the individual to conduct a lifetime collection of data and documents in a partly pre-structured file.

The European Union itself has established the 'Europass'[18] program in 1999, originally aiming for a pan-European accreditation instrument for job-based trainings and internships. Acceptance and value of the document in commerce and public is currently comparably low. Nonetheless, for the following years the European Union has pursued the goal of making the Europass the user-side part of a 'single framework for the transparency of qualifications and competences'. The corresponding proposal[19] is close to becoming official and determines the inclusion of vocational certificates, higher education diplomas and certificates of transnational mobility, internship records, as well as the European CV[20] and the European Language Portfolio (ELP)[21] into the new Europass. The latter two are structured self-assessment tools for writing Curriculum Vitae and document language skills that initially were developed by separate European institutions. The European CV contains an elaborate self-description of personal skills, ranging from social skills, which include 'living and working with other people (...) for example culture and sports, multicultural environments' (ibid., p. 27), to organizational skills acquired 'at work, in voluntary work (...) and at home etc.' (ibid.), to artistic skills and competences: 'music, writing, design etc.' (ibid.) and asks the applicant to 'describe these competencies and indicate where they were acquired' (ibid.).

The Diploma Supplement of the Europass will include the ECTS credit scheme established with the Bologna process, positioning it to become a key instrument in the pan-European mobility between universities. The Europass framework is also open to the voluntary inclusion of further documents by member states, such as profession specific 'skill-passports' (ibid., p. 7). Finally the Europass is projected to be available in an electronic form (ibid., p. 39), storing all data digitally, eventually allowing access and editing through the Internet. The implementation of the Europass as a Smart Card, tailored to interact with other Electronic Government processes is also being discussed. Here a pan-European interoperability is explicitly required:

> All Europass documents issued by authorized bodies are completed in electronic form and made available for retrieval—by their holders only[22]— throughout Europe. (...) The parts of the Europass information system managed at national level in different countries should be fully interoperable with each other and with the parts managed at European level. (ibid.)

Still, this part of the proposal merely outlines the prospects of such a system, while carefully avoiding touching on the delicate problems of national sovereignty concerning the management of individual data and educational policy. But it contains far-reaching consequences with hindsight to the development of a human resource management on the European level, because within this data, which are generated separately from statistical panels, comparability and therefore the possibility of evaluation and benchmarking is given. Within these datasets, fed by individuals in their own interests, a representation of a European population could arise, that is of strategic value for the EU policy makers. It is this knowledge of its people that is to become an asset for the EU, making 'government at a distance' possible. With this knowledge standards can be established that will influence learning opportunities and outcomes for the European population, despite vastly different settings throughout the EU in which its learning takes place.

It nevertheless has to be noted, that with hindsight to our assessment of earlier attempts of the EU to unify the different learning cultures of its member states given in the introduction of this text, the obstacles to success of this system are very high. Europass is the current political attempt to overcome these obstacles.

Our account of developing instruments of knowledge-generation in respect to lifelong learning in the European Union is far from exhaustive, but we intend to show that the individual is assigned a critical role in the whole process. In preceding educational organizations knowledge about the individual was predominantly generated outside and handled separately from the individual. The arrangement of lifelong learning in contrast seeks to animate the individuals to take a crucial part in the generation of knowledge of themselves. It furthermore builds conditions in which the individuals need to struggle to present their knowledge of themselves, making visible their capabilities. For the individuals the core challenge of lifelong learning is the internalization of the 'knowledge of the individual' into themselves, while simultaneously they need to tactically externalize it in order to make it recognizable. Reorienting oneself as a learner in almost every conceivable situation is not sufficient; the self performance of the new learner includes making one's efforts visible and recognizable. This translates into a new regime of documentation of oneself. While in the disciplines described by Foucault the individual was the object of documentary power exercised by institutions like the school (Foucault, 1977, p. 188), in lifelong learning the individual becomes the subject of its own documentation. One has to format one's situation in a form that is presentable. Official certificates of acquired knowledge need to be accompanied by comprehensive accounts of individual achievements. Portfolios of accumulated skills have to be generated.

A curriculum vitae is a basic part of such a self-representation, while on a more sophisticated level individual websites and web logs enable individuals to deliver near real-time assessments of individual situation awareness and judgment. Not merely institutions alone but the individuals are tasked to organize their situation, rendering it to an analytical space (Foucault, 1977, p. 143) by themselves, documenting that they are able to eliminate confusion (Foucault, 1977, p. 145). In conclusion this means that the individuals themselves are increasingly responsible for formalizing learning, especially when it occurred 'incidentally' or 'accidentally' or outside of defined institutional premises. The subject itself has to formalize the non-formal and informal by self-reporting skills and by self-describing its own condition. Self-assessment and concurrent self-profiling is the relationship one ought to have to oneself in a society of lifelong learning. Furthermore a limitless effort of translation arises, because with each new set of requirements encountered, one is obliged to name and communicate individual capacities accordingly. Factual knowledge and the competence to coin one's own condition as skills might become equally important, since only knowledge and skills made visible and communicable can be turned into an advantage. While 'in discipline, it is the subjects who have to be seen' (Foucault, 1977, p. 187), in this arrangement the individuals are urged to develop the wish to be seen. It is no longer the architecture of the enclosing institutions which exposes the individual to the gaze of power as described by Foucault (ibid.); the individual tries to attract the gaze in an open field of competitors, where everybody simultaneously tries to present him/her self as ideal for a given task. The first step in this development is that the individuals themselves contribute the critical data necessary to erect the 'regulated transparency' (Drummond, 2003, p. 59) that allows control in such systems. Inscribing oneself is the first sign of taking responsibility and the necessary precondition for later accountability. In their own interest, to gain recognition and advantages, the individuals have to become secretaries of their own being, diligently having to document their life-course. In the same time they are burdened with the decision to balance what to cover and what not, never sure what turns out to be a disadvantage and what not. In lifelong learning the individual becomes simultaneously subject and object alike of his/her learning documentation. These documents are a crucial part of the self-performance of lifelong learners, as they give evidence of the synthesizing abilities of the individual, ideally representing its learning abilities and unique personality in an accessible format.

This change in the mode of inscription of individuality is part of the bigger shift in responsibility from institutions to the individuals. While in the age of education the institutions had responsibility for providing circumstances for the learning of the individuals, in the age of lifelong learning the individuals increasingly have to present their circumstances as learning environments. The institutions do not primarily produce education anymore *ad loco*, they rather certify that learning has or has not taken place, regardless of the position in time and space that the individual occupied. The lifelong learning literature (see Bjornavold, 2000, p. 58) discusses this as the shift from input oriented to output- and efficiency oriented education.

While primary education is and will still be state provided—although to what extent may differ between nations—state subsidized secondary and tertiary education is comparably less laden with thoroughly pre-defined learning goals and forms—which at least were part of the right to be educated—but with assessments that oblige individuals to communicate the own status as learning. The final step of this process would be to detach the interfaces for documenting the own 'progress' from physical institutions that individuals have to visit, to interfaces that travel with the individuals and allow connection anytime, anywhere. The new field of learning and the individual as a learner as we described above become both reality and manageable with such a system. To designate events as learning anywhere and anytime presupposes tools at the disposal of the individual that allow him/her to label them as such. The closer in space and time that methods of inscription and storage are to the individual, the more likely is the chance that such a process of designation happens. The Europass proposals for a framework for transparency of qualifications and competences already contain the basic elements for such a system.

Conclusions

It might be too early to speak about an age of lifelong learning in contrast to an age of education, whose end we probably witness currently. However, our descriptions of the endeavors underway in the European Union were intended to outline critical features of the ongoing process of implementing lifelong learning. On the one hand we wanted to stress that this is a field where the EU increasingly gains leverage over its diverse people, having both instruments that affect whole populations, as well as establishing circuits at the individual level. On the other hand we wanted to show that within the arsenal of social technologies currently conceived by nation-states, lifelong learning promises to become one of the most universal tools. While other transitions in the life course where individuals link up to state entities, like joblessness or sickness, are comparatively temporal conditions, lifelong learning encompasses by definition the whole life. Furthermore learning is not a condition that has to be overcome; it is an activity that has to be conducted endlessly. The individual has to prepare for this: 'Learning to learn' is both an offer and an order to develop motivation and ability to do so. Among the 'strategies where the state enables rather than provides' (Edwards, 2004, p. 69) this is where the 'enabling' is practiced, starting in the kindergarten, overarching the whole life and extending—at least in the vision of some officials of the EU—well into retirement. While it seeks partially to overcome school, lifelong learning aims at rendering nothing less than the whole society into an omnipresent classroom where one is given the task to develop the 'responsibilized' self suitable for modern welfare regimes.

Notes

1. Overviews are given in *The Foucault Effect, Studies in Governmentality* edited by Graham Burchell, Colin Gordon and Peter Miller, as well as by Thomas Lemke in *Eine Kritik der politischen Vernunft, Foucaults Analyse der modernen Gouvernementalität*.
2. Between 1977 and 1979 Foucault's lectures were centered on the notion of governmentality. Parts of these lectures were gradually published during the 1990s (see e.g. Burchell,

1991) and have been completely available in French and German since 2004 (Foucault, 2004).

3. The theoretical framework built by Foucault originally for analyzing the state has been applied to other organizational entities like businesses as well, see for example Bröckling, 2000.

4. HTML-Document can be accessed here: http://europa.eu.int/european_council/conclusions/index_en.htm

5. For an introduction see the book by Gosta Esping Andersen *The Three Worlds of Welfare Capitalism* (1989).

6. This is also, but exclusively, the effect of the political compromise among the founders of the European Communities. Article 150 of the Treaty of Amsterdam (1997) explicitly states that the responsibility for content and organization of vocational training lies with the member states. See: http://europa.eu.int/eur-lex/en/treaties/dat/amsterdam.html#0145010077

7. OMC Processes have been initiated for social insurance, health care and labor market regulation.

8. The Term 'non-formal-education' was already coined in 1947 by the UNESCO in a report on education in the third-world: 'Fundamental Education: Common Ground for All People'.

9. The influential German neuroscientist Gerhard Roth even speaks of a 'natural will to learn' (*Weser Kurier* 14 September 2004).

10. The CEDEFOP is the European Center for the development of vocational training, a major think-tank involved in the development of European strategies on education. See: http://www.cedefop.eu.int

11. Further explanations of informal learning, especially concerning the relation of informal learning to—in the sense of being an umbrella term—experiential learning, everyday learning, implicit learning etc. can be found in Günther Dohmen's extensive work (2001).

12. We will spare the discourse on learning organizations here but would like to point out that there are similarities to the discourse of lifelong learning that deserve more attention. Both share a conception of ever-learning entities in an open field.

13. Straka, G. A. (in press) *Informal Learning, Conceptual Outline, Strategic Contexts: The demanding search for the lieu, direction and results of informal learning.*

14. For example to investigate the European Time Use Survey (TUS) in order to see how much time is dedicated to activities that can be described as education and learning.

15. See: Commission Regulation (EC) No 1313/2002
http://europa.eu.int/eur-lex/pri/en/oj/dat/2002/l_192/l_19220020720en00160021.pdf

16. See: Commission Regulation (EC) No 1313/2002
http://europa.eu.int/eur-lex/pri/en/oj/dat/2002/l_192/l_19220020720en00160021.pdf

17. See: http://www.ch-q.ch/

18. The Europass was initially outlined under the name 'Personal Skills Card' in the 1995 Whitebook by the European Commission called 'Lehren und Lernen—auf dem Weg zur kognitiven Gesellschaft'. The current Europass is administered by the member states, the German version can be accessed under: http://www.europass-berufsbildung.de

19. Proposal for a Decision of the European parliament and of the council on a single framework for the transparency of qualifications and competences (Europass): <http://europa.eu.int/eur-lex/en/com/pdf/2003/com2003_0796en01.pdf>

20. The European CV can be found here: Http://www.cedefop.eu.int/transparency/cv.asp

21. See: http://culture2.coe.int/portfolio/inc.asp?L=E&M=$t/208-1-0-1/main_pages/../&L=E&M=$t/208-1-0-1/main_pages/introduction.html

22. The clause 'by their holders only' hints at a complex problem underlying the whole effort of E-Government: the problem of authentication within open electronic networks like the Internet. Authentication means that a person can undeniably prove its legal

identity and therefore the right to access, alter or transfer a certain document, e.g. certain data. While in a real-world environment this can be achieved by personal signature, legal proof of identity within the digital domain is a non-trivial task involving major juridical and technical challenges. Since proof of identity is a necessary pre-requisite for many administrative as well as commercial processes, all E-government projects center on building an authentication infrastructure for the Internet. These systems usually consist of a government-approved smartcard that enables to verify the identity of transaction-partners on the internet. See Engemann, 2003.

References

Achtenhagen, F. & Lempert, W. (eds) (2000) *Lebenslanges Lernen im Beruf—seine Grundlegung im Kindes- und Jugendalter* (Opladen, Leske + Budrich).

Andersen-Esping, G. (1990) *The Three Worlds of Welfare Capitalism* (Princeton, NJ, University Press).

Aspin, D., Chapman J., Hatton, M. & Sawano, Y. (eds) (2001) *International Handbook of Lifelong Learning* (Hingham, Kluwer).

Baumert, J. & Deutsches Pisa-Konsortium (eds) (2001) *PISA 2000. Basiskompetenzen von Schülerinnen und Schülern im internationalen Vergleich* (Opladen, Leske + Budrich).

Beck, S. (2001) *Schlüsselqualifikationen im Spannungsfeld von Bildung und Qualifikation—Leerformel oder Integrationskonzept?* (Stuttgart, Kohlhammer).

Bjornavold, J. (2000) *Glossary*, in: CEDEFOP (ed.), *Making Learning Visible* (Luxemburg/ Thessaloniki, CEDEFOP).

Bretschneider, M. (2004) *Non-formales und informelles Lernen im Spiegel bildungspolitischer Dokumente der Europäischen Union* (Bonn, http://www.die-bonn.de/esprid/dokumente/doc-2004/ bretschneider04_01.pdf.).

Bröckling, U. (2000) Totale Mobilmachung. Menschenführung im Qualitäts- und Selbstmanagement, in: Broeckling, U., Krasmann, S. & Lemke, T. (eds), *Gouvernementalität der Gegenwart* (Frankfurt, Suhrkamp).

Burchell, G., Gordon, C. & Miller, P. (eds) (1991) *The Foucault Effect—Studies in Governmentality* (Chicago, IL, University of Chicago Press).

Dohmen, G. & Bundesministerium für Bildung und Forschung (eds) (2001) *Das informelle Lernen. Die internationale Erschließung einer bisher vernachlässigten Grundform menschlichen Lernens für das lebenslange Lernen aller* (Bonn, BMBF).

Colardyn, D. & Bjornavold, J. (2004) Validation of Formal, Non-formal and Informal Learning: policy and practices in EU Member States, *European Journal of Education*, 39:1, pp. 69–89.

Cropley, A. J. & Dave, R. H. (1978) *Lifelong Education and the Training of Teachers* (Oxford, Pergamon Press).

Cropley, A. J. (ed.) (1979) *Lifelong Education: A stocktaking* (Hamburg, UNESCO Institute for Education).

Cropley, A. J. (ed.) (1980) *Towards a System of Lifelong Education. Some Practical Considerations* (Oxford, Pergamon Press).

Dehnbostel, P. (2002) Modelle arbeitsbezogenen Lernens und Ansätze zur Integration formellen und informellen Lernens, in: Rohs, M. (Ed.), *Arbeitsprozessintegriertes Lernen. Neue Ansätze in der beruflichen Bildung* (Münster, Waxmann).

Deleuze, G. [1990] (1992) Postscript on the Societies of Control, *October*, 59, pp. 3–7 (first published in *L'Autre Journal*, no. 1, May 1990).

Delors, J. (1996) *Learning: The Treasure within* (Paris, UNESCO).

Döring, K. W. & Ritter-Mamczek, B. (1999) *Weiterbildung im lernenden System* (Weinheim, Beltz).

Drummond, J. (2003) Care of the Self in a Knowledge Economy: Higher education, vocation and the ethics of Michel Foucault, *Educational Philosophy and Theory*, 35:1, pp. 58–69.

Dutschke, R., Rabehl, B. & Semler, C. (1968) Ein Gespräch über die Zukunft, *Kursbuch*, 14:8, pp. 146–174.

Edwards, R. (2004) Intellectual Technologies in the Fashioning of Learning Societies, *Educational Philosophy and Theory*, 36:1, pp. 69–78.

Engemann, C. (2003) *Electronic Government. Vom User zum Buerger* (Bielefeld, Transcript).

European Network for SME Research (ENSR) (ed.) (2003) *Competence Development in SMEs* (Brussels, Observatory of European SMEs).

Erpenbeck, J. & Heyse, V. (1999) *Kompetenzbiographie—Kompetenzmilieu—Kompetenztransfer*, in: QUEM-report. Schriften zur beruflichen Weiterbildung 62. (Berlin, Arbeitsgemeinschaft Betriebliche Weiterbildungsforschung).

Erpenbeck, J. (2003) Modelle und Konzepte zur Erfassung non-formell und informell erworbener beruflicher Kompetenzen in Deutschland, in: G. A. Straka, (ed.), *Zertifizierung non-formell und informell erworbener beruflicher Kompetenzen* (Münster, Waxmann).

European Commission (2003) *A Memorandum on Lifelong Learning* (http://www.bologna-berlin2003.de/pdf/MemorandumEng.pdf.).

European Commission (2003) *Compendium European Networks To Promote the Local and Regional Dimension of Lifelong Learning (The 'R3L' Initiative)* (Brussels).

European Commission (2002) *14th CEIES Seminar Measuring Lifelong Learning* (Luxembourg).

European Commission (2002) *European Report on Quality Indicators of Lifelong Learning* (Brussels).

Eurostat (2001) *Document for Item 3.2 of the Agenda Statistical Programme 2003–2007*, DOC.EUROSTAT/E0/01/DSS/3/5/EN (Luxembourg).

European Council (2000) *Presidency Conclusion Lisbon European Council* (http://europa.eu.int/european_council/conclusions/index_en.htm).

Faure, E. *et al.* (eds) (1973) *Wie wir leben lernen. Der UNESCO-Bericht über Ziele und Zukunft unserer Erziehungsprogramme* (Reinbek bei Hamburg, Rororo).

Foucault, M. (1977) *Discipline and Punish* (New York, Pantheon).

Foucault, M. (2004) *Geschichte der Gouvernementalität*, 2 Bde. (Frankfurt, Suhrkamp).

Garrick, J. (1998) *Informal Learning in the Workplace: Unmasking human resource development* (London, Routledge).

Gerlach, C. (2000) *Lebenslanges Lernen. Konzepte und Entwicklungen 1972 bis 1997* (Köln, Boehlau).

Gordon, C. (1997) Governmental rationality: an introduction, in: G. Burchell, C. Gordon & P. Miller (eds), *The Foucault Effect—Studies in Governmentality* (Chicago, IL, University of Chicago Press).

Hager, P. (2001) *Lifelong Learning and the Contribution of Informal Learning*, in: D. Aspin, J. Chapman, M. Hatton & Y. Sawano (eds) (2001) *International Handbook of Lifelong Learning* (Hingham, Kluwer).

Höhne, T. (2003) *Pädagogik der Wissensgesellschaft* (Bielefeld, Transcript).

Howaldt, J. (2002) Lernen in Netzwerken—ein Zukunftsszenario für die Wissensgesellschaft, in: W. R. Heinz, H. Kotthoff & G. Peter (eds), *Lernen in der Wissensgesellschaft* (Münster, Lit).

Illich, I. (1973) *Entschulung der Gesellschaft. Entwurf eines demokratischen Bildungssystems* (Reinbek bei Hamburg, Rororo).

Kirchhöfer, D. (2000) *Informelles Lernen in alltäglichen Lebensführungen*, QUEM-report. Schriften zur beruflichen Weiterbildung 66. (Berlin, Arbeitsgemeinschaft Betriebliche Weiterbildungsforschung).

Kirchhöfer, D. (2003) Informelles Lernen—Legitimation für De-Institutionalisierung?, in: D. Hoffmann, K. Neumann, (eds), *Ökonomisierung der Wissenschaft. Forschen, Lehren und Lernen nach den Regeln des 'Marktes'* (Weinheim, Beltz).

Kommission der Europäischen Gemeinschaften (2003) *'Allgemeine und berufliche Bildung 2010'. Die Dringlichkeit von Reformen für den Erfolg der Lissabon-Strategie. Mitteilung der Kommission*, Brüssel, den 11.11.2003, KOM (2003) 685 endgültig (Brussels).

Kommission der Europäischen Gemeinschaften (2000) *Memorandum über Lebenslanges Lernen. Arbeitsdokument der Kommissionsdienststellen*, Brüssel, den 30.10.2000, SEK (2000) 1832 (Brussels).

Kraus, K. (2001) *Lebenslanges Lernen. Karriere einer Leitidee* (Bielefeld, W. Bertelsmann).

Lemke, T. (1997) *Eine Kritik der politischen Vernunft—Foucaults Analyse der modernen Gouvernementalität* (Hamburg/Berlin, Argument).

Lengrand, P. (1972) *Permanente Erziehung. Eine Einführung* (München, UTB).

Marsick, V. & Watkins, K. (1990) *Informal and Incidental Learning in the Workplace* (London, Routledge).

National Agency for Education (2000) *Lifelong and Lifewide Learning* (Stockholm, National Agency for Education).

Odih, P. & Knights, D. (1999) 'Discipline needs time'. Education for citizenship and financially self disciplined subject, *The School Field*, 10:3–4, pp. 127–152.

OECD/CERI (Ed.) (1973) *Recurrent Education. A Strategy for Lifelong Learning. A Clarifying Report* (Paris).

Overwien, B. (2002) Informelles Lernen und Erfahrungslernen in der internationalen Diskussion: Begriffsbestimmungen, Debatten und Forschungsansätze, in: Rohs, M. (ed.), *Arbeitsprozessintegriertes Lernen. Neue Ansätze in der beruflichen Bildung* (Münster, Waxmann).

Peters, M. (2001) Education, Enterprise Culture and the Entrepreneurial Self: A Foucauldian Perspective, *Journal of Educational Enquiry*, 2:2, pp. 58–71.

Reinmann-Rothmeier, G. & Mandl, H. (2000) Lebenslanges Lernen unter der Berücksichtigung des Themas Wissensmanagement, in: Achtenhagen, F. & Lempert, W. (Eds) (2000) *Lebenslanges Lernen im Beruf—seine Grundlegung im Kindes- und Jugendalter* (Opladen, Leske + Budrich).

Rose, N. (2000) Community, Citizenship and the Third Way, *American Behavioral Scientist*, 43:9, pp. 1395–1411.

Straka, G. A. (2005, in press) *Informal Learning, Conceptual Outline, Strategic Contexts: The demanding search for the lieu, direction and results of informal learning.*

Treaty of Amsterdam Amending the Treaty on European Union, The Treaties establishing the European Communities and related Acts 1997, http://europa.eu.int/eurlex/en/treaties/dat/amsterdam.html≠0145010077.

Tuschling, A. (2004) Lebenslanges Lernen, in: U. Bröckling, S. Krasmann & T. Lemke, (eds), *Glossar der Gegenwart* (Frankfurt, Suhrkamp).

UNESCO (1947) *Fundamental Education: Common Ground for All Peoples* (Paris, UNESCO).

Voß, G. (1998) Die Entgrenzung von Arbeit und Arbeitskraft. Eine subjektorientierte Interpretation des Wandels der Arbeit, *Mitteilungen aus dem Arbeitsmarkt- und Berufsforschung*, 31:3, pp. 473–487.

Wellhöfer, P. R. (2004) *Schlüsselqualifikation Sozialkompetenz. Theorie und Trainingsbeispiele* (Stuttgart, Lucius & Lucius).

4
Voluntary Self-Control: Education reform as a governmental strategy

LUDWIG A. PONGRATZ

1. PISA as 'Power Stabiliser'

When people in Germany first started hearing about PISA, they most probably thought of the leaning tower beloved by holidaymakers in Italy. Today, however, what PISA primarily brings to mind is the low ranking of the German education system. The current results of the international longitudinal study PISA (Programme for International Student Assessment; Deutsches PISA-Konsortium (Deutsches PISA-Konsortium, 2001) have stirred up the German education policy landscape as never before. No other empirical study of the German school system has been able to register as much public resonance. The flood of discussions, controversies and reform plans that has accompanied PISA is a reminder of earlier crisis scenarios, particularly the 'education catastrophe' that shook up German education policy in the 1960s (Picht, 1964). This crisis signaled the beginning of a profound transformation of the German education system, and its legitimate successor is today's 'PISA shock'.

But what does this shock consist of? The first, most immediate answer relates to the study's results themselves: the 'nation of poets and thinkers' seems to have been awoken from its educational half-sleep. The misleading illusion that 'Modell Deutschland' could establish itself at the top of the class in international comparison has vanished into thin air. The organiser of the PISA study is the OECD—an economic entity—that began a pilot study in 2000 with around 180,000 school pupils aged 15, in 32 countries. Already the preliminary results of this pilot study found enormous resonance in Germany, not only in professional spheres, but more broadly in the public consciousness. The results appeared to be simply staggering: in reading, mathematical and scientific literacy the performance of German school children lies below the international average. Further, the distribution of performance is particularly wide in Germany. In relation to reading literacy, this means, for example, that: in Germany the gap between the weakest 5% and the strongest 5% of readers is greater than in any other country. If one just compares the top groups, only 9% of German school students fall into that category, compared to 15% and more in other countries. Further, the results show that the differences in performance are determined more strongly by social origin in Germany than in any other country. For example, in Germany the gap between students from the upper and lower social classes is 111 points—while in Korea, Finland and Japan it is between 25 and 50 points. In other words, in other countries the school has a stronger impact on social disadvantage. This constitutes the real scandal for teachers and educational scholars: 'The German school system is comparatively very socially selective—and this despite education reform and expansion' (Terhart, 2002, p. 27).

This result is clearly cause for critical self-reflection, but it is not in itself a sufficient basis for the frantic radicalism of the resultant reform measures. It seems that something is operating through reform strategies of diverse types that has the capacity to exercise enormous pressure. This pressure functions as a strategic element within a currently active global transformation process driven by a wide variety of organisations and actors. One is led to suspect that it was not (or not only) academic interests that brought PISA to life. It is more the case that political instances (at the national level) and (at the international level) major organisations like the OECD (Organisation for Economic Cooperation and Development) put the PISA study to work within the framework of their global political agenda; one can already see that they will continue to exercise 'lasting influence on the research agenda and the implementation of the studies' (Lange, 2002, p. 461). It is thus hardly surprising, that among the global institutions (OECD, WTO, World Bank or IMF) one finds more or less the same objectives with respect to privatisation and language policies. They are: implementation of private sector management principles in the public sector, restructuring of education and research institutions according to business principles, introduction of market and management elements to all process levels. The consequences of these transformation processes can already be clearly seen in other countries.

> Even when particular results diverge in some cases—the world-wide neo-liberal restructuring of education has these three effects in every case: everywhere where it takes hold, first, the state financing of the education sector declines; second, social inequalities in relation to access to knowledge increase drastically; third, middle-class parents conclude that they would prefer it if their sons and daughters didn't share the classroom with every Tom, Dick and Harry. (Lohmann. 2002, p. 103)

Given the problematic effects of the forced restructuring of the education system, political shadowboxing between neo-liberal modernisers and welfare-state defenders of public education is not very helpful. On the contrary: the disputes create the impression that the PISA study has suffered the fate of so many reform projects: namely, being put to the service of a variety of interests which—depending on their perspective—read into the study's results what is opportune for them. However, considering the global strategies exercising their influence through the PISA study, it seems sensible to reverse this view: it is the global strategic situation that codes our perception through the PISA lens. The current process of reformation of the education system is based on implicit standards and orientations that had to have been already generally accepted before it stimulated the controversy around PISA.

All the complaints about how badly Germany has fared and all the well-intentioned reform proposals which are meant to restore Germany to 'the top', implicitly accept the disciplinary procedures set in motion by global testing, ranking and control. Rather than functioning as a 'neutral' instrument of scientific objectivity, PISA establishes its own standards of normality. All the resulting reform initiatives remain within a strategy of coordination of this power-based normalisation process, through which the disciplinary society extends its influence to the farthest corners of the education system. This applies *mutatis mutandis* to both variants of education reform currently in fashion: the conservative, 'which attempts, through more intense selection, to reinforce the three-tiered school system, promote elites and thus reinforce the legitimacy of the education system', as well as the progressive, 'which, with the help of the market and management, attempts to introduce cost-effective forms of administration' (Klausenitzer, 2002, p. 53).

Seen in this way, PISA can be seen as a nodal point in a disciplinary network, using an extensive arsenal of partly familiar, partly innovative modes of intervention. This apparatus extends from new modes of administration through budgeting, sponsoring and privatisation to certification, centralised performance control, credit-point systems, Total Quality Management, and not least, PISA. In a certain sense it remains irrelevant whether one supports the new reforms (more selection, more encouragement of elites, more performance, more competition, more control) or their philanthropic opponents (more self-organisation, more individual profiles, more (school) autonomy, more (self) responsibility, more democratic participation). In each case one can see a disciplinary strategy at work in the wake of the current educational reforms.

The PISA study and the reformist drive that it encourages indicate the central position that testing occupies within this apparatus. Tests are probably the most effective means of realising disciplinary procedures, of which the PISA study is an elaborate example on the basis of its broadly based framework. More than this: tests can be understood as the 'switching point' between strategic power relations and technologies of the self. They are the exemplary case of the governmental strategies that Foucault concentrated on, especially in his later work. Foucault's studies of governmentality pursue an analytical connection between 'techniques' and 'logics' of government.

> While government today has an exclusively political meaning, Foucault is able to show that up to the 18th century, the problem of government was framed in a more general way. Government was a topic not only in political, but also in philosophical, religious, medical, and educational texts. Beyond the control of the state or administration, 'government' also referred to the problem of self-control, the guidance of the family and children, the management of the household, the guidance of the soul, and so on. This is why Foucault defines government as conduct or, more precisely, as the 'conduct of conduct', which encompasses a continuum running from the 'government of the self' to the 'government of others'. (Lemke, 2002, p. 46)

Particularly with the rise of 'governmental states' in the 16th and 17th centuries (no longer determined by territory, but by a mass, the mass of the population) the problem of 'techniques of government' gains its own particular significance. For, in order to govern this mass, it requires a specific technology of security. Liberalism, as the governmental form of modern states, develops this technology of security by organising the conditions under which individuals can be 'free'; it 'fabricates' or 'produces' freedom (Lemke, Krasmann & Bröckling, 2000, 14). Liberalism does not simply guarantee individual legal freedoms, it governs them.

This distinction becomes important in order to understand the current shift from liberal to neo-liberal strategies: while 'liberal rationalities are characterized by the surveillance and organisation of "freedom's conditions of production", and thus also the market, this now itself becomes the state's organisational and regulatory principle' (Kessl, 2001, p. 6). The neo-liberal restructuring of state and society is more than ever concerned with inventing technologies of the self, which can be coupled with governmental aims. In the context of neo-liberal governmentality, self-determination, responsibility and freedom of choice indicate 'not the boundaries of governmental action, but an instrument and vehicle for the transformation of the relationship of the subject to him or herself and to others' (Lemke, Krasmann & Bröckling, 2000, p. 30). Following this shift, pedagogy acquires enormous significance: schooling and further education, educational institutions and social work are gathered together in a strategic complex which aims to recode relations of power on the basis of a new neo-liberal topography of the social. The question of the function of pedagogic institutions thus leads directly to what is currently the centre of the analytics of power.

2. Flashback: School as an Apparatus of Power

Foucault himself marginally treated central pedagogic questions (Foucault, 1987, p. 253), but they remain present throughout his study of the prison (Foucault, 1976) or his examination of the apparatus of sexuality (Foucault, 1977). In any case, the meaning of the concept 'apparatus' is not self-evident. Foucault summarises it as follows:

> What I am trying to pick out with this term is, ... a thoroughly heterogeneous ensemble consisting of discourses, institutions, architectural forms, regulatory decisions, laws, administrative measures, scientific statements, philosophical, moral and philanthropic propositions—in short, the said as much as the unsaid. Such are the elements of the apparatus. The apparatus itself is the system of relations that can be established between these elements. (Foucault, 1980, p. 194)

Its central function is to respond to a 'strategic imperative' in a given historical situation. The apparatus of the prison arose as a historical response to the disciplinary problem of criminality; the apparatus of sexuality as historical response to the disciplinary problem of reproduction and physical desire; the apparatus of schooling as historical response to the disciplinary problems of tutorable bodies.

School as apparatus thus refers to the theoretical horizon of disciplinary power. German educational history is characterized by two clear breaks in the process of formation of the school apparatus: an early phase (in a sense an initiation into the disciplinary society) represented, for example, by the Prussian gymnasium reform or Pestalozzi's elementary method, and a transition phase (to 'soft' panoptic disciplinary techniques), characterizing German reform pedagogy in the early 20th century.

2.1 Initiation into the Disciplinary Society

Foucault's 'analytics of power' makes it possible to rethink the history of pedagogy. The particular position granted to pedagogic heroes like Pestalozzi can be attributed, from this perspective, not to his undisputed engagement with the poor of his time, but to the methodological repertoire of disciplinary techniques which his 'elementary method' demands and establishes in society (Pongratz, 1989, p. 183ff.). The elementary method not only establishes a new and enduring pedagogic discourse, but also functions—in metatheoretical terms—at the same time as an early introduction to the disciplinary society. The fascination for Pestalozzi's contemporaries probably lay not only in the promise of an efficient and stable fabrication of knowledge through systematic teaching, but also in its inner affinity with the technique of disciplinary power itself, that is, with disassembly, arrangement and productive reorganisation. The elementary method does not simply make it possible, but necessary to subdivide the teaching process in terms of content and time. It results necessarily in the composition of compulsory, structured teaching plans and an improved, more even sequencing of the learning process. The new temporal regulation of teaching also generates a new image of the school pupil: the image of the 'normal pupil' (Kost, 1985, p. 39). The subdivision of teaching into its elements and the corresponding techniques of exercise and examination make it possible to characterize the pupil in terms of the overall aim, the other pupils, and a particular method. The division of classes according to age and learning ability goes hand in hand with this normalisation effect in accordance with the fictional 'normal pupil'. All of this makes the elementary method an integral part of a new technique of power focusing on a differentiated treatment of tutorable bodies in order to increase their utility and compliance (Foucault, 1976, pp. 220–250). And this technique meshes silently with architectural and organisational arrangements: with a particular ordering of space in the school, which installs what Foucault called the 'compelling gaze' (Foucault, 1976, p. 221), with the introduction of gendered code, with a 'micro-justice' which regulates proper behaviour in the classroom, with a minute control of the body, beginning with the fixing of seating and overseeing the posture and technique of writing.

These techniques, with which physical violence is implanted, so to speak, in the fabric of everyday school life, in order to subtly penetrate the school pupil, constitute the early forms of disciplinary power. Their introduction into the school system took place over a long period, and by the end of the 18th century the foundations had been laid for the 19th century establishment of the school as an apparatus of disciplinary power—first for the privileged bourgeoisie, later for the rest of the population (Pongratz, 2004a).

2.2 Soft Control and Panopticism

Towards the end of the 19th century the school is well established in the social body as a central apparatus and—in a first step—already supplied with possible articulations with further 'intersection points' in the disciplinary network (youth welfare and the juvenile court, family and social welfare). It is at this stage, as the school apparatus has become widespread and lost its exclusiveness as a former essentially bourgeois social formation, that new, class specific differentiations are introduced into the school apparatus, which allow for a reinterpretation of the apparatus as a whole.

This is the real innovative achievement of the 'reform pedagogy movement' around the turn of the 20th century. The reformation of the school apparatus which it set in train can be analysed at a variety of levels: at the level of the subterranean, local functioning of disciplinary power, the early 20th century constitutes a transition from the old learn-and-drill school to more dynamic, inner-directed methods aiming at an early transformation of external into internal regulation. The focal point of pedagogic discourse then moves to a certain extent inwards: attention is now paid less to external arrangements for the regulation of tutorable bodies (school bench, school hygiene, regulation of time and space in the classroom, etc.), and much more to internal arrangements (motivation structures, psychic dispositions, 'school life', panoptic methods of control) securing the school pupil's attention and autonomy.

Teaching becomes 'community education', the class becomes a 'living and working community', education turns into 'self-education'. In this way, it becomes possible to integrate school pupils into the school's institutional framework more effectively than ever before. Kost has illustrated this transformation of the old drill pedagogy into reform pedagogy with the example of the relationship of teachers to the school pupil's trouser pocket:

> If the 'old' pedagogy controls the trouser pockets to establish that they contain clean handkerchiefs, the 'new' pedagogy does exactly the opposite, turning their contents out onto the table, in order to gain insight into the student's inner life and to make this pedagogically useful. (Kost, 1985, p. 190)

In this way the learning situation is reorganized according to the principle of 'panopticism', in which the disciplining network no longer functions through administrative decrees, but more through flexibly managed mechanisms for steering 'school life'. Individuals are thus placed in a dual position: they can experience themselves as the subjects of processes of which they simultaneously remain the objects (Pongratz, 2004b).

3. Education Reform as a Governmental Strategy

It is in these terms that the analysis of the school as an apparatus of power needs to be analysed today. What is currently being discussed under the headings of 'self organisation' or the 'learning organisation' turns out on closer inspection to be part of the governmental strategy characterizing the current educational reforms as a whole. A range of indicators show this (Helsper, 1990, p. 31, 85, 186f.): ideals of partnership and the greater attribution of self-responsibility to students means that what used to be achieved through direct external constraint or internalised authority, now has to be attained through self-constraint.

> These relations of coercion disguise themselves as egalitarian communication between students, teachers and school administrators, which frequently obscures the fact that the real decision-making field is contained (through bureaucratic guidelines, administrative and economic structures) within narrow boundaries. (Boenicke, 1998, p. 178)

At the same time the distance in the face of school processes is made more difficult. An inconsistent proximity emerges which binds students more closely to the school. They are meant to see themselves as part of 'learning organisations'; further still: they are to consider themselves as 'autopoietic, self-organizing systems'. The discourse of self-organisation, constitutes, so to speak, the heart of the power-knowledge complex which links neo-liberalism and the economisation of education with systems and constructivist theory, in order to assimilate the education more thoroughly than ever before into the network of disciplinary procedures. The linkage of technologies of the self with new governmental strategies of control, the 'voluntary self-control' of individuals, manifests itself at all levels of the education system (Pongratz, 2005):

Just as wage labourers are to become 'labour entrepreneurs' (Voß & Pongratz, 1998), 'I Ltds' or 'intrapreneurs', students are redefined as knowledge self-managers, autopoietic 'learning systems', for whom success is held out particularly when they acquire the qualities of modern management: acquiring the means of production for the creation of knowledge (learning to learn), subjecting themselves to the self-constraint of permanent quality control and optimisation (motivation management), learning to see themselves as both clients and private suppliers on the education market (self-management), exposing themselves to permanent control, examination and certification (self-optimisation), and so on. Every student and every teacher becomes their own 'competence centre'; accordingly, the concept of competence moves to the centre of pedagogic reflection. Competence is here understood as the individual disposition towards self-organisation, as the totality of the 'requirements of a person, a team, an organisation or an enterprise to act with some level of certainty in situations with guaranteed uncertain outcomes' (Erpenbeck, 2001, p. 206). Competencies are meant to secure the possibility of self-managed learning in the 'jungle of the globalised market' (ibid., p. 206). Learning becomes self-managed when 'the learning goals and the operations and strategies which lead to those goals are determined by the learning system itself' (ibid., p. 204).

Implicitly the concept of self-management makes it clear that there is no longer anything the self can hold on to, other than itself. Given the uncontrollable relationships that gather around it, that is precious little. The fact that in the jungle of market relationships there are no more securities that can guarantee success with one's chosen strategies, is echoed in the constructivist thesis of the 'unintendedness' and contingency of learning. The fact that everyone has to give their all, so as not to lose their place, is expressed in the maxims of 'viability' and 'receptiveness', against which the outcomes of learning processes are measured. At the level of the teaching process, a new vocabulary is thus set in motion, which constructs teaching as a sort of learning management, as the arrangement and steering of learning situations, in which it is ultimately up to the individual to make the best of it (or to fail to do so). In a direct translation of the enabling strategies of private enterprise management, pedagogic approaches informed by systems theory and constructivism propagate a new sort of 'enabling didactics' (Arnold & Siebert, 1995). They sanction at the didactic-methodological level the transition from Fordist forms of educational production (with operationalised guidelines, defined elements of the curriculum and a corresponding set of methods) to post-Fordist steering models. The mode of social steering is shifted from an expert-oriented regimentation to a mobile adaptation strategy oriented to subjects as clients. Uncertainty and contingency are thus subjectively redefined. They are perceived 'no longer simply as threat ... but as a field of freedom and thus as a resource to be exploited' (Bröckling, 2000, p. 133). Corresponding learning arrangements have the task of both enabling the desired practices of subjectification and placing functional limits around them. Use is then made of older reform pedagogic models.

> All the pedagogic elements which were once considered in terms of the formation of autonomous subjects: project learning, situation learning, complex learning and much more, resurface as a new means by which ultimately the entrepreneurial construction of a more comprehensively needed subject can be realised. (Röder, 1989, p. 186)

The same aim is pursued at an institutional level by the reorganisation of the school as a market-oriented service centre. Its goal is no longer 'education' but the privatisation and commercialisation of knowledge; educational processes are transformed into private property transactions with knowledge as a commodity. What used to be understood as the genuine pedagogic task of the institution (from teaching and examination to drug prevention or the organisation of school holidays) is now dealt with formally according to the framework of enterprise project development. Running a school becomes a project management task, with the aim of introducing new products and guiding internal restructuring. 'The school leaver as branded product—this is how one could capture the secret program of current concerns with education reform in a concise formula' (Fischbach, 2002, p. 11). The teacher disappears in a corresponding way, to reappear as project leader or evaluation manager (Schirlbauer, 1998, p. 56). The modern form of enterprise management in education is meant to develop a 'corporate identity'—a unique school profile—which corresponds at the level of action with 'corporate behaviour', and at the structural level with 'corporate design'. Nevertheless the effectiveness and efficiency of the enterprise as a whole is no longer to be ensured through partial measures, but produces a manifest demand for organisational and personal development. It establishes a 'permanent quality tribunal' (Simons, 2002, p. 617ff.) that brings in tow its own rhetoric of 'liberation', a sort of smooth-talking the mechanisms of disciplining. 'There is a whole game with the connotations and associations of words like flexibility, capacity for adaption, deregulation, promoting the belief that the neo-liberal message is one of general liberation' (Bourdieu, 1998, p. 50). Intensified competition among teachers and students is presented as 'achievement equity'; the introduction of school fees becomes 'cost-sharing' and the plea for new structures of control turns into 'cooperative autonomy' (Bennhold, 2002, p. 293). This suits the cynical undertone with which Bertelsmann-Company—spiritual father and promoter of the CHE (Centre for University Development) presented its motto for 1999: 'Everyone makes our own (*not their own, L. P.*) fortune'. The motto unintentionally deciphers the sophisticated combination of external- and self-subjection characterizing the current restructuring of the education system. Its essential effect consists of producing what Simons (following Foucault) calls the 'will to quality'. It brings together 'advanced liberalism, the permanent economic tribunal and the enterprising self' (Simons, 2002, p. 619). The advanced form of neoliberal governmentality in the education system arises from the linkage of the school apparatus with the incessant demand for self-management. 'Referring to Foucault, we could define actual "managementality" as management of self-management, with the constitution of an economic tribunal as the permanent point of reference' (ibid., p. 622).

Total quality management, which has established itself as the driving motor of the transformation of teaching and the school, is entirely true to its totalitarian claims: while it demands incessant procedures of individualisation (of organisations as well as individuals), at the same time it promotes 'totalisation through modern power mechanisms' (Foucault, 1987, p. 250). The freedom of the enterprise 'I & Co.' (Bridges, 1996) consists of the voluntary self-control and self-subjection to a permanent and comprehensive economic tribunal (put into practice by management consultants). They correspond to a permanent self-examination and evaluation. The contemporary 'microphysics of power' leaves the old techniques of surveillance and punishment behind; instead its works with benchmarking, quality audits, empowerment and tests (Lemke, Krasmann & Bröckling, 2000, p. 35).

Accordingly, the PISA test is a striking demonstration of the mechanics of governmental strategies:

• PISA is no traditional test of performance; PISA does not test students' personality characteristics, but rather their performance in dealing with future tasks. This is why the test items are overwhelmingly oriented not towards the school curriculum, but towards what are seen as constituting the students' future (one could also say 'virtual') job profiles. The foundation is a narrow, psychologically determined understanding of 'self-regulated learning' focused primarily on the capacity for the development of 'learning strategies' and 'strategy utilization'. A future-oriented test-construction means that there is no longer any conclusion to the testing process, there are only 'preliminary results' which form the basis of the next round of testing. Once this line of inquiry has begun, it demands follow-up tests generating yet more demands for qualifications. In this way an individual's biography becomes an ongoing testing ground, and schools become subjected to permanent reform pressure. Learning now *has* to be 'life-long' learning.

- PISA does not test norms defined in advance, but concentrates on statistically averaged values: those being tested lie on a continuum between 'normal' and 'abnormal'. 'The statistical average is not the desired value which the tested person approximates, but the norm to be surpassed' (Lemke, 2004, p. 266). This shows how the PISA test strategically couples diagnostic inquiry with normalising selection. Whatever the test results represent, they lead to correcting (self-) practices, to incessant 'care for the self', to continual 'deciphering of the self'. In this sense one could also say that PISA is—like all tests—a 'truth machine', that does not simply bring to the surface an already existing, hidden but not yet known truth, it actually produces the 'truth' concerning the tested person. PISA constitutes primarily the 'field of reality', which then becomes the point of departure for new strategies of control.

- As a 'truth machine', PISA lies 'in the tradition of the Enlightenment and shares its dialectic' (ibid., p. 267). On the one hand, PISA stimulates permanent critique (and self-critique). It scrutinizes the production of self-defined 'competencies' and critically examines their presumed meaning. At the same time, however, this critical self-reflection is instrumentalised in the context of the testing procedure, in order 'to immunise itself against objections and reservations. Critique can be directed at a test's concrete benchmarks, but not at the practice of testing itself. The results may be provisional, but the premises are not' (ibid., p. 268).

- The fact that the PISA test both advances the 'Dialectic of Enlightenment' and, in the context of its normalising practices, refines it, is made clear by the contradiction between, on the one hand, the incessant demand for standards of normality and, on the other hand, the constant identification of ongoing divergences and differences. In this way, the uniqueness of the individual is both constantly affirmed, but at the same time systematically repudiated; the uniqueness of the school (its unmistakable profile, its corporate identity) is constantly asserted—but at the same time it is obliged to orient itself to generalised (educational) standards.

- The present German discussion of 'educational standards', which the highly-charged PISA debate now joins up with, also reveals the changed role of the state in the context of neoliberal practices of regulation. The state does not withdraw completely from events to become the 'night watchman' and leave the field to competing (educational) actors. It is more that it pushes the privatisation of the education sector, in order to control this field more intensively than ever with a specialised, concentrated distribution of functions.

- The PISA study draws its attraction and its shock value from a power network in which PISA itself functions as a switching point as well as a driving force. PISA can thus rightly be interpreted as a 'power stabiliser', which extends disciplinary procedures across a timeless horizon. PISA establishes not just a normalising practice that sets standards that can be achieved or missed. It is more the case that it concerns a dynamic form of quality measurement, which, in the framework of benchmarking or the invitation to quality prizes (best practice institutions) unleashes the never-ending hunt for new records. Although one's own position in the quality ranking is always only relative to one's competitors, the push for improved performance never stops. Everyone occupies simultaneously and to the same extent the role of the competition judge and contestant, the winner and the loser, the self-entrepreneur and the serf. Where the dictatorship of comparison reigns, there—adapting Hegel—the world market becomes supreme court (Bröckling, in: Bröckling, Krasmann & Lemke, 2000, p. 162).

From this perspective, it may become possible to understand what the 'PISA shock' had actually unleashed. The world market and its reform-pedagogic instruments—internationally implemented batteries of tests—establish themselves as a supreme court. The next tests have already been announced, and the OECD, an ideational executive manager, will do everything to continue the process. Before us lies the empty transcendence of the 'will to quality'.

References

Arnold, R. & Siebert, H. (1995) *Konstruktivistische Erwachsenenbildung* (Hohengehren, Schneider).

Bennhold, M. (2002) Die Bertelsmann Stiftung, das CHE und die Hochschulreform: Politik der 'Reformen als Politik der Unterwerfung', in: I. Lohmann & R. Rilling (eds), *Die verkaufte Bildung* (Opladen, Leske u. Budrich), pp. 279–299.

Boenicke, R. (1998) *Bildung, absoluter Durchgangspunkt. H.-J. Heydorns Begründung einer kritischen Bildungstheorie*, Habilitationsschrift Thesis (TU Darmstadt, Darmstadt).

Bourdieu, P. (1998) *Gegenfeuer* (Konstanz, Edition Discours).

Bridges, W. (1996) *Ich & Co. Wie man sich auf dem neuen Arbeitsmarkt behauptet* (Hamburg, Hoffmann u. Campe).

Bröckling, U. (2000) Totale Mobilmachung. Menschenführung im Qualitäts- und Selbstmanagement, in: U. Bröckling, S. Krasmann & T. Lemke (eds), *Gouvernementalität der Gegenwart* (Frankfurt/M., Suhrkamp), pp. 131–165.

Deutsches PISA-Konsortium (ed.) (2001) *PISA 2000. Basiskompetenzen von Schülerinnen und Schülern im internationalen Vergleich* (Opladen, Leske u. Budrich).

Erpenbeck, J. (2001) Selbstorganisiertes Lernen—Ausdruck des Zeitgeistes oder Ausdruck der Zeit?, in: D. Hoffmann & K. Maack-Rheinländer (eds), *Ökonomisierung der Bildung* (Weinheim, Beltz), pp. 199–214.

Fischbach, R. (2002) Die Wissensgesellschaft. Maßstab oder Phantom der Bildungsdebatte?, *Widersprüche*, 22:83, pp. 9–22.

Foucault, M. (1976) *Überwachen und Strafen* (Frankfurt/M., Suhrkamp).

Foucault, M. (1977) *Sexualität und Wahrheit, Bd. 1: Der Wille zum Wissen.* (Frankfurt/M., Suhrkamp).

Foucault, M. (1978) *Dispositive der Macht. Über Sexualität, Wissen und Wahrheit* (Berlin, Merve).

Foucault, M. (1980) The Confession of the Flesh, in: C. Gordon (ed.), *Power/Knowledge. Selected interviews and other writings 1972–1977* (New York, Pantheon), pp. 194–228.

Foucault, M. (1987) Das Subjekt und die Macht, in: H. L. Dreyfus & P. Rabinow (ed.), *Michel Foucault—Jenseits von Strukturalismus und Hermeneutik* (Frankfurt/M., Suhrkamp), pp. 243–264.

Helsper, W. (1990) Schule in den Antinomien der Moderne, in: H.-H. Krüger (ed.), *Abschied von der Aufklärung? Perspektiven der Erziehungswissenschaft* (Opladen, Leske u. Budrich).

Kessl, F. (2001) Von Fremd- und Selbsttechnologien—mögliche Perspektiven einer Gouvernementalität der Gegenwart, *Sozialwissenschaftliche Literaturrundschau*, 43, pp. 5–13.

Klausenitzer, J. (2002) Altes und Neues, *Widersprüche*, 22:83, pp. 53–65.

Kost, F. (1985) *Volksschule und Disziplin* (Zürich).

Lange, H. (2002) PISA: Und was nun? Bildungspolitische Konsequenzen für Deutschland, *Zeitschrift für Erziehungswissenschaft*, 5:3, pp. 455–471.

Lemke, T., Krasmann, S. & Bröckling, U. (2000) Gouvernementalität, Neoliberalismus und Selbsttechnologien. Eine Einleitung, in: U. Bröckling, S. Krasmann & T. Lemke (ed.), *Gouvernementalität der Gegenwart* (Frankfurt/M., Suhrkamp), pp. 7–40.

Lemke, T. (2002) Stichwort: Gouvernementalität, *Information Philosophie*, 30:3, pp. 46–48.

Lemke, T. (2004) Stichwort: Test, in: U. Bröckling, S. Krasmann & T. Lemke (eds), *Glossar der Gegenwart* (Frankfurt/M, Suhrkamp), pp. 263–269

Lohmann, I. (2002) After Neoliberalism, in: I. Lohmann & R. Rilling (eds), *Die verkaufte Bildung* (Opladen, Leske u. Budrich), pp. 89–108.

Picht, G. (1964) *Die deutsche Bildungskatastrophe* (Freiburg).

Pongratz, L. A. (1989) *Pädagogik im Prozeß der Moderne. Studien zur Sozial- und Theoriegeschichte der Schule* (Weinheim, DSV).

Pongratz, L. A. (2004a) Critical Theory and Pedagogy: Adorno und Horkheimer's contemporary significance for a Critical pedagogy, in: G. Fishman, P. McLaren, H. Sünker & C. Lankshear (eds), *Critical Theories, Critical pedagogies and global conflicts* (Boulder, CO, Rowman & Littlefield).

Pongratz, L. A. (2004b) Freedom and Discipline: Transformations in pedagogic punishment, in: M. Peters (ed.), *Why Foucault?* (New York, Lang).

Pongratz, L. A., Nieke, W., Masschelein, J. & Wimmer, M. (eds) (2004c) *Nach Foucault— Diskurs- und machtanalytische Perspektiven der Pädagogik* (Wiesbaden, VS-Verlag für Sozialwissenschaften).

Pongratz, L. A. (2005) Subjektivität und Gouvernementalität, in: B. Hafeneger (ed.), *Subjektdiagnosen* (Schwalbach/Ts., Wochenschau-Verlag).

Röder, R. (1989) Funktionalisierung von Bildung im Bereich informations- und kommunikationstechnischen Lernens, in: W. Gieseke, E. Meueler & E. Nuissl (eds), *Zentrifugale und zentripetale Kräfte in der Disziplin Erwachsenenbildung* (Mainz), pp. 157–190.

Schirlbauer, A. (1998) Vom Verschwinden des Lehrers in der 'Neuen Lernkultur', in: H. Giesecke *et al.* (eds), *Der Lehrer—Hoffnungsträger oder Prügelknabe der Gesellschaft* (Innsbruck, Tyrolia).

Simons, M. (2002) Governmentality, Education and Quality Management, *Zeitschrift für Erziehungswissenschaft*, 5:4, pp. 617–33.

Terhart, E. (2002) Nach PISA—Bildungsqualität entwickeln (Hamburg).

Voß, G. G. & Pongratz, H. J. (1998) Der Arbeitskraftunternehmer. Eine neue Grundform der Ware Arbeitskraft?, *Kölner Zeitschrift für Soziologie und Sozialpsychologie*, 50, pp. 131–58.

5

Education or Service? Remarks on teaching and learning in the entrepreneurial university

ANDREA LIESNER

Introduction: German Universities and the European Higher Education Area

Since the end of the 1990's, education has become an issue of great interest in the German public sphere. Spurred on in large part by both national and international rankings, a significant portion of this discussion has focused on the field of Higher Education. Especially in the contemporary political debates, the German universities are considered to be old-fashioned, sluggish and inadequate in meeting the perceived future needs for competitiveness. Looking back through history, such critical statements are nothing new. Already in the 19th century, the 'crisis of the university' seemed to be its 'usual condition' (Schelsky, 1963, p. 33).[1] Thus, the claims of decay, the corresponding reform debates as well as the political restructuring of the university can be viewed as 'part of the process of a politically framed "normal science"' (Kimmich & Thumfart, 2004, p. 8).

However, there are indications that the present debates as well as the reforms already implemented possess a qualitatively new form. The current political programs mean a fundamental change in the German university structures, and they threaten to overload an already heavily burdened system. The newly introduced BA/MA programs exceed teaching capacities, and have already led to the closure of several degree programs. In addition, the implementation of new management structures coupled with the tendency towards the separation of teaching and research constitutes a radical break with the Humboldt University Model, which was highly acclaimed and internationally exported 150 years ago.

The basis for these reforms stem from the so-called 'Sorbonne Declaration' signed by the education ministers of Germany, France, Italy, and the United Kingdom in 1998. The declaration intends a 'harmonisation of the architecture of the European higher education system' and precedes the Bologna Conference, which is to date the most influential political program involving European universities.[2] At the Bologna Conference in 1999, 29 ministers of education agreed upon creating a shared European Higher Education System by 2010 (EME, 1999; eurActiv, 2003). Six objectives guide this initiative designed to make the various European universities more compatible and comparable with each other. With the aim of increasing the international competitiveness of the entire European system of higher education, these objectives concentrate on three points: They shall enable (a) 'easily readable and comparable degrees', (b) studies 'based on two main cycles' and the acquiring of 'credits' as well as (c) the promotion of 'mobility', of a 'cooperation in quality assurance' and of 'European dimensions in higher education' (ibid.).

Two years later in Prague, the themes 'lifelong learning', 'Involvement of students' and 'attractiveness and competitiveness of the European Higher Education Area to other parts of the world' were incorporated into the current program. At the following meeting in Berlin 2003, 33 education ministers agreed upon the introduction of 'effective quality assurance systems', the 'implementation of BA/MA programs' as well as improving 'the recognition system of degrees and periods of studies' by 2005 (eurActiv, 2003). In the meantime also Albania, Andorra, Bosnia-Herzegovina, the Vatican, Serbia and Montenegro, the former Yugoslavian Republic of Macedonia and Russia declared willingness to follow, and the latter alone will effectively double the size of the European Higher Education Area.

Since Germany was one of the founding members of the Bologna-Process, and its university reforms are already in the more advanced phases, the German government was prepared to submit preliminary results. In the following, I would like to take a look at how these reforms affect the university. The point of departure for this reflection is the thesis that the discussions concerning quality, efficiency and excellence aim at a new mode of social regulation. As such, the political 'Europeanization' program of the universities demonstrates a new mode of government, which is described by Foucault as a neoliberal governmentality (Foucault, 1994, 2004).

In the first part of my paper, I will focus on the field of academic teaching and learning and ask, how these reforms are at the same time related to specific regimes and imply a specific arrangement of education. What does teaching and learning mean in the newly structured university? In what way are the managerial oriented political reforms objectifying these activities?

The second part inquires how the university itself objectifies academic teaching and learning. The example of the so-called 'entrepreneurship-education' shows that the political reorganization of formal university structures is linked with a specific reorganization of the curriculum offered by the university itself. In other words, how does the university conceive of itself, if higher education were to restrict itself to an entrepreneurial environment, where students are considered customers and teachers as service personnel?

In order to systematize this reflection, the third section examines the premises of subjectivity within the present renewal of the Higher Education system. The model of politically promoted subjectivity already creates its own reality, and even if the subject is considered dead in specific areas of educational science, it should not be overlooked that its political constitution enjoys excellent health. Translated into terms of a neoliberal call to be-oneself and to self-agency, the subject is transformed into an entrepreneurial self; a self-understanding comprised of future university 'customers' (students) and 'service-providers' (instructors), which, according to my thesis, should come to the critical attention of scientific investigations.

From Self-Government Towards Management: The Rise of the Entrepreneurial University

As previously mentioned, many different sectors within the public and political discourse agree with the statement that German universities, in their current form, have become antiquated. One characteristic feature that has come under fire is the outdated form of self-government via committees. It is precisely the democratically constituted administration, in which every group affiliated with the university is represented, that is presently criticized for its unacceptable inefficiency. Proponents of the current self-administrative structure have increasingly become the target of political attacks, and publicly branded as 'Humboldt's gravediggers' and the destroyers of 'Germany's future' (Spiewak, 2003).

In 1997, German university chancellors agreed upon the following recommendation: 'Regarding the participation of university members in reference to groups', a distinction should be made 'between issues of fundamental importance, where the broader participation of university members is required', and those issues whose 'executive and operative' character should be left to authorities 'with the appropriate experience and expertise' (HRK, 1997). At the moment, this drive towards efficiency and quality has been realized throughout the country by implementing an entrepreneurial model of management; a model, already practiced in many European countries under the heading New Public Management (Hoffacker, 2001).

It should be noted that the following critique of this model is by no means an endorsement of the current administrative structure. There are complaints from within the ranks of the university itself about the endless counsel debates and committee sessions, the general demeanour of which many, including myself, perceive as ambivalent. Although the importance of these meetings is rarely questioned within the university, there are ever fewer individuals willing to take an active role. Contributing to this situation is the undifferentiated mass of tasks assigned to committees; an aspect that would fall in line with the political recommendation for streamlining.

One need not be an economist in order to estimate the costs, if a significant number of highly paid experts have to actually analyze, discuss, and then reach a consensus on the entire departmental agenda. Such tasks can include everything from building and development planning to issues of legal liability and insurance. Structural questions and those concerning research, curriculum and course of study are transferred to the corresponding committees. Their findings, however, rarely ever provoke sustained discussions at the departmental level and are increasingly superseded by decisions at the political level.

So what would be new about the decision-making processes in a 'more efficiently' organized university? Would we find, for instance, many of the issues important to students still considered? Or would they be seen as 'non-foundational', and thus fall under the jurisdiction of the new administrative 'organ'? And if so, would such issues simply be declared non-economically viable, and therefore left neglected? Or would it be viewed as economically feasible, because such issues could serve as incentives in the competition to attract new students?

According to Hoffacker, what is new about the new management model is that for the first time in the institution's history, it proposes the removal of the university from a cooperative state system of administration. As a result, it is 'not about the financial transformation of the university system into an entrepreneurial system. Rather, a "systematic" compatibility between university and enterprise is produced by the application of managerial principles in such a way that both systems equally orient their organized activities towards a shared economic calculus' (ibid., p. 3).

An important aspect of this alignment of universities with enterprises is the production of instruments in order to measure their efficiency. Since 1998, German universities are required by law to ensure quality, and in connection with the Bologna-Process most European countries have meanwhile established autonomous quality assurance agencies. According to the preliminary report issued by the Danish Institute for Evaluation appointed by the European Network for Quality Assurance in Higher Education (ENQA), 'the preferred method' in Europe 'is still the traditional evaluation used in combination with different foci' (with as many as 49 variations possible). However, not all countries utilize the same evaluative methods: While 'accreditation is most often used in newly associated countries as well as in Dutch and German speaking countries', English speaking countries tend to favour an 'institutional audit' type of evaluation (ibid., p. 8). Whether these differences will continue in the future is unclear; for the meeting of education ministers in Berlin 2003 entrusted the ENQA, among other things, with the task 'to develop a common set of standards, procedures, and guidelines for quality assurance' (EME, 2003, p. 3).

Another system of quality assurance is Total Quality Management (TQM). As an instrument taken over from private business, TQM is part of the New Public Management now widely used in European public administration, but still relatively uncommon in the field of higher education. Nevertheless, first impressions of the 'adaptation of business instrumentality for quality management' as applied to education in Germany, have been submitted for examination (Tenberg, 2004). Because the reconfiguration of teaching and learning is linked to the providing of a service, and because the principle of market orientation also dominates the reform politics within the university, it is worthwhile to examine Total Quality Management more closely.

In its actual form, it is a style of management that suggests normalizing modes of social conduct and no longer aims solely at ensuring the technical quality of products. The strategy underlying the motto 'customer orientation' is to control the rules of conduct that ultimately constitute a company's corporate identity. The concept of totality at work here, can 'only be realized in a "Top-down-process"', as Bröckling elaborated on in his article on the economization of the social (Bröckling, 2000, p. 139). As such, upper management takes on 'the role of the philosopher king'; for despite lean management and deflated hierarchies, it remains the one to determine 'the course taken in the politics of quality and the vision of the enterprise'. The manuals associated with this movement advise 'to focus on short, pregnant slogans that, everyone can identify with, and which evoke a competitiveness and sense of "we"'. In other words, a certain kind of collective identity is promoted, from which even its originators are not exempt; for now the prevailing theme is: 'Not: getting completely behind something, rather: blaze a trail forward' (Frehr, cited in Bröckling, 2000, p. 139).

As a result, 'the era of disciplinarian management structures' are replaced by mottos, 'in offices and work areas' that are meant as forms of visual reinforcement 'in the sense of a 'visible management'. The following example with the acronym-intensified principles makes TQM's way of governing people more approachable:

> **C**are about customers as individuals; **U**nderstand their point of view; **S**erve their human and business needs; **T**hank them for their business; **O**ffer to go the extra mile; **M**anage their moments of truth; **E**mphasize and listen to their concerns; **R**esolve problems for them; **S**ee customers as the reason for your job. (Townley, cited in Bröckling, 2000, p. 137)

The conviction expressed, here, that each and every single principle is responsible for the success of the company corresponds to the certainty presupposed by the TQM discourse, i.e. that the principle of the free-market rewards those prepared to excel, which means not only waging the same risks, but, more so, waging the same chances. Both correspond to the political rhetoric regarding the competitiveness of universities, thereby striking a certain resonance. If the universities take up models without even being compelled to do so, or request course evaluations from the students/customers, it could very well become increasingly difficult to fend off politically motivated cost reducing measures (including position cuts) based on competitiveness profiles, rankings or even a 'satisfaction barometer' (Bröckling, 2004, p. 81).

Uneasiness within the Entrepreneurial University

In my view, it goes without saying that universities should be offering a demanding curriculum. However, the question is what would actually change at the participatory level within a system completely oriented around the principles of supply and demand. What characterizes the self-conception of teachers, who view themselves as service providers and students as customers? Does this way of understanding oneself differ from, perhaps, that of teachers, who see themselves as being part of a research community involving students?

The example mentioned above dealing with proper employee attitudes towards customers will serve as the starting point for a short thought experiment.

'**C**are about customers as individuals': Among today's teachers, who would not emphasize the importance of individual advising and supervision of students as well as the room for improvement given the current situation? '**U**nderstand their point of view': Here, I do not wish to enter into a discussion concerning the didactics and the relation to students' life experiences. Yet, confronted with well-founded and clearly thought out student positions, what teacher would blindly maintain that their own standpoint is the only truly valid one? '**S**ervice their human and business needs': It is not necessary to take over the rhetoric of needs in order to suppose that a not insignificant number of teachers understand the university as a social sphere, where a less anonymous interaction would be desirable and a consideration for individual abilities, interests, and knowledge is taken. The next requirement, 'Thank them for their business', might be more difficult to imagine, but are we dealing with something essentially different than the present practice of many colleagues who expressly recognize the interests of students? And who is not pre-pared—with some exceptions taken—to do more should the need arise? How is this to be distinguished from 'Offer to go the extra mile'? What is the difference between dealing with student contributions in seminars that are oriented towards claims of validity and the recommendation, 'Manage their moments of truth?'

Continuing on, 'Empathize and listen to their concerns': Whether empathy will ever belong to the important motives of university didactics, is not of the utmost concern here. But, what teacher honestly believes that listening and advising students during difficult times does not belong to their duties? 'Resolve problems for them': this might prove difficult to bring into accord with the dominant para-digm of self-engagement and activity. However, if one understood this to mean something along the lines of 'helping someone to help himself', then perhaps it does not seem quite so exotic. Finally, 'See customers as the reason for your job': Keeping in mind that most researchers in German universities today (still) have the dual tasks of research *and* teaching, it is inevitable that some identify them-selves more closely with the latter rather than the former. For the majority, how-ever, these two tasks are indispensably linked at the university level, and therefore, it is nothing new that their positions have something to do with students being there to study.

To summarize, if important aspects of teaching are, *at first sight*, subsumable under the heading of 'providing services', then the question arises, what is the reason for the diffuse uneasiness that is—beside explicit critique (Hoffmann & Rheinländer, 2001; Hoffmann & Neumann, 2003; Lohmann & Rilling, 2002)—articulated within the political reformed universities in Germany?

At this point, it is instructive to revisit Heydorn's lectures on educational theory, which were at odds with the recommendations of the German Educational Counsel in the 1970's (Heydorn, 1972/1995). His critique against the reformation of insti-tutional learning focused on the enormous importance attributed to *method*, and precisely this preference for method returns in the contemporary discourse con-cerning the idea of life long (autonomous) learning. There seems to be a politically construed structural analogy between the selling of goods or services and the providing of lectures. In this simultaneously objectified analogy, the absolutization of method functions as a replacement for the content of teaching, because it makes the process of intellectual argumentation disappear in favour of a particular dispo-sition of conduct. Heydorn wrote: 'The material content is relativized, the material components of education appear as (ever) changing film content; what is taught today is already outdated tomorrow … . Education orients itself towards the moment that immediately plunges into emptiness; the moment acquires the char-acter of an absolutely sensual determination' (Heydorn, 1972/1995, p. 119).

Only if questions about such things as content and truth in reference to the future of the university are suspended can learning ever appear as something barely distinguishable from other services. The market principle obliterates all differences and makes it possible to overlook that, perhaps, it is not so much knowledge that is outdated, but rather its economic application. Therefore, it might well be that the uneasiness within the newly structured university results from the *universality of conduct codes* recommended to teachers. It evokes the question, whether their activities are in any way different from those of arms dealers or aerobic studio owners, i.e. the sale of products to anyone, anywhere, and for any reason as long as the demand exists.

Universities Between Contentment and Indolence

The uneasiness could be dissolved, if teachers and students were simply more familiar with this calculated style of thinking offered by the neoliberal reform-strategies. Within the framework of a program that promises and even requires self-optimization (or pedagogically speaking, *perfectibilité*), this demand represents a technology bearing 'its own materiality', a technology that is oriented towards the individual's activities (Lemke, 2000, p. 43). The Me-Inc., a form of an entre-preneurial subjectivity that both teachers and students are encouraged to pursue, 'already has an effect on the social relationships and a "use" within them'. As an ambivalent mode of leadership, it hands down conceptions of an autonomous subject and an autonomous state, both of which are simultaneously undermined (ibid.).

As a result, the problem of critique becomes increasingly difficult to focus on. Today, what would be described as the 'de-socialization of the society' (Hirsch, 1998, p. 104) or as 'de-individuation' (Helsper, 1989) accompanied by escalating possibilities of individuation, is an erosion of the conditions for critique; a critique that resists the widely accepted model of a completely compliant, market oriented and flexible subject. To speak of 'the' society insofar as it attempts to criticize the status quo regarding human relationships or the 'objectified consciousness' that extends 'to totality' (Adorno, 1970, p. 488), increasingly loses credibility in com-parison to the conception of 'the' knowledge- or 'the' information-society. This holds especially true, if the power relations within nation-states, which strongly encourage the 'economic restructuring process' in reference to 'locally determined constraints' in times of globalization, become increasingly abstract (Hirsch, 1998, p. 120).

The German university chancellors interpret one of these constraints, related to this focus on university teaching and learning, as follows: 'In the future, the demand for self-initiative will increase: part-time activities and professional inde-pendence will occupy a much larger part of the business world. As such, university graduates should orient themselves, either in the short- or long-term, towards an independent professional existence' (see HRK, 1997). This prognosis could very well prove correct. Keeping in mind Foucault's characterization of neoliberal gov-ernmentality, it can be asked, whether the above reasoned recommendation, indeed, arises out of a critical situation or whether it is, rather, more strategically intended: an attempt to ride on the back of the independence theme currently buzzing in the political realm and to provoke the acceptance of new forms of work. The imperative use of the concept 'orienting-oneself-towards' is, here, very telling.

Using the previously cited recommendation of the university chancellors, it is possible to sketch out, what the corresponding demand placed upon the student mindset confronted with its own professional future might look like. I will do so utilizing the example of the so-called entrepreneurship-education; a concept that can be found in economic sciences of European universities. However, the claims of entrepreneurship-education far exceed this field and there are remarkable political efforts to support them. Both bear witness to the fact that the figure of the entrepreneurial self is inextricably tied to it.

In Germany, students are made familiar with this process via courses focused on business establishment. According to the curriculum developer Ripsas, the first of three phases should involve 'an obligatory meeting for all students', when 'entrepreneurial education is finally recognized as a general task of the university' (Ripsas, 1998, p. 224). The 'basic courses' should, above all, serve to motivate the dissemination of 'information regarding the function of business in the economy as well as its process'. Furthermore, a sense for the 'general economic market processes' should be fostered, in order to show students different 'ways to increase individual prosperity that are in harmony with social norms and capitalistic processes'. Yet, precisely this mindset presents a significant difficulty for teachers. The course participants are primarily interested in planning their own business projects, while 'little attention remains for the function of the entrepreneur in economic theory or for economy at the global level' (ibid., p. 223). Although entrepreneurial education holds the latter to be indispensable, it would be naïve to assume that these courses confront students with different theories to enable well-informed decisions regarding economic issues.

The object is not to engage in reflection, but rather merely the installation of a particular set of beliefs. As Ripsas sees it, 'a brief representation of the market philosophy can increase the comprehension of the entrepreneur's function within the economy, and consequently increase the estimated value of this function, in effect, increasing the perceived attractiveness of the business' (ibid.). Therefore the students are not encouraged to form a differentiated, substantiated judgment; they are simply tuned into an affirmative approach to entrepreneurial thought.

Entrepreneurship-education, thusly conceived, has the task of assisting students in attaining a specific attitude, in which the legitimacy of all factual issues is reduced to the personal estimation, whether something is profitable or not. If teachers turn this into a contemporary requirement for student independence, they will be effectively covering over the fact that certain choices have already been stripped away: Most importantly, what has been taken away is the possibility of confronting competing theories, effectively blocking any attempt to investigate the matters more thoroughly. Regardless of how finite and provisional these judgments may be, they form the indispensable presuppositions for judgment that desire to be more than mere opinion or—to use the more antiquated concept— ideology. The revival of an indoctrinal pedagogy,[3] like that of entrepreneurial education, might be an exaggeration of today's tendency towards economization within the existing university curriculum.[4] And—moreover—it serves as a reminder that we cannot have a structural reform without reforming the content of curriculum as well. When the university chancellors criticize that 'the majority of the course syllabi are still geared according to the ever increasing *thoughts of security and care in our society*' (HRK, 1997, p. 97, my italics), it becomes clear that what is at stake, here, is a revision of thought; a thought that is idle, anti-risk, and passively or consumption oriented. Because this imperative of a new mental 'autonomy' is being endlessly repeated within the present political reform discussion, it would be prudent to look more closely at its meaning for this new way of governing. I would now like to sketch out at least three points:

As a reaction to the severe problem of structural unemployment, focus is placed *firstly* on the subject, who now has the full burden of responsibility for his or her professional future. Within this power relation, the path to success is certainly less interesting than its opposite. Students who exercise autonomous learning, but later fail their exams (the selective function of university learning), have to attribute this failure exclusively to themselves. The same holds for graduates that turn towards philosophical, rather than economically oriented research areas: they are responsible for lowering their own market value.

The multiplicity of reasons why students fail in their courses of study (including reasons specific to the university) is reduced to a singular dimension of blame. It is a self-induced insolvency that necessarily becomes an existential issue for subjects believing in their autonomy. They cannot bring themselves into view as objects of their own or outside investment; a perspective which would partially release them of their responsibility (Bröckling, 2003).

Secondly, the grounding of the political program of independence bears collective functions (Liesner, 2002, pp. 131–144). Understood as belonging to a productive community, each individual citizen is called to self-initiative, in order to keep Germany internationally competitive. The old target for the new 'we' continues to be the nation-state. The recommendation to take one's life into one's own hands is combined with the request to conceive of the social security systems as a heteronymous and unreasonable demand. The combination of these imperatives legitimates the neoliberal 'withdrawal' of the state, and at the same time, strengthens the state by preventing the subjects from misinterpreting their newly obtained freedom. In the realm of possibilities to take on more self-responsibility, egocentric or even anarchic forms of individualization are not intended. Similarly, one cannot conclude from the diminishing rights correspondingly diminishing duties. Hirsch maintains that 'the more uncertain social bonds, in the sense of material standards of life or political participation, become, the more compelling the picture of society as a "ship", in which "we" (whoever that is) supposedly sit together' (Hirsch, 1998, p. 120). His prediction could also prove correct that 'threats and angst serve as the legitimation of a politics always striving to push further onwards' (ibid., p. 104). As a result, the focus on a self, who is responsible for the national collective in current reform discussions, does not appear paradoxical, but rather right on target; for it is—as an accompanying technique of leadership—able to raise the acceptance of more economic forms of government. For each individual, self-responsibility becomes a 'wandering line; people are pushed to the very edge, and those, who inadvertently stray too far, are allowed to fall over this edge' (Fach, 2004, p. 234).

Thirdly, the current mobilization of both a self and nationally obligated individual appears to reinforce the constant 'elitist tendencies' in educational institutions (Herrlitz, 1998, p. 6; Sünker, 2004; Kincheloe & Sünker, 2004). This new orientation, proclaimed as a necessary condition for globalization, is questionable because it proposes that elitism and democracy are in no way at odds with one another. The controversial debates of the 1970's regarding equal opportunity, for instance, are not even consulted in the present discussion regarding the 'justice of opportunity'. More prevalent today are statements to the effect that it is already an accomplishment 'when professionals as well as the public at large recognize that an elite education as well as the support of the greater public, do not contradict one another' (von Saldern, 1997, p. 153). Quite the contrary, the two are said to 'guarantee a positive development for Germany' (ibid.).

With respect to the universities, one finds a great deal of enthusiasm for this 'turn', where the new concept of autonomy is related to the demand that universities should be allowed to pick their students. Further implications can be illustrated by a passage from the previously cited newspaper article:

> The dream that two million students will receive a comparable education is over. It is not necessary that everyone experience the unity of teaching and research as Humboldt ideally conceived of it. Neither must every university necessarily have to offer every course of study, nor does every professor have to be a great researcher. With a corresponding increase in teaching load, a good teacher will suffice. What is needed are different opportunities in competition with one another, i.e. *universities for those professors and students at the very highest levels of research and others that serve their own regional turf.* In other words, universities to compete at the world level and universities to serve their respective regions. Therefore, it is clear that the respectively categorized universities must be able to pick the students that fit them best. (Spiewak, 2003, p. 1, my italics)

Aided and encouraged by this kind of journalistic support, the current politics attempts to widen the scope of the practicable. After a decade of abstinence, it again lends credibility to theories of natural talent, which in turn, makes the public task of elite recruiting acceptable, and thereby leaves behind the idea of a 'democratic university' (Brunkhorst, 2004, p. 88). The restructuring process tends to transform the present German system of Higher Education into a service providing business and structurally contributes to the ever-widening gap between publicly and privately organized science. To put it bluntly, there is reason to fear that apart from a few elite-institutions most of the universities will favour the employment of teachers enthusiastic for fashionable methods and lacking research interests (or forced to suffice without them). The assumption that these 'good teachers' will be in demand is dependent upon the number of students who are already considered provincial racehorses:[5] All of the students, whose self-initiative, and especially, personal capital is sufficient only for a Ltd. Company, but not for a Me-Inc.

This possibility could only be ignored if one is not disturbed by the fact that the education of Me-Inc.'s also has end consumers. In the educational sciences, students as well as other 'clientele' do *not* have a choice regarding the refusal or acceptance of the services provided; for they, analogous to medical patients, the unemployed or also criminals, reside within 'asymmetrical power relations' (Voswinkel, 2004, p. 149).

An open and critical dialogue concerning the issues *within* the university would require that a significant number of colleagues are interested in the political reform programs. However, those affiliated with the university hardly ever protest against the university's reconfiguration into a service provider: The overwhelming reaction within the institution appears to be one of indolence.

This might indicate that the political dissatisfaction and 'latent anti-intellectualism' (Bourdieu, 2001, p. 35) are not phenomena found exclusively outside the university. Or does the lack of reaction mean that these questions are no longer relevant to those teaching and researching at the university? Could the wide spread indolence mean that the new modes of governing have already entered the university and shaped a new kind of academic subjectivity? At a time, when this institution is one of the few places where one can freely and openly question what neoliberal government, market globalization and the new forms of capitalism actually entail for our lives, such apathy would lay stress upon the necessity to look for points of resistance and to find suitable forms of analysis and critique.

With regards to the current situation, what seems to be important is the need for a committed reflection. This is to say a reflection that can discuss issues like democratic theory, theories of power, governance and education as well as economic theories *without* serving as a political advisor and *without* giving up rigorous scientific standards. This form of discussion does not shy away from the disconcertment of some (potentially influential) individuals in comparison to the breaking of the so-called 'axiological neutrality' (ibid.). It would openly point out the pitfalls of rigorous thinking, and is willing to subject itself to critique in order to avoid 'the use of intellectual authority as a political weapon'. Correspondingly, this reflection prevents the confusion of the 'things of logic with the logic of things', and it is capable of communicating itself outside the walls of the university (ibid., p. 36). Without an engagement like this, the university runs the risk of losing the condition for the possibility to be sceptical or critical at all.

Notes

1. All citations have been translated from the German.
2. Due to constraints, the significance of the WTO organized *General Trade Agreement on Trade in Services* (GATS) cannot be more thoroughly examined. See Lohmann (2004/ 2002) for more on this topic.
3. Here, the term 'indoctrinal' refers to all of these directions in the German history of educational thinking that react on efforts towards uncompromising theory with an appeal to ties, values and unreflective attitudes.
4. See Kent's compilation (1990) in reference to the realization of entrepreneurial education at schools and universities in the USA.
5. The term 'racehorses' plays on the 'turf' mentioned in the preceding paragraph. 'Turf' is used in German almost exclusively in reference to horseracing, and thus lacks the broader applications and associations found in English. Utilizing these two terms, I wish to draw attention to *how* students are conceived of in this perspective.

References

Adorno, T. W. (1970) *Ästhetische Theorie* (Frankfurt/M., Suhrkamp).

BWF (2003) *Strukturreform für Hamburgs Hochschulen (Bericht)—Entwicklungsperspektiven 2003 bis 2012. Empfehlungen der Strukturkommission an den Senator für Wissenschaft und Forschung. Ausgabe Januar 2003* (http://fhh.hamburg.de/stadt/Aktuell/behoerden/wissenschaft-forschung/service/buecher-und-broschueren/strukturreform-fuer-hamburgs-hochschulen-kommissionsbericht-pdf,property=source.pdf).

Bourdieu, P. (2001) *Gegenfeuer 2. Für eine europäische soziale Bewegung* (Konstanz, UVK).

Bröckling, U. (2000) Totale Mobilmachung. Menschenführung im Qualitäts- und Selbst-management, in: T. Lemke, S. Krasmann & U. Bröckling (eds), *Gouvernementalität der Gegenwart. Studien zur Ökonomisierung des Sozialen* (Frankfurt/M., Suhrkamp).

Bröckling, U. (2003) Menschenökonomie, Humankapital. Eine Kritik der biopolitischen Ökon-omie, *Mittelweg*, 36:12, pp. 3–22.

Bröckling, U. (2004) Evaluation, in: U. Bröckling, S. Krasmann & T. Lemke (eds), *Glossar der Gegenwart* (Frankfurt/M., Suhrkamp).

Brunkhorst, H. (2004) Die Universität der Demokratie, in: D. Kimmich & A. Thumfart (eds), *Universität ohne Zukunft?* (Frankfurt/M., Suhrkamp).

European Ministers of Education (1999) *The Bologna Declaration of 19 June 1999. Joint declaration of the European Ministers of Education* (http://www.bologna-berlin2003.de/pdf/bologna_declaration.pdf).

European Ministers of Education (2003) *Realising the European Higher Education Area. Commu-niqué of the Conference of Ministers responsible for Higher Education in Berlin on 19 September 2003* (http://erzwiss.uni-hamburg.de/personal/lohmann/datenbank/index.html).

ENQA (2003) *Quality procedures in European Higher Education. An ENQA survey by The Danish Evaluation Institute* (http://www.enqa.net/texts/procedures.pdf).

Fach, W. (2004) Selbstverantwortung, in: U. Bröckling, S. Krasmann & T. Lemke (eds), *Glossar der Gegenwart*, (Frankfurt/M., Suhrkamp).

Foucault, M. (1977–78/1978–79/2004) *Geschichte der Gouvernementalität* (Frankfurt/M., Suhrkamp).

Foucault, M. (1994) Das Subjekt und die Macht, in H. L. Dreyfus, P. Rabinow (eds), *Michel Foucault. Jenseits von Strukturalismus und Hermeneutik* (Weinheim, Beltz).

Helsper, W. (1989) *Selbstkrise und Individuationsprozeß. Subjekt- und sozialisationstheoretische Entwürfe zum imaginären Selbst der Moderne* (Opladen, Westdeutscher Verlag).

Heydorn, H.-J. (1972/1995) Zu einer Neufassung des Bildungsbegriffs, in: Heydorn, H.-J., *Bildungstheoretische und pädagogische Schriften 1971–1974* (Vaduz, Topos).

Hirsch, J. (1998) *Vom Sicherheitsstaat zum nationalen Wettbewerbsstaat* (Berlin, ID).

Hoffacker, W. (2001) *Reform oder Systemänderung. Zur Übertragung betriebswirtschaftlicher Steuerung-skonzepte auf das Hochschulsystem* (http://www.forschung-und-lehre.de/archiv/08-01/hoffacker.html).

Hoffmann, D. & Maack-Rheinländer, K. (eds) (2001) *Ökonomisierung der Bildung. Die Pädagogik unter den Zwängen des 'Marktes'* (Weinheim and Basel, Beltz).

Hoffmann, D. & Maack-Rheinländer, K. (eds) (2001) *Ökonomisierung der Wissenschaft. Forschen, Lehren und Lernen nach den Regeln des 'Marktes'* (Weinheim and Basel, Beltz).

HRK (2000) *Evaluation der Lehre—Sachstandsbericht mit Handreichungen. 190. Plenum am 21./ 22.02.2000* (http://212.79.160.110/beschluesse/1885.htm).

HRK (1997) *Organisations- und Leitungsstrukturen der Hochschulen. 183. Plenum am 10.11.1997* (http://www.hrk.de/beschluesse/2018.htm).

Kent, C. A. (1990) *Entrepreneurship Education: Current developments, future directions* (New York, Quorum).

Kimmich, D., Thumfart, A. (2004) Universität und Wissensgesellschaft: Was heißt Autonomie für die moderne Hochschule?, in: D. Kimmich & A. Thumfart (eds), *Universität ohne Zukunft?* (Frankfurt/M., Suhrkamp).

Kincheloe, J., Sünker, H. (2004) Begabungsideologie, Hegemonie der Eliten und Bildungspolitik, *Widersprüche*, 93, pp. 29–44.

KMK, HRK, BMBF (2003) *Realisierung der Ziele der 'Bologna-Erklärung in Deutschland. Sachstandsdarstellung* (http://www.erzwiss.uni-hamburg.de/personal/lohmann/datenbank/index.html).

Lemke, T., Krasmann, S. & Bröckling, U. (2000) Gouvernementalität, Neoliberalismus und Selbsttechnologien. Eine Einführung, in: T. Lemke, S. Krasmann & U. Bröckling (eds), *Gouvernementalität der Gegenwart. Studien zur Ökonomisierung des Sozialen* (Frankfurt/M., Suhrkamp).

Liesner, A. (2002) *Zwischen Weltflucht und Herstellungswahn. Zur Ambivalenz des Sicherheitsdenkens von der Antike bis zur Gegenwart* (Würzburg, Königshausen & Neumann).

Lohmann, I. (2002) Bildungspläne der Marktideologen. Ein Zwischenbericht, *Vierteljahrsschrift für wissenschaftliche Pädagogik*, 3, pp. 267–279.

Lohmann, I. & Rilling, R. (eds) (2002) *Die verkaufte Bildung. Kritik und Kontroversen zur Kommerzialisierung von Schule, Weiterbildung, Erziehung und Wissenschaft* (Opladen, Leske & Budrich).

Lohmann, I. (2004) *Tektonische Verschiebungen. Neue Weltmarktordnungen, Globalisierungspolitik und die Folgen für die nationalen Bildungs- und Sozialsysteme* (http://www.erzwiss.uni-hamburg.de/Personal/Lohmann/Publik/zuerich-sy-19.htm).

Schelsky, H. (1963) *Einsamkeit und Freiheit* (Reinbek, Rowohlt).

Siewak, M. (2004) Humboldts Totengräber. Mit der Universität fällt Deutschlands beste Tradition- und Zukunft, *Die Zeit*, 19:1 (30.04.2003).

Sünker, H. (2004) Elitendiskurse und politische Kultur in Deutschland, *Widersprüche*, 93, pp. 3–12.

Tenberg, R. (2004) *'Dienstleistung' Unterricht? Unstimmigkeiten beid der Adaption betrieblicher Instrumente von Qualitätsmanagement an Schulen* (http://www.lrz-muenchen.de/~tenbergpublikationen/pdf/Dienstleistung%20Unterricht.pdf).

Voswinkel, S. (2004) Kundenorientierung, in: U. Bröckling, S. Krasmann & T. Lemke (eds), *Glossar der Gegenwart*, (Frankfurt/M., Suhrkamp).

6
Participation for Free. Exploring (limits of) participatory government

KERLIJN QUAGHEBEUR

Introduction

Whereas in international development participation has been recognised as an important end and means—in participatory projects—for a couple of decades, since the early 1990s education and educational contexts are also increasingly adopting its principles, stakes and approaches.[1] In both contexts participation is first of all promoted as an answer to problems of exclusion, of insufficient or biased accessibility, indicating participatory measures as possible solutions, striving for more or better numeric inclusion. Besides its numeric understanding participation, however, also represents and promotes a specific way of being involved, not only enabling participants to be included, but also to acquire skills, knowledge and experience to take greater responsibility for their own development and education and, ultimately, to be empowered to transform their lives and their environment. Especially in this second interpretation, participation assumes a learning process: participative learning, and learning to participate, is assumed to provide the individual with desirable and even necessary capacities and skills to survive in and to co-construct today's and the future's unpredictable and constantly changing society. Offering an alternative to dominating and top-down approaches participation, moreover, assumes an increased motivation, to contribute to the internalisation of learning contents, and entails more efficiency and effectiveness in the learning and development process.

Participative learning and participatory development are often justified by arguments concerning freedom: freedom from dominance or external dependencies, freedom or autonomy as self-development and self-realisation, or freedom for children or for the most disadvantaged to (learn to) act for themselves. Participation and participatory approaches as such claim to contribute to (an increase of) freedom or to processes aimed at freedom such as emancipation or liberation, not by imposing liberative or emancipatory measures or by enforcing the individual to free oneself but by offering opportunities for the individual to freely practice one's own freedom. Participation and participatory approaches, in other words, intend to create possibilities for the individual to become or to be free, to bring one's freedom into practice, more specifically by stimulating or instigating the development of those skills and capacities that enable participants to create for themselves certain spaces of freedom, as possibilities for freely determining their own lives, their worlds, their identities.[2] In this paper, we want to scrutinize this argument of freedom. We therefore explore participation as it appears in a particular learning and development context. For this exploration and questioning of the emphasis on freedom we rely on Foucault's perspective of governmentality. This perspective enables us to consider participation, participatory training, participatory techniques and practices as elements in a regime of government, whereby freedom is, on the one hand, conceived as a condition (and not an opposite) of government and, on the other hand, also as a specific effect of productive (governmental) power exercises. Via that perspective we analyse how freedom is produced as an effect (not a product) of participatory practices as power exercises referring to different converging rationalities, techniques and instruments.

1. Participation as a Specific Practice of Freedom

First we explore how participation or participatory approaches intend to provide circumstances in which the subject is enabled to practice freedom. We expose a concrete case, combining educational and development aspects, to investigate how participation and its approaches intend to open up opportunities for the subject to 'freely and creatively' determine oneself, to enact freedom, to be or become a 'free' individual or participant.

Participative Training on Participatory Management for Development Workers[3]

The concrete case we discuss concerns an international training programme on 'management and evaluation of participative projects', organised for local NGO development workers involved with the management of projects, who are qualified and experienced, and proficient in English.[4] The training consisted of several modules and work forms, presented by different teachers and trainers and running during 13 weeks. The training committee and sponsors provided for 12 scholarships of which 11 were occupied by six women and five men, from 11 different countries and two continents (Africa and Asia). Our analysis is based on research within two of the training modules entitled 'participatory context analysis' and 'participatory planning'.

  With these modules, as we read from the programme description,[5] trainers envisioned introducing 'Project cycle management' (PCM) as a framework for improving the quality of development projects; they aimed at clarifying the concept of participation and at examining its different interpretations; they aimed to situate the development of participatory approaches and to expose a variety of participatory tools and principles. They furthermore intended to present the logical framework approach as a method for participatory analysis and planning, considered as 'a participatory process involving different stakeholders, providing and presenting essential information in a logical and transparent way, being object/result oriented and enhancing transparency in decision-making, in setting goals, etc.'. From an overview of the basic structure of the entire programme we read participation indeed to be a basic aspect, not only in the content but also in the methodology of the programme (situated at the bottom of the visual scheme, supporting and backing up, crossing all other themes and work forms). This means that the training of development workers in participation, participatory tools and approaches was itself intended to proceed according to participatory principles, to apply participatory approaches. In the programme brochure examples are given of how the training was intended to be participative: by 'translating aspects of PCM into concrete examples to enhance their comprehension', whereby also 'a practical example will demonstrate how each of the phases of the project cycle could look like'. Besides practical examples, the programme also invites participants to apply participatory tools 'to their new context in Belgium, to their working environment at home, etc.', enabling them to 'discover opportunities and difficulties related to the tools' and during the exercise also 'to exchange experiences with other participants and to learn from them'. Other participatory exercises proposed in the programme brochure are so-called role plays, whereby participants identify with stakeholder roles and 'analyse an existing, problematic situation' by means of different tools and frameworks and according to the different phases of the log(ical) frame(work) approach. These exercises, in which participants were asked to apply what they were taught or to experience (and exchange experiences about) how certain tools, concepts or approaches work, were thus presented as practices of participatory learning or also, in more official or at least more commonly known terms, of experiential learning or 'learning by doing'.[6]

From the presentation of the programme, we infer participation to constitute the object as well as the approach of the learning process that the training intended and proposed to instigate. In other words, the training can be described as a place or occasion that proposed offering possibilities to development workers for learning participation and learning to participate in a participatory way. Or more concretely, in the training programme, development workers were to be given opportunities for learning how to handle participatory tools, how to manage (i.e. approach, consider, but also analyse, programme, identify, plan, monitor, evaluate)[7] participatory projects. They were intended to acquire experiences with participatory acting, thinking and behaving, or also to become 'participants' and to be enabled to identify, address and involve target groups as participants in participative development processes. In the practices and discourses that constituted the training different arguments and justifications for participation and for the participatory approach can be distinguished.

Participation for Free

Without exploring in detail all arguments in favour of participation (the literature extensively reports on the advantages and necessity for participation),[8] we assess some of the most prominent motivations justifying the participatory approach, promoting participatory learning and participation itself as a desirable behaviour, attitude and/or object of knowledge. Making trainees participate, by inviting them to apply participatory tools to concrete situations, by making them experience what they learn, reflects the assumption that knowledge could be at best internalised, that attitudes could be induced and skills acquired best through 'live' experiences, by addressing trainees as 'participants', by inviting them to behave, think and act in a specific participatory way. Trainees themselves[9] argued that they learn better and more when treated as participants or *'what I really like, personally I like 'learning by doing' because I feel I understand better ... if I learn in practice here, it is easier for me to transfer the knowledge from myself to other trainers using the same 'learning by doing' approach ...'* or, in other words, *'yeah, for this course ... I think participation is a very good word. Ever since we started, we have seen different issues and the trainers have always given time for the participants to be active, ... the approach is different. Mostly school is more lecturing, but this training makes you ... move ... do things yourself, which is more practical and which implies that I will always remember what we have seen'.* Not only the participatory character of the training, but also the content of participation, framed to enable trainees to organise development projects in a participatory way, was positively motivated by the development workers. Or as one of the trainees testified: *'For me ... participation in development ... I like the sentence: 'development is not having a Mercedes, but knowing how to drive Mercedes'. Without participation ... of the people, we can give the Mercedes, we can give the driver, we can give the mechanics ... to the community ... but the community never knows ... how to drive Mercedes. But if I introduce development with participation, it means that I will involve the community to know how to drive the Mercedes ... to know how to ... repair if there is something broken ... like that. And when they understand the system, then maybe, they can make their own consciousness!'.* The testimonies of trainees resonate with the assumption (and the trainees' beliefs in, their reproduction or adoption of that assumption) that participation enables them to learn 'from the inside', stimulating internalisation of contents and attitudes, increasing motivation and, hence, ensuring and enhancing the effectiveness and efficiency of education and development.

Apart from efficiency and effectiveness, arguments of freedom also take a prominent place in the motivation of participation and participatory approaches. The last quote, for instance, indicates how participation is assumed to contribute to freedom, as independence, self-reliance or also empowerment, by offering people the possibility to do it (by) themselves, 'to drive the Mercedes themselves', free or also emancipated or liberated from external dependencies. This relation between participation and freedom as self-reliance and independence is actualised in exercises such as the assignment to trainees of tasks applying acquired skills, knowledge and capacities or techniques to an individual case: a real-life situation from their working context at home which trainees were asked to prepare and elaborate for the selection procedure, as one of the criteria on the basis of which trainees were selected for a scholarship. The individual case exercises, mediated via tutorship, were set up as areas in which trainees learn to work independently, without direct control of the trainer, in which they learn to take responsibility for their own case and for their learning process, as they were mandated by the tutors to time and organise this work according to their own mood, rhythm and opinion. Addressing the need for trainees to take responsibility, to organise their learning, such exercises reflect an aspect of freedom or emancipation, first of all, in the relationship of participants to trainers, to people who determine 'from above' (or top-down) what they should do and how to do it. The approach of tutorship, for instance, represents that argument in the way in which it 'frees' participants from such control by leaving the initiative for tutorship to them[10] or as a participant argued: '*When I was going to university … I had to sit in the classroom … but here … in the programme, it's different … We are used to that system of classes: professors come to give, you are going to cover this, this, this … but here it is important how WE do it (…) that has been very nice*'. This argument of freedom in relation to external control or support is also reflected in the programme announcement where training in participatory management is promoted as follows: 'the training of local staff is crucial for the success of development projects. This is in particular the case in the long run, once foreign support is withdrawn and local organisations are supposed to continue the project on their own'. Besides freedom for participants in their relation to others, participatory practices are also justified or legitimated for their link to freedom as self-determination or freedom in the way in which a participant can determine her own actions, can express her own opinions and interests. In other words, participatory practices are not only assumed to offer opportunities for participants to be self-responsible and independent from external control, but also to determine oneself, to express one's opinions and interests, to gain self-esteem, to feel empowered and to enhance one's well being. This freedom to express (and negotiate) one's opinions is instantiated in the three evaluation sessions, organised in the beginning, in the middle and at the end of the programme, in which participants were anonymously consulted to give their opinions about the support for the course preparation in their home countries, about the organisation of their stay, their relationship with teachers and staff, the sessions, the visits, the workload and some other miscellaneous activities.[11] The work plan candidates were also ordered to provide an example in the application form of a possibility for participants to 'freely' express their opinions, interests and ideas, to 'freely' determine what they expected, what they wanted to do, how they saw their realisation of the training. More informal (i.e. less planned and monitored in advance) examples of opportunities in which participants were enabled to practice freedom in the expression of their opinions, in the determination of their own ways of acting and behaving, were given throughout the sessions, in, for instance, the daily evaluations,[12] in decisions left to the participants about the afternoon programme, about group formations etc. Also, when indicating, while the trainees were assigned to draw two maps, the importance of possibilities and opportunities, of feelings of comfort and ease, of learning and discussion rather than of results, aesthetics, accuracy or preciseness, the trainer emphasised the same argument of freedom,[13] thereby placing a higher value on freedom (or opportunities and possibilities) of self-expression (through discussion) and self-determination (related to positive feelings) than on a correct representation (in maps) or an adequate mastering of techniques. This means that through such interventions, in interactions with the trainer, participants learn that freedom is rather related to

self-expression, to their determination in terms of opinions and to their responsibility for expressions and determination than to an adequate mastering of techniques
or, as in this case, to a correct or truthful representation in maps of a certain
reality.

The exploration of arguments and more specifically of the argument of freedom
in participatory practices and in their discourses as such indicates how participation is assumed to or is justified in opening up possibilities or opportunities to
practice freedom or how, in other words, participatory practices actually are displayed as practices of freedom. In the next paragraphs we argue how practices of
freedom opened up through participation are in fact determined or conditioned
or also, how participants practicing freedom are governed in a very specific way,
described and prescribed by practices of participation, by the tools and exercises,
by the rationalities that accompany their realisation. We do not mean to say that
participation might be imposed, that participants might be forced to take part, to
practice participation and as such also freedom: participation is rather presented
as an invitation, an opportunity, which the individual is free to take up or to refuse.
However, we argue that participation does not imply 'general' or 'neutral' opportunities, that participants are not enabled to practice freedom in a 'natural' or
completely arbitrary way. We argue that the opportunities for practicing participation, and as such also freedom, are governing participants to behave and to think
in a very particular way, to practice their freedom in a specific way. Freedom
practices appear to comply more with an obedience of the subject to a certain
participatory norm, with its subjection and subjectification[14] along a participatory
profile, than with arbitrary or 'natural' practices of subjectification or even with
resistance. This implies that from our analysis we aim to indicate that (and how)
participatory freedom practices relate to a particular understanding of freedom,
which we investigate through a more detailed exploration of participatory practices, exercises and interactions that displayed during the participatory training
programme.

Practicing Freedom Through Participation

A first example of a participatory exercise indicating participatory government,
suggesting conditions for participatory practices of freedom, can be found in the
elaboration of a 'problem tree'.[15] Initially the problem tree was presented (by slide)
as a framework and procedure for 'analysing an existing situation; identifying key
problems in its contexts and; visualising the problem in the form of a diagram
(cause-effect relationships)'. Then, trainers further introduced the presentation of
the procedure and framework as a workshop to which all participants of the training were invited. The topic of the workshop was a problem analysis of an imaginary
'culturally neutral' model project,[16] described by the trainers in a document of 17
pages. At first the participants were asked to identify stakeholder groups and then,
divided into subgroups for the different stakeholders, to symbolically (indicating +
or −) 'score' their stakeholder group in terms of characteristics, interests and
expectations, potentials and deficiencies, implications for the project, power and

influence.[17] Thus taking the position of or identifying (as) stakeholders, participants were asked to indicate and formulate project problems, a process initially facilitated by the trainer. This meant that the trainer wrote down problems suggested by the participants on yellow cards ('green is for objectives', FNII25) and attached them to a poster on the wall ('with long and slantwise attached pieces of tape, to avoid the paper coming off from humid walls', FNII26). The problems were thereby ordered in the format of a tree, with a starter problem on top and causally related, clearly defined singular problems attached gradually descending down the wall. After a while roles changed and trainees alternately represented stakeholders and facilitator, while the trainer commented, directed and re-directed what was happening, what should be taken care of and what were the eventual problems to be solved. The example illustrates how the exercise of problem analysis, taking the format of a problem tree, relied upon or was constituted by clearly formulated rules, advice and conventions. Through the exercise it became clear that partici- pants were intended to learn those rules, that they were supposed to follow them, as a condition for a good course of the exercise and training and as a condition for analysing situations in a participatory way (with all participants, also the poorest, also women and children), in terms of problems and in view of an analysis of objectives (in an objective tree) and of strategies, interventions, activities, monitor- ing and evaluation. The conditions for participatory behaviour, for participative analysis and actually also for practicing freedom, were in this example clearly indicated on slides, in general remarks of the trainer or directly deduced from actions or expressions during the exercise, for instance: write one problem per card (in a maximum of 3 lines); connect different problems with cause-effect arrows; respect everyone's view, never ask who wrote the card (cards are anonymous); don't tear up 'wrong' cards, people would be offended; identify real existing problems, not future or imaginary ones; don't use 'lack of a solution' as a problem, or a problem should not be shown as the absence of a solution but as an existing negative situation.

Besides the direct and clearly formulated suggestions, the practice comprised many more indications, transmitted through the behaviour of the trainer or, indi- rectly, through the actions or thoughts that were avoided or the assumptions that were taken for granted. One such assumption, governing or determining how to proceed, is, for example, implied in the typically participatory principle of visuali- sation,[18] indicated as 'an important aspect of participatory approaches; not merely because it results in a tangible item that can be left in the village but especially because visualisation encourages participation, discussion and dialogue'. This prin- ciple, argued 'to enhance comprehension, to remove boundaries, enabling to make problems more concrete, to explain them, to discuss and negotiate opinions' (FNI10), tells participants to draw their opinions, to 'translate' their thoughts or ideas about themselves, their communities, their environment in visual signs (symbols, arrows, lines), with materialised objects (seeds, stones, sands, leaves). An example of government or conditioning through visualisation was given with the exercise in which participants were summoned to leave the room and go outside to design (on the ground, with differently coloured chalk) a chapatti or Venn diagram representing the groups, persons, institutions, their relations and their relative importance for decision-making in the organisation of the training programme in which they participated.[19] Eliciting heated discussions among the participants about, for instance, the size of the circles and the legitimacy of the accompanying argumentations for this size, the trainer explained how indeed discussions were important, because they bring out the 'true' or 'real' opinions of those involved, including local knowledge otherwise difficult to retrieve, and also because they add a 'genuine' (i.e. shared by all participants) representation of reality, to an under-standable picture of complex and difficult issues. Although trainees in the pro-gramme were assumed to be literate, so the trainer explained, the design of a diagram, the representation of reality in terms of circles is also feasible and prac-ticable for illiterate people, for the poorest, those who cannot read, for women and children. And, so the trainer added, sitting on the ground (which they didn't do for the exercise, but which was recommended in 'real contexts', in villages), at the same level of the others, also 'makes it difficult for any one person to dominate', or 'eases contact; erases differences between poor and richer people' (FNI12).[20] The legitimisations that are given for visualising data or, more specifically, opinions or ideas and for behaviours or physical attitudes such as sitting on the floor, again reveal how trainees in participatory exercises submit to particular rules and norms determining behaviour, but also physical attitudes, ways of thinking or at least of presenting one's thoughts. The description here shows, not how partic-ipants are enforced to behave, act, think in a specific way, but how in participatory practices the opportunities participants can grasp are determined or conditioned, how participants are governed in the ways in which they deal with the participatory opportunities, in which they practice freedom. Through the exercises, participants not only learn to participate or to practice freedom: they learn that freedom practices are compliant with practices of self-determination and self-expression of oneself as a self-responsible subject, expressing and negotiating one's opinions in visualised schemes, behaving as equals by sitting on the floor, in circles, identi-fying in terms of power and influence, interests and expectations or potentials and deficiencies. Also, participants actually learn to behave, to think, to act in particular ways; they learn that the possibilities for practicing freedom are very specific, implying an equally specific understanding of freedom and freedom practices.

Exploring how participatory practices govern the ways in which participants can behave, can practice their freedom, we see that besides self-responsibility, expression of opinions and needs (problems) in visual or other predetermined schemes, identification of oneself and others in stakeholder categories, and self-screening and transparency about oneself are assumed to contribute to freedom, to enlarge one's opportunities to practice freedom and participation. A nice example of the importance of transparency and screening has been provided with a role-play exercise in which participants were asked to play four typical workshop situations, sketched by the trainer, from which observers were assigned to detect the do's and don'ts in the behaviour of the facilitator (who in the exercise played the person introducing or representing the project workshop):[21]

DO's	DON'Ts
respect local customs of greeting	being rough or rude
be humble, really concerned	one-way communication
listen actively	using difficult words
make effort to involve participants	being too directive/impose
reconcile	rushing
keep a good atmosphere	making a business of presents
try to find right balance with presents	showing off, creating gaps
look for key person (for entrance to the community)	making judgements
establish eye contact (following local customs)	misusing power
respect time	discriminating
be flexible	creating conflicts
sit and talk at the level of the participants	being too defensive
allow mistakes	
respect dress code	
introduce yourself, your organisation	
be careful with taking pictures	

Table 1: Facilitator's behavioural code

This table (attached on the wall for further completion during the rest of the training) shows how specifically the rules and norms for the government of conduct can be posited and how participating involves self-screening (making oneself trans-parent) of the participants, often also implying self-evaluation as an identification, presentation and evaluation of one's behaviour or a critical attitude towards one's own way of participating. This self-screening, self-expression and self-evaluation also appeared in the application and selection procedure, where participants were asked to express themselves or to explain themselves about, for instance, their proficiency in English, degree of higher studies, relevant work experience,[22] but also about marital status, children, plans to bring spouse and/or children, complete education, scholarship history, professional experience, extracurricular record, motivation and future plans ('to see if expectations correspond to objectives and contents of the programme'),[23] motivation for applying for a scholarship, any useful additional information, work plan, referees, concluding with a word of honour ('I thereby declare on my word of honour that this information is correct and com-plete') and a signature of the candidate-participant. Besides this information that had to be written down the candidate, moreover, had to submit, translate (into English, French or Dutch, which is not that evident and which asks a lot of Asian or African people)[24] and/or legally validate diplomas, their birth certificate, a letter of good conduct, a visa for travelling. The candidate was expected to provide two referees, preferably a colleague or superior of one's current working context and an independent and relevant authority. This means that candidates had to be capable of finding their way through administration and also that they have at their disposal the necessary networking skills for arranging the necessary documents, for finding and 'activating' some good referees. Once passing all these criteria and require-ments, candidates were finally selected in view of their continent and gender balance for scholarships. All requirements indicated in the selection procedure point out not only many rules and norms of conduct but also a very specific profile to which the candidate or participant had to conform in order to have a chance to be selected, to 'participate'. Our exploration of the selection practice, in other words, shows how participation (in the training) as an opportunity for the subject to practice freedom, involves not only a specific behaviour, but how it represents a (more general) normative profile, a profile to which a subject should respond in order to be able to participate, in order to be a 'good' participant. The selection procedure for participation reveals a certain kind of subject, projects a certain participant profile, indicates how and who a participant should be, how a subject should 'style' oneself in order to be a participant, what a subject should do, feel, think, assume in order to get a chance, to take an opportunity to participate and, as such, to practice freedom. From the descriptions more generally we see that these participatory freedom practices also project a specific understanding of freedom referring to practices of self-expression, self-responsibility, self-knowledge, respect (for oneself and for others), problem analysis. In learning terms, this means that through participation, through the training, through different practices participants are assumed to learn certain rules and norms and to learn how to behave according to these rules and norms, to learn (how) to meet the 'participatory' norm. They learn the norm according to which they can practice their freedom.

2. Who is the Free Participant?

The foregoing exploration pointed out how participatory practices, techniques, exercises project or consolidate around a specific norm, a particular profile that indicates how subjects, as participants, are addressed, what kind of subjects are considered (selected) for participation, what subjects (are assumed to) learn through participating, how subjects should behave, determine themselves for participation and as such also for practicing freedom. In this section we reconsider the participatory norm, the profile of the participatory subject. We indicate how this profile not only concerns behavioural codes, but how participatory government actually involves the whole being of the subject, the way in which the subject should think, act, feel, believe, the conduct of a participant.

As we infer from the exploration of the training, a profile of the participant and the codes, rules or laws from which it can be constituted, are not only becoming visible in direct hints or direct assignments, indicating for a subject-participant what to do, how to behave. Many clues or indications are also found in the ways in which participants are addressed (in e.g. application forms, by the trainers, in exercises), in documents or written material on participation (such as slides, practical and also theoretical literature), in the (expressed and unexpressed) assumptions that animate or determine what happens, what can be said and done but also (sometimes even more) what is or can not (be) said and done. A consideration of such indications yielded the following profile of the participant or, in its derived versions, of the facilitator, stakeholder or also beneficiary (a term somewhat avoided in current literature, in favour of the term stakeholder, considered to sound more neutral and less dependent, helpless or powerless). In profile the participant points out a subject that is or that has to become active, continuously activating or mobilising oneself for expressing and negotiating opinions: opinions about needs and interests or stakes, formulated in terms of simple, singular, visualisable, causally attributable actual problems. Many techniques, exercises and strategies are designed to realise this kind of activation, whereby the subject is assumed to strive for self-knowledge, for self-identification, for making oneself transparent. We thereby see how the transparency into which the participant is enticed, pointing at sometimes intrusive, personal private matters but also more generally local matters, local characteristics, features, customs or attitudes (indicating so-called 'local knowledge') is legitimised in reference to the identification and management of stakes. In other words, speaking out or expressing opinions, for the participant always relates to stakes, to needs (or problems, deficiencies) and interests (or expectations, potentials) and their possible satisfaction. The participant is someone who is continuously asked for her opinions, someone who has a voice and who is invited to use that voice: for indicating and defending her relevant (not future or imagined) stakes, her clearly and singularly definable, her causally retrievable or analysable stakes. The participant also takes other's stakes into account: in order to establish the relation to others, more specifically defined as a relation of networking and negotiation, the participant learns to position herself at the other's level, if necessary even by sitting on the floor with them, by wearing the same clothes, but also by submitting to the same standardised selection procedure. This characterisation implies that the participant has at her disposal specific skills and competencies: such as drawing, mapping and role-playing, discussing, scoring, evaluating, but also networking (in order to engage others in the realisation of one's planning), brainstorming (about possible problems, solutions, strategies), classifying and categorising. Most of these skills, which the participant is assumed to have or at least to be able to learn, are conceived of as capital, as resources to invest in the (circular) process of identification and satisfaction of needs and interests, for which the participant herself is held accountable and self-responsible. Accountability and responsibility thereby, assume very specific shapes or, in other words, they can be realised by the participant in different but particular ways: in the subscription of forms (declaring on one's word of honour) materialising a relation between words and an act of signing, in the exposition of personal information assuming a link between transparency and truthfulness (whereby participant's—visualised—opinions are considered or believed to offer true and genuine representations of reality), in the mobilisation of oneself to activate specific competencies (assuming a link between self-responsibility and one's engagement to lifelong learning and training). Such indications show how the government of the participant, the conditions of participatory freedom practices are not limited to just behavioural (or physical) aspects, but actually also concern or affect the participant's will, her rationality, her ways of thinking and believing, the connections that are assumed between certain words or expressions and certain actions. Participants for instance, learn that participation, and freedom, depend upon their will, that their (free) will is addressed as instigator of their participation, well-being, freedom, that they themselves have to orient their will toward achieving the norm, toward opening up their access to the opportunities of the participatory and freedom practices. Moreover, participants learn rationalities, they learn or are assumed to believe that local knowledge is best retrievable and representable in visual schemes, that difficulties and complexities can be logically analysed in several logical steps, that visualisation and sitting on the ground or in a circle neutralises (power, literacy) differences. Feelings and moods are also involved in participatory government. The participant harbours particular feelings and emotions. Participants for example are assumed and expected to respect themselves and others, to feel self-esteem, ownership, trust, belonging, to experience wellbeing as a result of participation. Specific urges and hopes are highlighted, are brought into relation to specific participatory conduct, such as the urge to be taken seriously (assumed to increase with the degree of transparency and of mobilisation) or 'the hope to win their hearts by making them participate in our activities'.[25] This last quote makes it very clear once more that participation, as a practice of freedom, is not an evident comportment of the subject, but rather a governed choice or option, an opportunity governing the participant in what she does, wants, feels and/or strives for. Learning to participate reveals itself to be also learning the norm and how to submit to that norm as a practice of freedom.

We don't want to question whether 'the participant' provides a good norm for a subject to practice freedom, for the development worker, or also for the child or student, for the poor and illiterate, for the villager who is offered opportunities to participate in his or her own development. We don't want to question the participatory tribunal of self-knowledge and self-responsibility. Because after all, *who are we* to question this norm or this tribunal? But maybe we could just ask, taking up Foucault's suggestion,[26] whether practices of freedom have to involve subjection to a norm or tribunal?

Notes

1. For development sources on participation, see e.g. Stiefel & Wolfe, 1994; The World Bank, 1996; for participation in education, see e.g. de Winter, 1995; Bellamy, 2002; Masschelein & Quaghebeur, 2005.

2. Robin McTaggart exemplarily describes the link between freedom, emancipation and participatory approaches as follows: 'Participatory action research *establishes self-critical communities* of people participating and collaborating in the research processes of planning, acting, observing and reflecting; it aims to build communities of people committed to *enlightening* themselves about the relationship between circumstance, action and consequence, and to *emancipating* themselves from the institutional and personal constraints which limit their power to live by their legitimate, and freely chosen social values' (Wadsworth, 1997, p. 79).

3. The discussion exposed in the following section is based on information and arguments gathered, in field notes, before and during the concerned training, from interviews, written documents and course material.

4. The programme announcement literally indicates that: '*The programme is destined for local staff involved in the management of development projects, in the bilateral, multilateral and non-governmental sectors; Candidates should have a degree of higher studies and have a relevant*

work experience of at least five years in the planning, monitoring, implementation or evaluation of development projects; Candidates must be proficient in English' (VLIR, 2003, p. 30).

5. See IDPM-UA, 2003, pp. 7–10, 16–17.

6. See, for instance, Kolb, 1984; Gee, 1997.

7. These indicate the different phases of project cycle management: programming, identification, formulation, implementation, monitoring and evaluation (see IDPM-UA, 2003, p. 7).

8. Some exemplary sources promoting participation are: Bellamy, 2002; Chambers, 1994; Hart, Newman, Ackermann & Feeny, 2004.

9. Trainees' opinions are literally quoted from interviews. We thereby remark that the language used for the interviews (as for the training) is English, although English is for most of the participants not their mother tongue. Therefore, quotations might sometimes sound odd. For reasons of honesty and authenticity, we did, however, prefer not to change odd expressions and left everything as originally expressed by the interviewees.

10. See FNI, pp. 38, 40–42; FN II, pp. 44, 63–65 where trainees at several reprises are reminded of the availability of the trainers to tutor.

11. See FNII, pp. 61–62.

12. See e.g. FNI, pp. 15–16.

13. See FNI, pp. 20, 22, 33; the mapping exercise which is referred to here consisted of an assignment to design a map of the city in which the training was taking place.

14. We use this term in line with Butler's interpretation of Foucault's perspective on governmentality, to indicate a process of subject-becoming (see Butler, 1997).

15. See FNII, pp. 22–49; Slides 19–22.

16. This project was described in different subdocuments, concerning 'general information', 'description of the context' of the country (Kamolia) and of two provinces (Atago and Borasule), 'situation at the end of phase I' and 'description of phase I'. Trainers indicated this document to be originally based on a real project; names were changed and physical and political backgrounds, population and society and economy (in the context description) were neutralised, i.e. 'described so that it was recognisable for Asian as well as African people from different contexts, cultures and backgrounds' (FNI, p. 39; FNII, p. 7).

17. See FNII, pp. 5–17; Slides 15–17: the definition of 'stakeholder' as well as the categories for stakeholder identification were presented on slides, followed by an invitation to the trainees to brainstorm about possible stakeholder groups for the documented project. After the brainstorming session, participant subgroups were asked to describe and categorise stakeholders and, finally, to delegate a member for the plenary presentation of their work.

18. See FNI, p. 10; see also Chambers, 1997, pp. 131–140, 159–161 where visual techniques, as participatory instruments, as instruments to involve the poor, 'the last', are praised and promoted for their neutrality and rigour, for their trustworthiness and relevance, for their leverage function in understanding and expressing difficulty and complexity. Besides appreciation of the participatory principle of visualisation, some authors also raised harsh criticisms, denouncing the principle for several reasons, see e.g. Francis, 2001, p. 81; Kapoor, 2002, p. 104; Rajar, 2001.

19. See FNI, pp. 28–29 and Rietbergen-McCracken & Narayan, 1998, pp. 147–148 for more information in the manual that was used by the trainers.

20. These arguments are also brought up for other participatory instruments, and are more than once repeated during the training, see FNI, more specifically also, pp. 44–45. Also in literature, Venn diagrams, as other (mostly visual) participatory instruments, are largely commented on and discussed from those same and even more elaborate points of view, see—among others—Chambers, Pacey & Thrupp, 1989, pp. 77–100; Clayton, Oakley & Pratt, 1997, chapter 3; Rietbergen-McCracken & Narayan, 1998, pp. 141 ff.

21. See FNI, pp. 12–14; see also FNII, p. 15 for a clarification on the role of facilitator, who can be a trainer, a technical advisor (providing resources for the process) or a moderator (keeping the time, regulating the training, 'usually someone who has practical experience and who, as such, is more than others entitled to provide for training').
22. These categories refer to the formal criteria that had to be satisfied for the candidate-participant to receive a scholarship. These criteria are, together with a programme description, presented in the training brochure. See also note 4.
23. Quotation from a telephone conversation with the secretary of the training programme.
24. See interviews.
25. See interviews.
26. See Foucault, 1984bb; see also Gros, 2001.

References

Bellamy, C. (2002) *The State of the World's Children 2003* (New York, UNICEF).
Butler, J. (1997) *The Psychic Life of Power: Theories in subjection* (Stanford, CA, Stanford University Press).
Chambers, R. (1994) Participatory Rural Appraisal; Challenges, potentials and paradigm, *World Development*, 22:10, pp. 1437–1454.
Chambers, R. (1997) *Whose Reality Counts? Putting the first last* (London, Intermediate Technology Publications).
Chambers, R., Pacey, A. & Thrupp, L. A. (1989) *Farmer First: Farmer innovation and agricultural research* (London, Intermediate Technology Publications).
Clayton, A., Oakley, P. & Pratt, B. (1997) *Empowering People: A guide to participation* (Oxford, INTRAC).
de Winter, M. (1995) *Kinderen als Medeburgers: Kinder- en Jeugdparticipatie als Maatschappelijk Opvoedingsperspectief* (Utrecht, De Tijdstroom).
Fieldnotes, part I & II [FN I&II] (unpublished research documents by Kerlijn Quaghebeur, August 2003).
Foucault, M. (1984) The Ethics of the Concern of the Self as a Practice of Freedom, in: P. Rabinow (ed.), *Michel Foucault: Ethics; Subjectivity and truth; Essential works of Foucault 1954–1984* (London, Penguin Books).
Francis, P. (2001) Participatory Development at the World Bank: The primacy of process, in: B. Cooke & U. Kothari (eds), *Participation: The new tyranny?* (London/New York, Zed Books).
Gee, J. P. (1997) Thinking, Learning, and Reading: The situated socio-cultural mind, in: D. Kirshner & J. A. Whitson (eds), *Situated Cognition: Social, semiotic, and psychological perspectives* (Mahwah, NJ, Lawrence Erlbaum Associates).
Gros, F. (2001) Situation du Cours, in: Foucault, M. *L'Herméneutique du Sujet; Cours au Collège de France 1981–1982* (Paris, Gallimard/Seuil).
Hart, J., Newman, J., Ackermann, L. & Feeny, T. (2004) *Children Changing their World: Understanding and evaluating children's participation in development* (Surrey/London, PLAN).
IDPM-UA (2003) *Management and Evaluation of Participatory Projects 2003* (Antwerpen, Institute of Development Policy. and Management, University of Antwerp).
Interviews (unpublished, written out notes of interviews with trainees by Kerlijn Quaghebeur, Mai 2003).
Kapoor, I. (2002) The Devil's in the Theory: A critical assessment of Robert Chambers' work on participatory development, *Third World Quarterly*, 23:1, pp. 101–117.
Kolb, D. A. (1984) *Experiential Learning: Experience as the source of learning and development* (Upper Saddle River, NJ, Prentice Hall).
Masschelein, J. & Quaghebeur, K. (2005) Participation for Better or for Worse, *Journal of Philosophy of Education*, 39:1, pp. 51–65.

Rajar, D. (2001) *From Verbal to Visual: The politics of pictures in participatory rural appraisal (PRA)* (unpublished research document, Institute of Development Studies, Brighton, UK).

Rietbergen-McCracken, J. & Narayan, D. (1998) *Participation and Social Assessment: Tools and techniques* (Washington, DC, The International Bank for Reconstruction and Development, The World Bank).

Slides (unpublished course documentation by the trainers of the international programme, April–June 2003).

Stiefel, M. & Wolfe, M. (1994) *A Voice for the Excluded: Popular participation in development: utopia or necessity?* (London & NJ, UNRISD/Zed Books).

The World Bank (1996) *The World Bank Participation Sourcebook* (Washington, DC, World Bank).

VLIR (2003) *Advanced University Education: Flanders-Belgium in the heart of Europe* (Brussels, Flemish University Council).

Wadsworth, Y. (1997) *Everyday Evaluation on the Run* (Sydney, Allen & Unwin).

7
On Creativity: A brainstorming session

Ulrich Bröckling

Theological Niceties. Creativity is a concept with metaphysical subtleties and theological niceties. *Creatio ex nihilo* only exists as a divine act. To insert something into the undefined or empty, amounts to generating a miniature world. Even in creativity's form as a secularised human capacity, its religious roots have not been severed. True, we can formulate conditions more or less propitious for new things to emerge; we can analytically reduce the process into increasingly tiny units and describe what is taking place in the brain; but inevitably, an inexplicable 'leap' remains: a 'miracle' when expressed theologically. Even though, as the well-known formula has it, creativity involves 99% perspiration, we are still left with one per cent inspiration. This is revealed not least of all in a metaphorical terminology recalling the Pentecostal advent of the Holy Spirit: from the 'flash of insight' and the 'stroke of genius' to 'brainstorming', where 'the wind bloweth where it will' (John 3,8). Invocations of creativity always have something of the supplicatory prayer about them: *Veni creator spiritus.*

Potential. Creativity is tied to the human potential to bring into being something new. Its basis is, first, the power of imagination as the capacity to make the absent present; and second, building upon this, fantasy as the capacity to realize the (as yet) inexistent. Following the distinction suggested by the German sociologist Heinrich Popitz, generating the new can transpire along three paths: firstly, that of exploring (discovery and invention; the search for new knowledge); second, that of shaping (the production and formation of artefacts); third, generating meaning (interpretation, philosophical justification) (Popitz, 1997). This distinction is ideal-typical. In reality the three dimensions of action intersect, as do the social functions and role models deriving from them.

Mirror game. The effort to pin down creativity culminates in an infinite regression. Something old lurks within everything new; the new builds on the old, modifies it, distances itself from it. The closer one looks, the more familiarly it stares back. Inversely, a moment of creative variation lurks within every repetition. One does not step twice into the same brook. For this reason, it is just as easy to confirm or deny that an artefact, discovery, or interpretation is creative. Those wishing to establish the old's present in the new will prove just as successful as those seeking the new in the old. What decides is the angle of vision.

Contingency. Creative acts do or do not take place. They can be enticed into being through work or enthusiasm, and above all through both, but they cannot be forced. As Max Weber wrote, 'ideas occur to us when they please, not when it pleases us' (Weber, 1946, p. 136). The entire realm of human knowledge, of artefacts and interpretations, hence all products of creative investigation, formation, generation of meaning, possess no necessary existential grounding. They could also be otherwise or not be at all (Makropoulos, 1997). In its contingency, creativity is ambivalent to a high degree—at one and the same time a desirable resource and a threatening potential. Consequently, with the experience of contingency comes a need to direct it, that is, to render its productive aspects useful and its destructive aspects null and void. On the one hand, creativity is meant to be mobilized and set free; on the other hand, it is meant to be controlled and reined in, oriented toward the solving of certain problems while kept at a remove from others. Liberation and domestication are here inextricably tied together. Phantasms of complete controllability must necessarily end up shattered, because creativity cannot be shoved into the domain of compliance—with absence of the anarchic moment, it is never present. Regimes of control change; what remains are attempts to steer the course of creativity.

Historical a Priori. What constitutes creativity has not been determined once and for all, but rather emerges from the various ways it has been attributed, evoked, and catalysed throughout history. This fact comprises determination of those capable of and called on for creative action (the gods or God, and human beings as well? which of the latter should be included or excluded?). It also comprises definition of the realms in which creativity can manifest itself; the shifting nature of the strategies and tactics through which it is governed; and both the final purpose of the creative action and the sources of its legitimacy (in the name of which authority does the call go forth to encourage or control creativity?). A genealogy of creativity would have to explore its historical semantic elements; the disparate technologies involved in forming the human capacity to discover and shape, and to generate meaning; the various models of creative accomplishment and self-accomplishment (from genius embraced by the muses to unorthodox mind-mapping thinkers); finally, both the heterogeneous creativity specialists and various justifications of creative action: pedagogic (the personality's unfolding), therapeutic (fantasy's healing powers), economic (competitive advantages through innovation), and political (the well-ordered commonweal).

Metaphors. Because what creativity is cannot be precisely defined, metaphors run rampant. Described roughly, six associative field are at work here (Joas, 1997), a specific anthropological or conceptual tradition corresponding to each. The dividing lines are hazy, the overlaps many. Firstly, creativity is associated with artistic action, with the moment of expressivity occupying the foreground. Human beings are here defined as expressive beings, both in terms of capacity and innate nature; the embodiment of this approach is the artistic genius, with lines of tradition reaching back to the Italian Renaissance and to Herder and German Romanticism, but also to the philosophical anthropology of Max Scheler, Helmuth Plessner, and Arnold Gehlen. Second, creativity is conceived in terms of production. The focus here is on individuals as beings who realize and objectify themselves through work and its products; the craftsman is here an exemplary figure. The roots of this conceptual model extend back to Aristotle's distinction between praxis and poiesis; one of its most prominent formulations is the ontology of work formulated by the young Marx. With their concept of 'immaterial work', the Italian postoperaists offer a contemporary variant of the model (Lazzarato, 1993). It contrasts with, third, the concept of creativity as problem-solving action, with stress being placed on invention and innovation. The anthropology implied here is along the following lines: human beings are beings who master their lives, being able to rely neither on instinct-bound reactive patterns nor on simple behavioral routines. For this conceptual model, creativity is concretely situated; it responds to challenges demanding solutions that are both new and fitting: an approach exemplarily embodied in the figure of the inventor. It has been extensively formulated by American pragmatism as a theory of cognition and action, and by Jean Piaget in his theory of cognitive development. A fourth metaphoric field is that of revolution. Creativity here means liberating action, a radical new invention of social structure: the human being confronts the world as a border-transgressor, a 'creative destroyer'. Prototypes for this dimension of creativity are, naturally, nonconformists and dissidents *de tout couleur*, with manifestos of various artistic and political avant-gardes offering relevant programmatic statements. Creativity evokes, fifth, life-connected associations: metaphors of birth and generation, but also of biological evolution. In general, what is here being centred on is the phenomenon of emergence, creativity manifesting itself as personal or supra-personal energies even—and particularly—clearing new ground when encountering resistance. At this model's centre we find, on the one hand, the individual's drive-related dimension—the creativity of what Deleuze and Guattari called 'machines of desire' (Deleuze & Guattari, 1988); and, on the other hand, the non-intentional processes of adapting to one's environment through natural selection. Theoretical efforts in this direction have been offered by Nietzsche, Bergson, and Freud, as well as by Darwin and various neo-Darwinists (Simonton, 1999). Sixth and last, the probably most familiar creativity metaphor is that of play, identifying creative with purposeless activity. The paragon for *homo ludens* is the child. This model can be traced back to Plato's ideal of 'spend[ing] life in making our *play* as perfect as possible' (Plato, 1966, VII, 803 C); Schiller's declaration that 'the human being plays only when he is human in the full sense of the word; and he is only fully human when he plays' (Schiller 1795/1954, p. 601) moves in the same direction. Whether this or that metaphor or several at once are evoked depends on which creative potentials happen to be required and are meant to be furthered. That such varied associations can be linked to creativity is not the least of the reasons no one wishes to see them go. In the flurry of metaphors, each person discovers his or her own.

Common coinage. The heroic productive powers of the genius were only reserved for a few; everyone can and should be creative. Where geniality was exclusive, bestowed on some and not others, creativity has gradations—some have more of it, others less. Genius belonged in a sphere beyond the norm, common sense thus locating it in the vicinity of madness. Creativity is normal; it is distributed in conformity with the curves of Gaussian norm-distribution. Geniuses distinguished themselves through extraordinary accomplishments in the arts and sciences, perhaps also in politics and warfare. The attribute 'creative' ennobles even the most banal activities—from the washing-cutting-drying of the creative coiffeur around the corner to the creative bookkeeping of someone faking a balance. 'Every man is an artist' propagated Joseph Beuys in *documenta* 5 of 1972, and this is the legitimating ideal behind every extension school's program. Creativity-promotion is democracy's cult of genius.

Interpellation. One is creative starting from birth—and is never finished with becoming so over a lifetime. This is the source of the implicit Rousseauism of most creativity programs: they offer cultural techniques meant to lead one back to a nature putatively buried by the process of cultural formation. Appeals ('be creative!') and self-understanding ('I'm myself to the extent I'm creative') here come together. The unity of description and prescription corresponds to a paradoxical temporal structure that fuses the 'always was' with the 'not yet': According to this schema, creativity is firstly something everyone has—an anthropological capacity; second, something one ought to have—a binding norm; third, something one can never have enough of—a telos without closure; fourth, something that can be intensified through methodological instruction and exercise—a learnable competence.

Political economy. Creativity is an economical resource that the market both mobilises and consumes: creative destruction is the entrepreneur's economical function; his profits result from 'carrying out new combinations' (Schumpeter, 1926, p. 110). In order not to go under, he must offer other commodities than the competitors, or the same commodities in better quality or at a more appealing price, more speedily furnished, and so forth. And success here is only for the moment. As soon as competitors catch on, the advantage vanishes. Entrepreneurial action thus demands permanent innovation—and consequently ceaseless creative exertion. Everybody not only has to be simply creative, but more creative than the others; and nobody can be sure of finding takers for the new combinations. Despite all efforts to objectify or subjectify the conditions for success by market research or entrepreneurial intuition, individual economic subjects have only the principle of trial and error at their disposal. As the competition's products, ever-more artefacts, reserves of knowledge, and interpretations are piled up by the society as a whole. In this sense, creativity is 'general labour', the innovative side of general intellect and, as such, a direct productive force (Marx, 1894/1969, p. 114).

Spirit of Enterprise. To the extent that nowadays everyone is expected to act, in all life circumstances, as his or her own entrepreneur, the mobilization of innovative potential is itself privatised and individualized. Entrepreneurship not only forms the goal of all interpellations of creativity, but its privileged means as well. In contrast, the state appears as the great institutionalised hindrance to creativity. The individual who proceeds creatively resembles the successful investor: he speculates on the future and seeks his chances outside the beaten path. 'Buy low and sell high' is his principle. Today he lays his stake on offbeat ideas, hoping that tomorrow they comprise the norm. The market decides which creations yield effective interest. The remainder fizzles. The opportunity for success only waves a hand at those incurring the risk of failure upon their shoulders. Whether or not something is creative only emerges afterwards, when it appears pleasing, illuminating, or useful to others, in short: when it experiences valuation, or at least attracts attention. In the presence of disinterest, simply travelling other paths than the masses is useless—what is creative is the new that prevails (Sternberg & Lubart, 1991).

Distinction. The new is a relational category, existing through demarcation from the old. What is new is what was not there. (As soon as it is there it stops being new.) Being creative thus means drawing distinctions. This can involve the invention of previously unknown artefacts, insights, or interpretations; but it can also involve the recombination or variation of what is already present, the privileging of previously devalued or devaluation of previously privileged artefacts, insights, or interpretations (Groys, 1992). The possibilities for creating something new are unlimited; what is decisive is the moment of difference—creative persons thus being always already postmodern. The creative imperative necessitates permanent deviation; its enemies are homogeneity, compulsory identity, standardization, repetition. Attributes of being apart and special are only enjoyed by those who do not fit in. But within the promise of alterity, a threat is lurking: 'be someone select ... or you'll be a reject' is the way it is put in a guide to constructing 'Me Inc'. (Peters, 2000, p. 8).

Ambiguity. Like every order, societal order needs constant renewal in order to deal with changing circumstances. Creativity is thus a civic responsibility, its promotion a political duty no less important than street-maintenance or preserving public safety. But creativity is also a subversive force, a force threatening every order. Celebrating the great negation, Russian anarchist Mikhael Bakunin exclaims that 'the passion for destruction is a creative passion, too!' (Bakunin, 1842/1969, p. 69). Hence political rhetoric either alternates between appeals to freedom and postulates of loyalty or has recourse to oxymorons such as 'creative obedience' and 'revolutionary discipline'. The political Janus-face has its counterpart in moral ambivalence: creative achievements are both the directing of a military campaign and the negotiation of a peace treaty.

Technologies. The appeal to be creative is no less paradoxical than the legendary appeal to be spontaneous. Creativity can neither be ordered into existence nor pressed into study plans or work contracts. One cannot command something indefinite. In any event, factors can be specified that make creative acts more likely. Creativity-promotion involves controlling contexts—it creates nothing, but makes things possible. Nevertheless, programs of 'innovation gymnastics' thrive (Hentig, 2000, p. 60)—and these have of course moved far past the stage of home prescriptions. An army of scientific specialists is investigating the relevant terrain, furnishing those hungry for creativity with ever-new training methods (this itself a creative accomplishment under the sign of the market). The specialists base their work on everyday forms of idea-production, these assimilated into systematically derived, often professionally run and institutionally supported strategies for innovation management. Precisely this constitutes the leap from technique to technology. Contemporary creativity programs thus make use both of inventories from the communication and information sciences (neurolinguistic programming) and of discoveries in cognitive research (activation of the brain's right hemisphere); they adapt formerly 'alternative' educational concepts ('open space', learning through projects, 'future factories'), therapeutic techniques (free association), and practices of artistic avant-gardes (*écriture automatique*).

Performative contradiction. The creative imperative demands serial singularity, ready-made difference. Creativity-training standardizes the breach with standard solutions. It normalises deviations from the norm, instructing us not to rely on what has been learned. The paths to the particular should be the same paths for all. For this reason, they are as general as possible: an irritation of certainties and of conceptual and behavioural patterns that have been hammered in from birth (*lateral thinking*); an exclusion of both inner and outer censoring instances (a doing away with 'creativity killers'); artistic naivety (being dumb as a creative strategy); associative leaps and analogy-formation (synectics); the systematic exploration and grasping of possible solutions (brainstorming, mind-mapping, and similar procedures). Being creative means hard work yet demands the lightness of play. The realm of necessity forces what can only thrive in the realm of freedom.

Fun-culture. Being creative is fun. Joy at individual or common activity and its results is not the least of the motivations for creative action. Psychologists name this 'intrinsic motivation', and it serves as one of the main sources tapped by the ubiquitous appeals to creativity. People in a good mood are more productive. Because not so much occurs to the unhappy and depressed, our fun-culture blossoms. Gone are the times when carnivalizing daily life was still a subversive project and the Munich Situationists in the SPUR group could declare that 'being creative means pleasure playing with everything through permanently new creation'; in the Bavarian German original: '*Schöpferisch sein heißt: durch dauernde Neuschöpfung mit allen Dingen seine Gaudi treiben*' (The SPUR group, 1961, pp. 16/17). Today this is taken care of by comedy shows on all channels, and firms engage professional fun-makers who place clown-noses on staff members in order to ready them for new business strategies through 'motivational theatre'.

Speed of circulation. Creativity needs leisure, the market forces speed. Creativity released by the economic imperative thus undermines the basis of its existence. The higher the pressure to innovate, the shorter the half-time of the new and the greater the corroding of creative potential. To be sure, everyone can be creative, but no one can be so constantly. 'If I were only free for a few days or weeks from the need to always offer something new', complains the creative individual, 'then I'd certainly come up with some truly new ideas'. To which his manager offers the crushing reply: 'without deadline-pressure you'd end up producing nothing'. When leisure-time is systematically shortened or functionalized into a catalyst for innovative processes, only the simulation of creativity remains. (Doubtless, such simulation also requires a fitting measure of fantasy.) Perhaps this is the reason why nothing seems more antiquated than what just seemed so trendy. Progress—the return, once again, of what has often seemed new.

Les misérables. That necessity is invention's mother is only maintained by those not in need. Those tormented by hunger or anxiety seek bread and shelter; they are not inclined towards creative experiments. Creativity requires free spaces in which the pressures of self-preservation have been at least temporarily suspended. But necessity itself knows no imperative. Those living in misery cannot afford to always stick to the straight path. The adroit hand-flick into the stranger's wallet, the beggar's pity-evoking story, opening the clasp of the passer-by's purse, the less ambitious and more ambitious tricks for gaining what one needs but cannot afford, for making money through whatever can be sold—all of this demands the highest possible degree of innovation, improvisational talent, and deviation from the norm. The art of survival is the poor man's creativity.

Beyond the imperative. In face of the exactions of the creative imperative, neither the pathos of refusal nor the furore of raising the stakes will prove sufficient. When deviance becomes a normative demand, flagrant non-conformism emerges as absolute conformity. But when renunciation of the new is inflated into a principle, this itself marks a creative difference, with the concomitant hope of gaining distinction. Originality- and repetition-compulsion are two sides of the same coin. Freedom that deserves the name only begins where neither one nor the other prevails. The negation of the ubiquitous creativity postulate is not 'Don't be creative', but rather a turn away from speaking in the imperative. One cannot not be creative, but perhaps one can stop wanting to always be creative.

Social Fantasy. The 'creative moment', the 'eureka', may be the individual's prerogative, coming over him in the proverbial quiet little room, but one is never creative when alone. Creative action is always addressed somewhere and is always 'an action upon an action, on possible or actual future or present actions' (Foucault, 2000, p. 340). There are no creative monads. The creative individual lives face to face with others, whose recognition he hopes for and whose displeasure he fears, with whom he forges common ideas or whom he avoids, who furnishes him with problems or whose solutions are not satisfactory to him, whose footprints he steps into or out of, and so forth. Like Nietzsche's 'chain-thinker', 'every new thought that he hears or reads of' appears to him 'immediately in the form of a chain' (Nietzsche, 1969, p. 864). One of creativity's main objects is the social self. Like the ego, society is always invented, formed, established anew. To show that social fantasy can be more than the sum of efforts to contain it in truth-regimes, behavioural codices, and Weltanschauungen would be a truly creative project.

Addendum—a test. Theories of creativity unfailingly soar to the highest heights of philosophical abstraction while simultaneously landing in the most awful aporias. In response to the questions of what creativity is and, above all, who is creative, they furnish nothing but contradictory answers. For this reason, in conclusion let us look at a creativity test as simple as it is unerring. It was devised by Niklas Luhmann:

> The test involved here is a self-test that, however, can be derived from a survey-procedure. It is likewise a two-stage test. The first stage involves following a very simple behavioral rule: The subject must take his conscience into his neighbor's room. Whenever he sees that the neighbor is reading books he himself has not yet read and then has a bad conscience, he is not creative—he simply wishes to imitate his neighbor. Whenever, to the contrary, he sees that the neighbor is reading the same books as he is and then has a bad conscience, he is presumably creative. For in the latter case he is—perhaps unconsciously—seeking new paths. Hence creativity is here tested in terms of the way guilt-feelings are steered. This is, however, only the first stage of the test. The rule applied in the second stage is as follows: Whoever carries out the creativity test is not creative for just that reason, since this shows he is interested in being creative. And in the end everybody wishes to be so (Luhmann, 1988, pp. 18, 19).

translated by Joel Golb

References

Bakunin, M. (1842/1969) Die Reaktion in Deutschland, in: *idem, Philosophie der Tat* (Köln, Verlag Jakob Hegner).
Deleuze, G. & Guattari, F. (1988) *Anti-Oedipus. Capitalism and schizophrenia* (Minneapolis, MN, University of Minnesota Press).
Foucault, M. (2000) The Subject and Power, in: *Essential Works of Michel Foucault, Vol. 3: Power*, J. D. Faubion, ed. (New York, New Press), pp. 326–348.
Groys, B. (1992) *Über das Neue. Versuch einer Kulturökonomie* (Munich & Vienna, Hanser Verlag).
Hentig, H. v. (2000) *Kreativität. Hohe Erwartungen an einen schwachen Begriff* (Weinheim & Basel, Beltz Verlag).
Joas, H. (1997) *The Creativity of Action* (Chicago, IL, University of Chicago Press).
Lazzarato, M. (1993) Immaterielle Arbeit, in: T. Negri, M. Lazzarato & P. Virno, *Umherschweifende Produzenten. Immaterielle Arbeit und Subversion* (Berlin, ID Verlag), pp. 39–52.
Luhmann, N. (1988) Über 'Kreativität', in: H.-U. Gumbrecht (ed.), *Kreativität—Ein verbrauchter Begriff* (Munich, Wilhelm Fink Verlag).
Makropoulos, M. (1997) *Modernität und Kontingenz* (Munich, Wilhelm Fink Verlag).
Marx, K. (1894/1969) *Das Kapital*, Vol. 3, *Marx und Engels, Werke*, Vol. 25 (Berlin, Dietz Verlag).
Nietzsche, F. (1969) Menschliches, Allzumenschliches, in: *idem, Werke*, Vol. 1 (Munich, Hanser Verlag).
Peters, T. (2000) *TOP 50 Selbstmanagement. Machen Sie aus sich die ICH AG* (Munich, Econ Verlag).
Plato, *Laws* (1966) in: E. Hamilton & H. Cairns (eds), *Collected Dialogues of Plato* (New York, Princeton University Press).
Popitz, H. (1997) Wege der Kreativität. Erkunden, Gestalten, Sinnstiften, in: *idem, Wege der Kreativität* (Tübingen, Mohr & Siebeck), pp. 80–132.

Schiller, F. (1795/1954) Über die ästhetische Erziehung des Menschen in einer Reihe von Briefen, in: *idem, Werke*, Vol. 2 (Munich, Droemersche Verlagsanstalt), pp. 563–641.

Schumpeter, J. (1926) *Theorie der wirtschaftlichen Entwicklung* (Munich & Leipzig, Verlag Duncker & Humblot).

Simonton, D. K. (1999) *Origins of Genius: Darwinian Perspectives on Creativity* (New York, Oxford University Press).

Sternberg R. J. & Lubart, T. L. (1991) An Investment Theory of Creativity and its Development, *Human Development*, 34, pp. 1–31.

The SPUR group (1961/1968) Januar-Manifest, in: A. Goeschel (ed.), *Richtlinien und Anschläge. Materialien zur Kritik der repressiven Gesellschaft* (Munich Hanser Verlag), pp. 16, 17.

Weber, M. (1946) Science as Vocation, in: H. H. Gerth & C. W. Mills (eds), *From Max Weber: Essays in sociology* (New York, Oxford University Press), pp. 129–156.

8

Learning as Investment: Notes on governmentality and biopolitics

Maarten Simons

> Human beings are unique among all living organisms in that their
> primary adaptive specialization lies not in some particular physical
> form or skill or fit in an ecological niche, but rather in identification
> with the process of adaptation itself—in the process of learning. We are
> thus the learning species, and our survival depends on our ability to adapt
> not only in the reactive sense of fitting into the physical and social worlds
> but in the proactive sense of creating and shaping those worlds.
>
> (Kolb, 1984, p. 1)

Introduction

Europe is in need of space. Some initiatives at least point in that direction. With
regard to the Lisbon-strategy and the European knowledge society the importance
of a 'European research area' is stressed. Another project is the creation of a
'European space of lifelong learning'. The most famous area, at least in educational
circles, is the 'European space of higher education'. This space should be focused
on international competitiveness, mobility and employability.

An analysis based upon Foucault, and more specifically inspired by studies
of governmentality, has pointed at the specific type of inhabitants of this space.
Entrepreneurial selves and institutions *need* a global network environment or
infrastructure (Masschelein & Simons, 2002; 2003). The infrastructure is *needed*
in order to be able to employ one's human capital, to make choices taking into
account information about the added value or quality, to make investments in
additional human capital and to use one's learning force in a productive way.
As a result, the European space of higher education can be described as an
infrastructure for entrepreneurial selves and institutions that look in an investing
way towards the future. And as far as we look at ourselves (as students, teachers,
and organisations) and our future in this way, the European infrastructure is not
just an option but a necessity.

The European space for higher education is a concrete illustration of what
Bröckling *et al.* have described as an 'economisation of the social' (Bröckling *et al.*,

2000). This formula refers to a main characteristic of advanced liberalism as a governmental regime. The term economic should be understood here in a rather specific way, i.e. it refers to entrepreneurship or a kind of freedom guaranteed through a submission to a 'permanent economic tribunal' (Foucault, 2004a, p. 253). Thus, the formula does not refer to the colonisation of the social by the economic (presupposing that the notions refer to two different domains), but to a governmental regime in which the economic has changed itself. In short, within this configuration of entrepreneurial government and self-government the distinction between the social and the economic (as two different domains, each requiring their own government) becomes obsolete.

This cartography of the present will be elaborated below by focusing on Foucault's notion of biopolitics. Foucault introduces the term in the middle of the 1970s to argue that the 'regulation of the population' (besides disciplining the body) is an important pillar of power relations within the modern nation state. Although recently the concept of biopolitics has been used in different places, with regard to studies of governmentality the concept has been of rather minor importance. Foucault's own use of the concept could help to explain this. Although the course at the *Collège de France* of 1978–1979 has the title *Naissance de la biopolitique*, he focuses mainly on the birth of liberal and neo-liberal forms of governmentality (Foucault, 2004a). Thus biopolitical issues are not extensively dealt with in his analysis of these economic regimes of government. However, according to us it is interesting to focus explicitly on the relation between political economy and biopolitics and to explore, using Bröckling's terminology and perspective, the 'intersection between a politicisation and economisation of human life' (Bröckling, 2003, p. 6). This exploration will give us the opportunity to argue that the 'economisation of the social' has a biopolitical dimension and that what is at stake is a 'bio-economisation'. The first part of this paper is limited to a general overview of the concept of biopolitics as used by Foucault and authors after him, in order to explore in the following parts—at a very general level—some biopolitical dimensions of the present and more specifically of the European space of higher education.

1. Ideas on Biopolitics

The notion biopolitics, used in accordance with Foucault, is not at all well defined. Nancy refers on this point to a kind of confusion due to a notion such as 'bio-ethics' (Nancy, 2000, p. 137). Bio-ethics is often used to talk about the ethical problems and moral decisions generated through new developments and possibilities of biotechnology. In this sense, it is not an 'ethics' that is completely determined or formed by 'bios' (a kind of vital ethics). Instead, it is a kind of ethical reflection about the consequences of new possibilities of biotechnology. The notion 'biopolitics'—in accordance with Foucault at least—should be understood in another way, i.e. it does not refer to a political reflection about biotechnology, but to a politics determined and steered by life.[1] Or to use Foucault's well known description: 'For millennia, man remained what he was for Aristotle: a living animal with the additional capacity for a political existence; modern man is an animal whose politics places his existence as a living being in question'. (Foucault, 1976/1979, p. 143)

Thus, with the term biopolitics Foucault tries to articulate how from the nineteenth century onwards politics understand itself not anymore (or only) in relation to subjects (in a juridical sense) or to a territory, but in relation to the life of an individual or species. This rather 'epochal' statement concerning the 'threshold of biological modernity' and the biopolitical era implies that politics and political forms of the exercise of power have changed in their essence (Donnelly, 1992, p. 200). In the following we will take a look at how Foucault looks at this global political change. Then, we will show how Agamben and Negri/Hardt take up and elaborate the term in their own, rather specific, framework. A short discussion of their use of the term biopolitics will enable us to explore how the term can be reintroduced with regard to studies of governmentality.

1.1 'The Threshold of Biological Modernity'

In order to explore the main features of biopower, Foucault contrasts this term with the features of sovereign power (Foucault, 1976/1979; 1997). The sovereign is someone who can decide upon life and dead. The right to kill can be used in an indirect way to hold power over life. The following formula expresses very well what is at stake in biopower: '(…) the ancient right to *take* life or *let* live is replaced by a power to *foster* life or *disallow* it to the point of death'. (Foucault, 1976/1979, p. 138) Thus, biopower is a kind of power directly focused on life, while death falls out of its scope. Moreover, in this power over life by taking life itself as a point of reference two poles are to be distinguished: an anatomo-politics of the human body (being shaped throughout the eighteenth century) in which the body is disciplined and a biopolitics of the human species (established at the end of the eighteenth century) and directed towards a regulation of the population. The notion biopolitics, thus, is reserved for the pole of biopower directed towards the collective body and operating through regulating the processes at the level of a population. In other words, problems such as the birth and death rates, health and aspects of economic production have an immediate political dimension. Biopolitics is about governing life, governing ways of life and regulating for example danger and accidents at the level of the individual and the species. What is at stake therefore, is to secure normality and order at the level of the population. And in order to achieve this, biopolitics can develop central mechanisms of control (campaigns on public health or central medical care) or can try to establish throughout disciplinary power a relation to the self (hygiene, frugality, providence) that promotes order at the level of the collective or population.

Within this configuration the family for example obtains a biopolitical dimension. The family does not refer any longer to a kind of governmental model, but is regarded as an important segment of the population. Foucault refers to this development as an 'instrumentalisation' of the family for the regulation of the population (Foucault, 1978a, p. 651). Closely related to this is the problematisation of childhood in biopolitical terms: it is regarded as a phase in life in need of a physical and moral environment to secure an optimal and healthy development (cf. Foucault, 1979a, p. 11). Donzelot has examined in detail how the family environment increasingly becomes the object of 'moralising' (providence, order) and 'normalising' (medicalisation of the family) interventions (Donzelot, 1978, p. 58). This concern for an optimal, educational environment does not only contribute to the individual child (a preparation for an optimal functioning as adult) but is regarded at the same time as a guarantee for order and prosperity at the level of the population. The family, thus, is functioning as a kind of intersection between the anatomo-political and the bio-political pole of biopower. Furthermore, this biopolitical problematisation and valuation of the family pictures very well how biopower is related to economical interests. Later on, we will deal with the relation between biopolitics and the economic in more detail. At this point, it is sufficient to state that an investment in a healthy population through acting upon the family is not only a condition for societal order and security, but at the same time for economic welfare.

This short contextualisation explains that what is at stake with the coming into existence of biopolitics (or the regulation of processes at the level of the population) is a kind of 'étatisation of the biological' (Foucault, 1997, p. 213). And this understanding of a collective of people as a population in need of regulation is, according to Foucault, a decisive step in the history of Western politics. In order to point at its importance we have to focus on a significant implication of this political turn.

Although Foucault distinguishes between classical sovereign power on the one hand and modern biopower and biopolitics on the other hand, he does not claim that sovereign power disappears. Instead, he indicates that sovereign power ('take life') is recoded in a specific way within modern biopower as 'state racism' (Foucault, 1997, p. 227). Modern racism makes distinctions within the biological continuum, i.e. it divides the population into subgroups or races and it places within the population groups against each other. Within this configuration 'take life' or 'make die' can be introduced as acts that follows a bio-logic: to make die inferior, dangerous or life threatening groups or individuals guarantees the life of a population. State-racism thus allows that a state that understands its role against a biopolitical horizon and thus that is focused on fostering life has given itself the right to eliminate others in the name of that life. In other words, after the biopolitical turn the state is only able to take a sovereign decision about life and death when racism is at stake. And this 'take life', according to Foucault, should be understood in a broad sense: the direct, physical death, but also exposure to death or enlarging the risk to die and even the political death, the negation or exclusion (Foucault, 1997, p. 228). The principle that the death of others is strengthening oneself in a biological sense, allows racism to assure the function of death within the economy of biopower.

This discussion of some features of biopolitical modernity helps us to understand in which way the term 'biopolitics' recently has been elaborated in a philosophical context by Agamben and by Negri and Hardt.

1.2 'Bare Life' and 'Empire'

A main theme in the (later) work of Agamben is biopolitics and more specifically the argument that politics has from the very beginning biopolitical roots (Agamben, 1998). Agamben reminds us that in Greek antiquity two notions were used to refer to life: *zoè* or naked life (common to all living beings, i.e. animals, human beings and gods) on the one hand and *bios* or a form of life (typical for an individual or group). The constitution of the polis, and more generally a juridical and institutional order, implies exclusion, 'ex-ception' or the banning of naked life: naked life is being included throughout an exclusion. *Homo sacer*, Agamben argues, is the name for someone whose life is reduced to naked life. It is the figure of someone who cannot be sacrificed and who can be killed without committing a murder. In short, the sovereign constitution of a political and juridical order is from the very beginning linked up with an exception and thus the production of naked life.

Against this background, Agamben argues that biopower does not succeed classical sovereign power (as Foucault seems to put it). Sovereign power instead has from the very start a biopolitical dimension. Agamben, therefore, claims that what is at stake from modernity onwards and within the modern nation state is the growing politicisation of naked life. Using the terminology of Benjamin he claims that the exception ('bare, naked life') is becoming the rule. The implication of this is that naked life being handed over to sovereign power potentially inhabits all citizens and that every one could be positioned in a state of exception. And that we, from modernity onwards, only have one notion for life and that this notion is often looked at from a biological perspective is, according to Agamben, exactly pointing at this state of exception (Agamben, 1995).

This challenging and in different respects 'fundamental' approach of politics as sovereign power over naked life, helps us to understand some 'exceptional' phenomena: the position of refugees, naked life in the camps of totalitarian regimes (Mesnard & Kahan, 2001). However, stressing the original relation between sovereignty and naked life makes it difficult to focus on new, modern conceptions about life (Larsen, 2003). In other words, it seems that Agamben is not only de-historicising sovereign power but also biopolitics. And in relation to this approach it is difficult to analyse how modern biopolitics for example has been developed in relation to populational reasoning and is embedded within governmental technologies. And furthermore, Agamben's analysis seems to be too 'fundamental' for a genealogical examination of how the political interest for the life of a population is related to the political interest for the economy (Lemke, 2002). Exactly this relation between biopolitics and political economy, as will be explored later, helps us to address some current developments (Bröckling, 2003). However, Agamben does help us to see that sovereignty in nation states did not at all disappear and that it has (the production of) naked life as its correlate.

While in Agamben's approach the modern relation between biopolitics and economy is not discussed in detail, this relation is in a rather specific way of central interest for Hardt and Negri (Hardt & Negri, 2000). These authors discuss how the global market and the global production-circuits have installed a new global order.

This global order, related to a new global form of sovereignty, is referred to as 'Empire': an immanent order without borders, without history and with transversal social relations. The structure of this global sovereignty is being described with two elements: biopower (Foucault) and the control-society (Foucault-Deleuze).[2] We limit ourselves to a short exploration of how the term biopower is being used here in reference to 'biopolitical production'.

'Biopolitical production' refers to processes of production and reproduction of life in all its forms (economical, social, cultural). These global networks of biopolitical production inaugurate, according to Hardt and Negri, the new, postmodern phase of capitalism. Essential for this phase is that not only is the labour force extracted from life (the disciplined body) and used for the economic production, but that life as a whole and in its totality is part of processes of production and reproduction. The result is that our social order, our body and affects and our subjectivity are always already the outcome of (material and immaterial) processes of production. And exactly the global networks of biopolitical production result in a situation in which life as a whole could become the object of (an immanent) regulation. To put it otherwise: '(...) Empire presents the paradigmatic form of biopower. (...) Biopower thus refers to a situation in which what is directly at stake in power is the production and reproduction of life itself' (Hardt & Negri, 2000, pp. xv & 24).

This analysis brings to the foreground the relation between biopolitics and the economic (and social) order and points at its functioning on a global scale. However, it is important to mention that the neo-Marxist focus does not allow us to make a distinction between economic power/exploitation and biopower. Power over life, here, is a power that immediately submits life to the capitalist process of production (Rabinow & Rose, 2003; Lemke, 2002). In this approach the spreading of power over life is regarded as a function of the further development of capitalism. Therefore it is difficult to analyse the coming into being (in a genealogical sense) of the relation between biopolitical and economic regulation. And more generally, the epochal statement on the disappearance of borders between life, politics and economy does not allow us to deal with concrete forms of self-guidance that are expected from us today. Certainly, Negri pays attention to this level of self-guidance when he refers for example to the 'biopolitical entrepreneur'. According to him, this entrepreneur is a (first) kind of resistance within and towards 'Empire'. It is an entrepreneurial militant transforming power over life into a vital critique.[3] Our aim however is to focus on the emerging relation between entrepreneurship and biopolitics, i.e. on how an entrepreneurial relation to the self implies a specific attitude towards and objectification of life and how this attitude is part of a governmental regime. In short, since Foucault's notion of biopolitics is situated at the level of a form of production and since it is used to point at the underlying principle of the capitalistic world order, the concept looses its analytical force.

In the previous paragraphs we mentioned two (fundamental) philosophical elaborations of the notion of biopolitics. Both elaborations however, seem to introduce the concept into a framework that is somehow strange to Foucault's genealogical perspective—although Foucault may have caused this himself in his statement about the 'threshold of biological modernity' and the epochal reversal of the Aristotelian definition of politics (Rancière, 2000). Agamben introduces the term biopolitics in a kind of 'onto-theologico-political domain' (Heidegger, Arendt, Bataille) and argues that the original relation between sovereignty and bare life is what remains un-thought in Western philosophy (and thus also in Foucault's own work). Hardt and Negri put the concept in an economic framework (and inspired by a kind of Marxist anthropology). Due to their 'ontologisation' of life (bios), however, the notion biopolitics looses its analytical potential.

Based upon these elaborations and revisions of the notion biopolitics we can take a step towards another line of thinking and study in which attention has been paid to biopolitics. This line of thinking is inspired by Foucault's ideas about governmentality. It is a perspective that could be fruitful to reintroduce the notion of biopolitics as well as to reintroduce some ideas of Agamben with regard to sovereignty.

1.3 Governmentality and Biopolitics

The course of lectures in which Foucault discusses in detail liberal and neoliberal forms of governmentality is titled 'The birth of biopolitics'. In the summary of the course he explains that he has not dealt in detail with the 'regulation of the population' (as suggested in the title) but with liberal and neoliberal governmentality (Foucault, 1979b, p. 818). The question coming to the foreground from the middle of the eighteenth century onwards is: how can government that wishes to govern by paying attention to the rights and (economic) liberties of citizens take into account the phenomenon of the population (and problems that arise at this collective level)? Although Foucault formulates this question as a starting point, he will focus mainly on (neo-)liberalism as an economic form of government. A short elaboration however will help us to understand that biopolitics play a role in this economic government.

Government in accordance with the reason of state used 'the police' as a general apparatus focused on the population and aimed at enforcing the state through detailed regulation (Foucault, 1978, 2004b; Gordon, 1991). The early-liberal form of governmentality becomes an economic government in a double sense. On the one hand, this kind of government discovers economy (and more general civil society) as an autonomous, natural domain, organising itself and asking for a rather specific kind of intervention (in accordance with the nature of the domain governed and inspired by political economy). On the other hand this kind of government is economic since it takes into account its own governmental costs. It is important to stress here that in this liberal configuration of government a rather specific form of freedom is required, i.e. it is a kind of freedom or self-government that is able to assure both individual and collective welfare (cf. Gordon, 1991, pp. 19–20; Rose, 1999, p. 63). An implication is that mechanisms are being used to assure this kind of freedom. At this point schooling, i.e. a disciplinarian-pedagogical milieu with its own historical roots and development, becomes of strategic importance at a governmental level. This milieu was thought to bring about the kind of freedom or self-government that is required for civil society; it assures the right form of freedom (cf. Hunter, 1994). However, liberal government should also bring about security at the level of the population in the name of freedom. Hence, 'social' intervention is possible and required with regard to social risks that transcend individual responsibility and harm order and welfare (Ewald, 1986, p. 185). What is required is a kind of 'vital politics' that is focused on the life conditions of the whole population and of subgroups within the population (children, workers, women, the unemployed …) and that is intervening in the name of general health and hygiene, reproduction and ecological problems (Osborne, 1996). In short, the liberal form of government can develop a biopolitics in the name of economic freedom and welfare and later on in the name of social security.

Within this governmental configuration, and in the beginning of the twentieth century, the population is becoming problematised in terms of race-hygiene and eugenics can become an active political intervention. As far as education is becoming part of these techniques of security, also children and parents become regarded from the perspective of 'biological selection' and 'eugenic selection' (Meyer-Drawe, 2000). In this regard, the educational milieu is a main domain of biopolitical intervention. Furthermore, it is important to stress that within this governmental configuration also the relation between the economic and the biologic can be reflected upon in a rather specific way.[4] Life, for example, can be seen in its totality as a function of economic development.

With regard to this Bröckling discusses the 'Menschenökonomie' as formulated in the beginning of twentieth century by Goldscheid: 'While the race hygienists reduce people biologically to their inheritance, Goldscheid reduces them economically to their economic value'. (Bröckling, 2003, pp. 8–9, my translation). Life is understood here as a kind capital ('organic capital'), it should be approached in a developmental-economic way and it should be regulated accordingly. As a result, the qualification of human life as a kind of capital and as a resource turns it into a governmental concern. Goldscheid argues for example for a general biopolitical administration. Investment in health and education, according to him, should be regarded as an investment in 'organic capital' and as a necessity in order to satisfy individual as well as social needs. And finally, it is within such a configuration (although not argued in this way by Goldscheid) that it is possible to think about the option of sacrificing life that is not worth living: 'Who is for a long period of time in need of care of others, without by herself being able to produce value throughout own work, is overloading the budget and has lost her right to existence'. (Bröckling, 2003, p. 16, my translation). The economic concern for life and the optimisation of organic capital here is being transformed into a sovereign power that 'makes die' or 'takes life'. Or to put it otherwise, when life is totally approached in economic terms, an economic calculation could question life itself.

This illustration of options within a liberal governmental regime illustrates that a biopolitical intervention is legitimised if life and conditions of life have an immediate economic value. However, there is not only room for central interventions directed towards the population and its conditions of life. Also each member of a population is addressed at an individual level to understand its freedom, rights and responsibilities in 'bio-social' and 'bio-economic' terms (Rose, 1999, p. 78). People are asked for instance to think about themselves as 'social individuals', i.e.

to admit that their freedom is only guaranteed within society and that their autonomy is not only a juridical matter but is linked up with social normality. In this regime of self-government, practicing freedom is from the very beginning a submission to what is normal within society and eventually to the biological fundaments of this normality. Furthermore against this background of social submission guaranteeing freedom and the relation between individuality and sociality, the connection between 'education' and 'society' can become a main governmental issue.[5] The same background is a condition to look at schooling as an instrument to bring about a social form of individuality, to bring about a self-understanding in which people see themselves as being part of a broader bio-social and bio-economic totality. This makes it also possible to start thinking about the reproduction of the order and norms of society (through education) or about its optimisation through biological and/or economic selection. Whatever option is taken, the horizon and governmental configuration remains the same, i.e. schooling appears as a kind of hinge point between (a specific kind of) freedom and security.

This sketch of biopolitical government and self-government in liberalism shows to what extent the 'regulation of the population' has a history. Furthermore, it indicates that an interesting element of this history is the way in which a politicisation of life is related with a economisation of life. Thus, the assurance and optimisation of processes of life is part of a political economy and life becomes a matter of investment and something to be judged upon using the criteria of economic return. To use the notion biopolitics in this way enables us to analyse the concrete mechanisms of biopolitical regulation and its relations with for example 'economic government'. Instead of regarding the growing 'power over life' as a phase in the 'logic of capital' (and as a prehistory of Empire, as Hardt and Negri seem to do), a governmental approach clarifies which specific forms of government and self-government are implied in this power over life (and its developments). Moreover, the introduction of biopolitical elements in the analysis of forms of government also enables us to reintroduce the problem of sovereignty (Dean, 2002; Bröckling, 2003). According to Foucault, the transformation of 'fostering life' into 'take life' (and to a certain extent within totalitarian regimes) is related to racist decisions/distinctions within the biological continuum. But as far as this 'fostering life' within liberal government has an economic function, it is an economic calculation that inaugurates the transition towards 'make die'.

In what follows, we will try to describe in a rather general way the present governmental configuration in order to deal with some biopolitical elements and to point at some economic manifestations of sovereign power (over life and death).

2. Government and Self-Government: The Permanent Economic Tribunal

The 'capitalisation of life' and biopolitics is developing in a specific way in the present, European regime of government and self-government. However, it is not our intention to present a detailed description of this regime.[6] Instead we will focus on the relation between education, biopolitics and economy and more specifically on how 'learning', 'living' and 'investment' are connected within the figure of the entrepreneurial self. An entrepreneurial relation to the self implies that who we are and who we will become is always the result of the informed choices we make and of the goods we produce in order to meet our own needs. The entrepreneurial relation to the self is a main component of the current regime of the self, i.e. a regime in which we are asked to judge what we are doing on the basis of a 'permanent economic tribunal' and to see in the submission to this tribunal the condition of our freedom (as self-realisation or self-development). A small cartography of this regime elaborated in detail elsewhere helps to illustrate this.[7]

An entrepreneurial attitude towards ourselves and others permits the appearance of some qualities of human beings as a form of capital or human capital. It is something for which investment was/is necessary, it represents a specific value and is the source of future income. As a consequence, since in education this form of capital is being produced, the choice for education is a deliberate, entrepreneurial choice: one expects that the choice will be a valuable investment and that there will a high return. But this 'capitalization of life' is also at issue in social life. An entrepreneurial attitude places someone into a position in which she thinks about norms, relations and networks as social capital that could contribute to the development of human capital or that could enlarge the productivity of someone's knowledge and skills.

This entrepreneurial, investing attitude towards oneself (and others) is related to a new way of thinking about time and space. The horizon is not longer the modern organisation of time and space in closed settings (factory, school, family …), with their rigid channels of interaction and in which human beings are positioned as individuals. The entrepreneurial self is not *positioned* in this space, but is *moving* in 'networks'. A network is an environment in which someone lives, in which someone confronts needs and in which human capital can be employed, circulate and become productive. Or to put it the other way round: a network environment asks to mobilise knowledge and skills. And mobilisation is about bringing knowledge and skills into a condition in which they can be 'putted at work'. It is about the employability of the reserve of human capital or potential. Paying attention to this (level of) employability is a permanent task of the entrepreneurial self.

This task of self-mobilisation is related to a specific meaning of risk. In the social state, risk is regarded as something that should be reduced. The entrepreneurial self in a market environment, however, thinks about risk as the condition for profit. Risk is not immediately understood as the chance that some problems will arise, but is instead a chance or opportunity (involving speculation): it is the condition for entrepreneurship, innovation and personal wellbeing. Certainly, the implication is not that the entrepreneurial self sees in every risk an opportunity. There is still a concern for the prevention of specific risks, but also with regard to this prevention an entrepreneurial attitude is required. To live an entrepreneurial life means that investment in health and security (and one's own responsibility with regard to this) is important because, and as long as, there is some profit. Risk-management, therefore, is part of managing one's entrepreneurial life.

But the figure of the entrepreneurial self, who is managing its own capitalised life, is not only part of a regime of self-government. At the same time, this new kind of self-government is the point of application for new governmental interventions. The 'social state' positioned itself towards an economic domain on the one hand and a bio-social domain on the other hand and it saw its task as governing in the name of bio-social welfare. Present governmental relations, and the 'enabling state', correlate with entrepreneurship. Of course, entrepreneurship can have social dimensions. However, the entrepreneurial self, and not the state, is regarded to be having the first responsibility for social inclusion. Therefore, what is occurring today is not a disappearance of central government but a changed configuration of governmental relations and a new understanding of the state. The example of schooling is interesting here.

For central government schooling is no longer problematised against the general background 'education and society'. The background to reflect in a governmental way about schooling is the 'network-environment' in which schools operate in an autonomous entrepreneurial way, i.e. following the laws of the economic tribunal. It is this background that allows to formulate rather specific problems (e.g. quality, performance) and to introduce new governmental instruments (e.g. audit). Therefore, we could say that central government sees it as her task to assure that there is a adequate infrastructure and environment for entrepreneurship and for its investing attitude. Or the other way around: entrepreneurship (at the level of schools, students, parents) asks central government to create an infrastructure to promote entrepreneurial freedom and informed choices.

Based on the features of this new governmental regime, supposed it actually is operational and supposed our relation to ourselves is an entrepreneurial one, we can take a closer look at what is at stake in 'life' and 'learning' today. We will argue below that the 'permanent economic tribunal' asks for an investing attitude towards 'life' and 'learning'. Or more precisely, it asks for an attitude for which the ideas of life and learning have a rather specific meaning. Moreover, this tribunal and the attitude of investment also imply a sovereignty through which the regime of (self) government can turn into a regime of economic terror.

3. Investment, Learning and Life

Both the enabling, entrepreneurial state and the entrepreneurial self can approach and problematise something in terms of its 'bio-value'. Originally, this term referred to the way bodies and organs of dead people can be used again to optimise or sustain the condition of the living. The dead body thus is regarded as a source for added value. In discussing 'biological citizenship' Rose and Novas elaborate the term (Rose & Novas, 2003, p. 30). With the introduction of entrepreneurship and the possibilities of genetic technology, bio-medicine and the neurosciences, 'biological citizenship' is not just about belonging to a 'race'. Instead, it refers for example to knowledge about the genetic characteristics of a population and about how these characteristics are related to the production of wealth and health. For central government these insights in genetic and vital characteristics of the population imply that they have insights in new sources for economic growth or in new risks. The genetic make-up of a population is approached here in terms of economic qualities and added value.

At this point it is interesting to refer briefly to Corning and his ideas about a 'bio-economy' or 'biopolitical economy' (Corning, 1997). According to him, this is a scientific discipline that can be very useful today. Bio-economy reflects upon the relation between economic activities and the satisfaction of our basic needs. These basic needs are termed 'basic survival needs'. Corning's point of departure is that society is a 'collective survival enterprise' and that it is possible and useful to make a list of 'survival indicators' and more specifically to construct profiles concerning 'personal fitness' and 'population fitness'. According to Corning this scientific discipline does not only offer theoretical opportunities, but he claims also: '(...) at this critical juncture in our evolution as a species, it is also an increasingly urgent moral imperative' (Corning, 2000, p. 77). Biopolitical economy therefore, does not only imply biopolitics in the name of the economic but also an economic politics in the name of survival.

However, in the actual governmental regime it is not just central government but foremost the entrepreneurial self that has to be concerned with its bio-value. The condition of the body and mental and physical health for example are being problematised in terms of investment, i.e. they are the source for added value and for the optimisation of entrepreneurial life. Habits, diet and lifestyle have a bio-economical dimension. Taking care of it is a matter of investment, it is the responsibility of the entrepreneurial citizen and it should be judged according to the value it adds. Furthermore, this attitude of investment can also be directed towards the bio-medical (neurological) condition or to the genetic pre-condition. Entrepreneurial citizens can organise themselves (in communities) on the basis of scientific insights in (the risks of) their common genetic make-up. These forms of 'bio-sociality' can invest for themselves in medical care or treatment, they can ask government to invest in them or they can organise a resistance to medical treatment itself (Rabinow & Rose, 2003). What these examples indicate is that what we regard as matters of life (dead, disease, genetic or neurological dysfunctions ...) is from the very beginning a correlate of an investing, entrepreneurial attitude. An interesting illustration is the capitalisation of procreation and how children are becoming the correlate of an attitude of investment.

Some time ago, the theory of human capital taught us to look at marriage and the choice for (and investment in) children as an economic activity (Becker, 1976, p. 172).[8] For entrepreneurial parents the 'production' of children is a well-considered choice. Children could be an enduring consumption good (and in this sense children produce satisfaction) or they can be an enduring production good (since children—even the 'rotten kid'—take care of additional income). Furthermore, the submission to the economic tribunal obliges us to regard children in terms of costs and prices: children have a (shadow-) price. Therefore a scarce item such as time and income play a role in the choice for children—children are a time intensive good. Additionally, Becker claims, what should be taken into account is the investment in human capital of children. Education, clothing and medical care are future costs and will determine the prize of children. Investment in human capital of children will also imply that parents have to invest their own time and also with regard to this the entrepreneurial parent is calculating the added value for herself and for the child. In this perspective, 'quality time' refers to using the scarce time in such a way that it is an optimal (given other needs) investment (in the human capital of the child). But entrepreneurial selves also know that investment in children (because one expects it is somehow an income) is always at the same time a risky business. Disabled children are more expensive; the gender as well can have an influence on the prize. From an economic entrepreneurial attitude pre-natal detection could be welcomed in order to minimise these risks. Thus with regard to children the entrepreneurial self is looking for an optimal investment and production and at this level genetic technology can become a productive instrument (Meyer-Drawe, 2000). Of course, as long as using genetic technology is a risky 'business' itself, it will not survive the economic tribunal and it will not be chosen and applied.

These illustrations explain that and how life (even at the genetic level) could become a correlate of an attitude of investment. All this often causes a kind of 'genetic unrest' and one often tries to point at the dangers with a warning reference to modern eugenics, modern racism and modern social hygiene (Foucault, 2004a). Although we will not claim there is no danger involved, we think it is important to frame the present dangers as precise as possible. Since biopolitics of the entre-preneurial self (and of the entrepreneurial central government) is governed by the economic tribunal it is *this* tribunal that can establish a regime of economic terror with regard to capitalised life. When life has an economic function, then 'let die', as Bröckling formulates clearly, is a consequence of 'disinvestment' (Bröckling, 2003). Or to put it otherwise: when 'fostering life' is guaranteed by an investment, then no longer investing disallows life to the point of death. Moreover dead itself can become the correlate of an investing attitude. Becker for example claims that most deaths—'if not all'—are in fact suicides for death could be postponed if there would have been more investment in life and in activities that could make it longer (Becker, 1976, p. 11). Thus if the entrepreneurial self (and entrepreneurial central government) is submitting everything to a permanent economic tribunal then it is exactly this entrepreneurship that has a sovereign force.

An enterprise invests in something if it expects it will produce an income. From this perspective, children, knowledge and genes exist because there has been invest-ment in them. If the expectation of possible incomes disappears, their very existence and survival is at stake. Entrepreneurship therefore, since it can decide upon investment, has a sovereign position: not only towards others, but maybe foremost and first of all towards itself. The existence of the entrepreneurial self is at stake if she does not want or is not able anymore to invest in her own human capital and therefore if she is not able to produce her own satisfaction. Thus one is entering the domain of 'letting die' (and even that of 'taking life') if the costs are higher then the expected incomes. At this point, and confronted with 'excluded' indi-viduals or individuals that have excluded themselves, central government can see investment and fostering life as its aim. Government for example can make a contract with people who are unemployed for a long time, with someone with a life that is not capitalised enough or with someone without an investing attitude (Dean, 2002, p. 133). But by doing this sovereignty is being reinstalled at the level of central government. In these kinds of contracts obligations are being enforced against the background of 'let live'.

4. Bio-Economisation of Europe?

Although it needs further research to establish whether a European bio-economical regime is being built, we will mention in conclusion some elements that point in this direction.

The European space of higher education can be regarded as a public infrastructure for entrepreneurial higher education. This infrastructure offers human capital to the entrepreneurial student in order to invest in. The student chooses training and invests in training if she expects future income. As a result, entrepreneurial institutions for higher education will do everything they can to offer human capital with an added value, they will strive for excellence and will make this value (quality) public in order to allow optimal choice. With regard to their internal organisation, these institutions will invest in the research and education for which they expect they will have customers. Researchers and teachers thus end up in a position in which their very existence (as researchers and teachers) depends upon this investment. A system of comparable degrees and a general system of quality assurance—components of the European space of higher education—could facilitate this turn towards a regime of economic terror: entrepreneurial higher education will only invest in training or in research centres if these have an added value on a European scale and in relation to the performance of comparable training and research centres. Of course, in such a regime one could search oneself (as a teacher or researcher) for sufficient means and thus one could ask the customer (business, students) for direct finance. The regime of economic terror, however, remains the same.

In entrepreneurial higher education in the European space of higher education it is up to each training and research centre to prove that education and training has its customers, that it is excellent or that it has an added value. In short, it is up to them to legitimate their existence. What is installed is a kind of regime of terror that, to paraphrase Lyotard, claims: 'take care of investment in yourself, or disappear' (Lyotard, 1979, p. 8).

But if learning is understood as the production of human capital, as the investment in competencies and as the construction of productive knowledge (in a knowledge society), it is also at this level that the economic tribunal can turn into a regime of economic terror. Learning, it is argued, has to enable us to develop the competencies in order to realise ourselves and to satisfy our needs in different environments. The permanent economic tribunal is decisive: we have to renew our human capital and competencies on a permanent basis. But it is not enough to keep them up-to-date. It is a necessity to compare oneself with others and to ask whether one has a better portfolio. The submission to a permanent economic tribunal therefore does not only condemn the entrepreneurial self to productive learning but also to a competitive process of lifelong learning. The learning process here is the condition for necessary added value and learning is investment in human capital (Masschelein, 2001). At this point, who we are and what we are is the result of what has been constructed throughout learning and is the result of a calculated investment.

One could reformulate this mode of reasoning as follows: being or what exists is a hypostasis of becoming and becoming is a learning process fed by a learning force. Learning is regarded as a fundamental process and force, as a kind of life force underlying everything that is. In other words, being or what is, is the result of a learning force. And this implies that who or what someone is, is the result of what has been learned. Against this entrepreneurial background it becomes a virtue to deal in a pro-active way with the learning process and the underlying learning force. One should orient the learning force towards the creation of the knowledge and skills that are expected to produce an income or to have an added value. Learning moreover is not just a process of production, it is always also a risky business. Thus from an entrepreneurial perspective, what is, has an added value and is as long as it has this value. Without this attitude of investment towards oneself and without a productive and pro-active use of one own learning force the existence of an entrepreneurial self is at stake. Finally, since that, who and what we are depends upon what has been learned and ultimately upon an investment, it becomes a necessary condition that we learn to learn and learn to orient our learning in order to be someone or something. As a result, schooling gradually defines her function in terms of 'learning to learn'.

Finally we could reformulate the citation of Kolb in the beginning of the article as follows: it is the entrepreneurial self (and the entrepreneurial society) that is identifying herself with the learning process and that is able to anticipate the demands of the environment. But we should add here: the entrepreneurial self is at the same time someone who decides upon the added value of the learning process. When the balance is negative, 'fostering life' turns into 'disinvestment', 'let die' and even 'to make die'.[9]

Notes

1. This is not to say that the notion biopolitics has no other meanings. There is for example the 'Journal for Biopolitics' focusing on the social and political consequences and dimensions of biology and biotechnology. In the USA the idea of biopolitics is related to a relatively autonomous discipline within political sciences (linked up with socio-biology, evolution-theory and aiming at a biological understanding of politics) (cf. Somit & Peterson, 1998). These usages of the term are not related to Foucault's use.

2. It is important to mention at this point that the term sovereignty, as being used by Hardt and Negri, is different from Agamben's use of the term. According to Nancy, it could be more exact to use in reference to 'empire' the notion 'domination' as the problem of sovereignty is exactly what is un-thought here. And thus Nancy asks: '*Et si la révolte du peuple était la souveraineté?*' (Nancy, 2002, pp. 170–173).

3. At this level, however, there seems to be a kind of ambivalence. On the one hand, Hardt and Negri try to argue that life as a whole is being captured within 'Empire' while on the other hand (and being inspired by a specific kind of vitalism of Deleuze) they look at life and the un-ordered multitude of (auto-affirmative) forces of life ('multitude') as the condition for new forms of political subjectivity. In short: the notion 'life' seems to

have in their analyses a kind of ontological meaning while at the same time being a product (Rancière, 2000; Lemke, 2002).

4. The governmental problematisation of the relation between the population and the economy is already articulated in the work of Malthus: 'Population, when unchecked, increases in a geometrical ration. Subsistence increases only in an arithmetical ration' (Malthus, 1798, I, p. 18). What is at stake here is the necessity to bring about a kind of balance between subsistence and the number of population.

5. Dewey, for example, states in 'My pedagogic creed': 'I believe that all education proceeds by the participation of the individual in the social consciousness of the race. (...) I believe that the only true education comes through the stimulation of the child's powers by the demands of the social situations in which he finds himself' (Dewey, 1897, p. 49).

6. An overview of studies of the actual regime of governmentality or so-called 'advanced liberalism': Barry *et al.*, 1996; Rose, 1999; Bröckling *et al.*, 2000.

7. For a more detailed cartography and especially focused on education: Masschelein & Simons, 2002, 2003, Peters, 2001.

8. We do not claim that the economic theory of Becker is a theory of the figure of the entrepreneurial self. It can be regarded as one component in the assemblage of the actual regime of governmentality. This paragraph therefore is not a detailed discussion of his theory but a sketch of a way of thinking. At this point we could also mention that 'entrepreneurship' has been elaborated explicitly by other economists. In order to understand 'entrepreneurship' Kirzner for example (and referring to von Mises) criticises the mechanic model of preferences and maximalisation since it does not deal with '*the very perception of the ends-mean framework* within which allocations and economizing is to take place' (Kirzner, 1973, p. 33). He claims that elements of alertness (and speculation) are essential for entrepreneurship.

9. This is an adapted version of the German article 'Lernen, Leben und Investieren: Anmerkungen zur Biopolitik' in Ricken & Rieger-Ladich, 2004.

References

Agamben, G. (1995) *Moyens sans fins. Notes sur la politique* (Paris, Payot et Rivages).

Agamben, G. (1998) *Homo Sacer. Le pouvoir souverain et la vie nue* (Paris, Seuil).

Barry, A., Osborne, T. & Rose, N. (eds) (1996) *Foucault and Political Reason. Liberalism, neo-liberalism and rationalities of government* (London, UCL Press).

Becker, G. S. (1976) *The Economic Approach to Human Behavior* (Chicago, IL, University of Chicago Press).

Becker, G. S. (1993) *Human Capital. A theoretical and empirical analysis, with special reference to education* (Chicago, IL, The University of Chicago Press).

Bröckling, U., Krasmann, S. & Lemke, T. (eds) (2000) *Gouvernementalität der Gegenwart. Studien zur Ökonomisierung des Sozialen* (Frankfurt am Main, Suhrkamp).

Bröckling, U. (2003) Menschenökonomie, Humankapital. Eine Kritik der biopolitischen Ökonomie, *Mittelweg*, 36, pp. 3–23.

Corning, P. A. (1997) Bio-political Economy. A trial-guide for a inevitable discipline, *Research in Biopolitics*, 5, pp. 247–277.

Corning, P. A. (2000) Biological Adaptation in Human Societies. A 'basic needs' approach, *Journal of Bioeconomics*, 2, pp. 41–86.

Dean, M. (2002) Powers of Life and Death Beyond Governmentality, *Cultural Values*, 6, pp. 119–138.

Dewey, J. (1897) Mijn pedagogisch credo, in: M. A. Nauwelaerts (ed.), *Opvoeding en onderwijs in het verleden. Teksten en documenten (3—hedendaagse tijd)* (Leuven, Acco).

Donnely, M. (1992) On Foucault's Uses of the Notion of 'Biopower', in: T. J. Armstrong (ed.), *Michel Foucault, Philosopher* (New York, Routledge).

Donzelot, J. (1977) *La police des familles* (Paris, Les Éditions de Minuit).

The European Higher Education Area (1999) Joint declaration of the European Ministers of Education Convened in Bologna on the 19th June 1999.

Ewald, F. (1986) *Histoire de l'état providence* (Paris, Grasset).

Foucault, M. (1976) *Histoire de la sexualité 1. La volonté de savoir* (Paris, Gallimard).

Foucault, M. (1978a) La 'gouvernementalité', in: D. Defert, F. Ewald & J. Lagrange (eds), *Dits et écrits III 1976–1979* (Paris, Gallimard).

Foucault, M. (1978b) Sécurité, territoire et population, in: D. Defert, F. Ewald & J. Lagrange (eds), *Dits et écrits III 1976–1979* (Paris, Gallimard).

Foucault, M. (1979a) La politique de la santé au XVIIIe siécle, in: D. Defert, F. Ewald & J. Lagrange (eds), *Dits et écrits III 1976–1979* (Paris, Gallimard).

Foucault, M. (1979b) Naissance de la biopolitique, in: D. Defert, F. Ewald & J. Lagrange (eds), *Dits et écrits III 1976–1979* (Paris, Gallimard).

Foucault, M. (1976/1979) *The History of Sexuality, vol. 1, an Introduction*, trans. R. Hurley (London, Allen Lane).

Foucault, M. (1981) 'Omnes et singulatim': vers une critique de la raison politique, in: D. Defert, F. Ewald & J. Lagrange (eds), *Dits et écrits IV 1980–1988* (Paris, Gallimard).

Foucault, M. (1997) *'Il faut défendre la société' Cours au Collège de France (1975–1976)* (Paris, Gallimard/Le Seuil).

Foucault, M. (2004a) *Naissance de la biopolitique. Cours au Collège de France (1978–1979)* (Paris, Gallimard/Le seuil).

Foucault, M. (2004b) *Sécurité, territoire, population. Cours au Collège de France (1977–1978)* (Paris, Gallimard/Le seuil).

Gordon, C. (1991) Governmental Rationality. An introduction, in: G., Burchell, C. Gordon & P. Miller (eds), *The Foucault Effect: Studies in governmentality* (London, Harvester Wheatsheaf).

Hardt, M. & Negri, A. (2000) *Empire* (Cambridge, MA, Harvard University Press).

Hunter, I. (1994) *Rethinking the School. Subjectivity, bureaucracy, criticism* (Sydney, Allen and Unwin).

Kirzner, I. (1973) *Competition and Entrepreneurship* (Chicago, IL, The University of Chicago Press).

Kolb, D. (1984) *Experiential Learning: Experience as the source of learning and development* (Englewood Cliffs, NJ, Prentice-Hall).

Larsen, L. T. (2003) Biopolitical Technologies of Community in Danish Health Promotion, Paper presented at the conference 'Vital Politics: Health, medicine and bioeconomics into the twenty-first century', September 5–7, 2003, London School of Economics.

Lemke, T., Krasmann, S. & Bröckling, U. (2000) Gouvernementalität, Neoliberalismus und Selbsttechnologien. Eine Einleitung, in: U. Bröckling, S. Krasmann, & T. Lemke (eds), *Gouvernementalité der Gegenwart Studien zur Ökonomisierung des Sozialen* (Frankfurt am Main, Suhrkamp).

Lemke, T. (2003) Biopolitik im Empire—Die Immanenz des Kapitalismus bei Michael Hardt und Antonio Negri, *Prokla. Zeitschrift für kritische Sozialwissenschaft*, 32, pp. 619–629.

Lyotard, J.-F. (1979) *La condition postmoderne* (Paris, Les Éditions de Minuit).

Malthus, T. R. (1798) *An essay on the principle of population* (London): at (http://www. faculty.rsu.edu/~felwell/Theorists/Malthus/Index.htm)

Masschelein, J. (2001) The Discourse of the Learning Society and the Loss of Childhood, *Journal of Philosophy of Education*, 35, pp. 1–20.

Masschelein, J. & Simons, M. (2002) An Adequate Education for a Globalized World? A note on the immunization of being-together, *Journal of Philosophy of Education*, 36, pp. 565–584.

Masschelein, J. & Simons, M. (2003) *Globale immuniteit. Een kleine cartografie van de Europese ruimte voor onderwijs* (Leuven, Acco).

Mesnard, P. & Kahan, C. (2001) *Giorgio Agamben à l'épreuve d'Auschwitz* (Paris, Éditions Kimé).

Meyer-Drawe, K. (2001) Erziehung und Macht, *Vierteljahrsschrift für wissenschaftliche Pädagogik*, 77, pp. 446–457.

Nancy, J.-L. (2002) *La création du monde ou la mondialisation* (Paris, Galilée).

Osborne, T. (1996) Security and Vitality: Drains, liberalism and power in the nineteenth Century, in: A. Barry, T. Osborne & N. Rose (eds), *Foucault and Political Reason. Liberalism, neo-liberalism and rationalities of government* (London, UCL Press).

Peters, M. (2001) Education, Enterprise Culture and the Entrepreneurial Self: A Foucauldian perspective, *Journal of Educational Enquiry*, 2:1.

Rabinow, P. & Rose, N. (2003) Thoughts on the Concept of Biopower Today, Paper presented at the conference 'Vital Politics: Health, medicine and bioeconomics into the twenty-first century', September 5–7, 2003, London School of Economics.

Rancière, J. (2000) Biopolitique ou politique?, *Multitudes*, 1, pp. 88–93.

Ricken, N. & Rieger-Ladich, M. (eds) (2004) *Michel Foucault: Pädagogische Lektüren* (Wiesbaden, VS Verlag Für Sozialwissenschaften).

Rose, N. (1999) *The Powers of Freedom. Reframing political thought* (Cambridge, Cambridge University Press).

Rose, N. & Novas, C. (2003) Biological citizenship, in: A. Ong & S. Collier (eds), *Blackwell Companion to Global Anthropology* (Oxford, Blackwell).

Somit, A. & Peterson, S. A. (1998) Review Article: Biopolitics After Three Decades—A Balance Sheet, *British Journal of Political Science*, 28, pp. 559–571.

9

The Power of Power—Questions to Michel Foucault

NORBERT RICKEN

> Nothing appears more surprising to those who consider human affairs with a philosophical eye than the easiness with which the many are governed by the few.
>
> David Hume, *On the First Principles of Government*

Power provokes—still today. Even if power in a lifeworld and theoretical sense is increasingly able to attract attention, its analysis is often criss-crossed by enormous simplifications and misleading contrasts which make understanding the term considerably more difficult: not only as the popularity and diffuse nature of the term effect each other, so that the supposed 'evidence of a phenomenon' only increases the raging 'uncertainty of the term' (Luhmann, 1969, p. 149);[1] but also because the idea of power, being deeply rooted in daily life, rarely escapes the predominance of lifeworld ascriptions of significance so that attempts at conceptual precision and systematic readjustment are often simply vain in the face of the persistence of familiar significance, but most of all because the familiar judgement 'that power is evil in itself' (Burckhardt, 1949, p. 61) still colours the discussion of the term and thus tempts us to support long outmoded views. Luhmann's familiarly sharp and accurate aphorism—'the power of power seems to be mostly in the fact that one does not really know what it is in the end' (Luhmann, 1969, p. 149)—may thus seem to be reasonable but may easily lead us to overlook that power evades a simple conceptual understanding and determination because its significance is dependent on far-reaching preconceptions and—finally—cannot be explained independently from human self-interpretation. But if that which may be understood as 'power' is and must often be presumed to be well known in some way, then it is just not possible to discuss power in an objective way; in each case it can only be sketched by way of interpretation. That which is viewed as a phenomenon is thus dependent on what is conceptually understood by 'power', so that particularly conceptual-systematic approaches towards power play a considerable role, just as on the other hand conceptual uncertainty and diffusion result in grave consequences.

But it is not only semantic difficulties which are a supposedly unnecessary burden on the idea of power; because the term is assumed to be clear, its very use causes problems, as that which is seemingly discussed only in an objective way or which is even meant to be depicted in a neutral way is actually put into practice (and claimed): whoever speaks about power in an analytical way and tries to name something by the term, does this (almost) always while claiming to show or uncover something which is just not obvious but hitherto unknown and to thus unmask something hidden. However, one who speaks of power is already using it—just by doing so—so that power can never be completely objectified but there also 'stays' an 'invisible' factor always 'with the act itself' 'referring to it as an object' (Röttgers, 1990, p. 28); thus, 'power' inevitably is a normatively loaded term. Just as 'symbolic power' cannot be selectively distilled out of the envisaged 'reality of power', obviousness and hiding are inevitably a part of the 'game of power', as are suspicion and exposure; every attempt at going back to a state before these only indicated—both semantic and performative—difficulties and of claiming that power is either impenetrable to insight or could be operationally determined by definitions is thus in danger of 'leading to a simplifying concept of power [...] in such a way that analyses of power would then hardly be worth the effort' (Röttgers, 1990, p. 29).

The involvement of the meaning of power in human self-interpretation shall thus be traced; this side of defining limitations, which only entice us into obscuring the problem of interpretability of power and discrediting it as an avoidable vagueness, I want to ask the question of to what 'power' may be considered an answer. While the question 'what is power?' focuses on power as an object and suggests rather simple answers, I am instead interested in the problem that is answered by help of power. By changing the question around, both what may be understood to be 'the power of power' comes into the view, as well as the 'how' of power. At the same time this may also—I hope—offer insight into that which makes us both 'governable' and 'govern'. Thus, questioning power in this way does not only include conceptual explorations and theoretical adjustments but also some explicit anthropological discussion of power, as every way of understanding and interpreting power in each single case is always dependent on how humans mutually understand themselves. Thus, my thoughts also aim at sketching a structural matrix of human self-understanding, in light of which power—and then also criticism—can be systematically reconstructed.

But such an attempt at discussing power anthropologically—particularly while reaching back to Foucault's thoughts—is confronted with a double objection: on the one hand, by adjusting the question of 'the power of power' the question of 'what is power' seems to be asked again, answering which Foucault considered both impossible and misleading and which he successfully discredited by the often quoted restriction to the supposedly more prudent 'how is power' (Foucault, 1982, p. 216; cf. Foucault, 1982, p. 208ff & 1999, p. 22ff). On the other hand, however, the attempt at taking up the question of the 'power of power' in an anthropological way meets resolute resistance in most cases today: not only because 'anthropology'—against one's own better judgement—is frequently understood within philosophy and the human sciences as giving an essential and substantial interpretation of what it means to be 'human'. This seems no longer acceptable, any interpretation being historically situated and contextualised. Only an historical anthropology seems possible, in the sense of a particular historical interpretation, rather than an a-historical, essential interpretation. Another reason is that such a power-theoretical approach is considered incompatible with some of Foucault's important views. In his various historic studies he pointed out the time- and power-bound nature of every kind of anthropology and he rejected anthropology itself by labelling it 'anthropological sleep' and an epitome of the modern way of seizing hold. The result is that Foucault's thesis—'strangely enough man, understanding of which is considered the oldest question since Socrates by naïve people, [...] is a young invention [...], a figure which is less than two centuries old' (Foucault, 1971, p. 26)—is interpreted as a verdict on any kind of future anthropology. But despite Foucault's warnings, this adjustment of the question—particularly while examining Foucault's theorems—will prove to be as inevitable as (hopefully) fruitful. Thus, my article is expressed as a question to Foucault (see Butler, 2003).

1.

If we have our first attempt of a conceptual exploration of power in a (more or less widely spread) everyday way of understanding and if we understand 'power' both as strength and possibility and as the right and authority of influencing other people and decide about them, in this everyday way of understanding, six aspects can be recognized as typical (see Luhmann, 1969; Röttgers, 1990) whose explication is as indispensable as it is already problematic and which thus leads towards significant philosophical problems:

First, power is mostly introduced as a substantially determinable possession, as a good or an ability being personally attributed, asymmetrically distributed, and which is seated at a centre or has its basis there (*substantiality* and *central nature*). *Second*, power is considered as *causality* and is understood to be a specific effecting power, as a cause which creates effects out of itself, so that power over other people's behaviour only exists if the latter would be different in case of the influence which is supposed to be its cause being non-existent (see Luhmann, 1969, p. 150). *Third*, an *intentionalist interpretation* of power is appropriate to this way of understanding power as a causality: if power in an everyday way of understanding means influence on or even determination and restriction of others, the intention of the supposedly influencing person is important for being able to recognize behaviour as powerful action. For, if this intention is missing, the idea of power does not seem to be appropriate (see Luhmann, 2000, p. 25ff), as coincidental effects of power are neither powerful nor clearly determinable regarding their causality. Thus, it is logical that power is generally considered a means for other purposes, so that whoever practices it only for its own sake must be aware of moral condemnation. Closely connected to this, there is *fourth*, a general *duality* and a *nature of opposition* regarding the logic of concepts: power is almost exclusively understood as 'restricting freedom' (Popitz, 1992, p. 17) and as a reduction definitely opposing freedom. Thus, it is placed into a continuum of more or less lack of freedom and is connected to rule, violence, and force and sometimes is even used as a synonym: violence—thus the employed logic—in this case is nothing else than 'increased power' (Schwartländer, 1973, p. 869) and 'the appearance of power or power as outer appearance' (Hegel, quoted in Röttgers, 1990, p. 524) while—on the other hand—'power is nothing else than alleviated violence i.e. violence restricted by justice' (Schwartländer, 1973, p. 869). In such a way, clamped between violence and rule, the idea of power comes *fifth*, into a rather political context which itself influences the term and suggests understanding power as a predominantly *political phenomenon* in the stricter sense of the word. Finally, power is *sixth*, in the context of a specific normative difficulty which as an ambivalent estimation is also expressed by way of the conceptual system: although it is considered a good hardly to be given up which (meanwhile) should also be positively strived for, power is still understood as a negative term having a pejorative meaning in most cases. Thus, discussing it all too easily takes on the character of unmasking, of uncovering power, so that, when used, the term gets a supposedly critical touch, while anyone who simply speaks of power—no matter in what way—believes himself entitled to refer it to himself. But regarding this ambivalence, the following definitely seems to be true: who 'has' power, speaks rarely about it, so that one who speaks about it is always suspected of wanting it for himself. This is also true in a conceptual-theoretical sense, so that the very definition of power is itself involved into that about which it is talking, at least performatively. Thus, one could at first formulate *as a summary* that in everyday life power means influencing others in one's own favour or to one's own purposes and even being able to enforce one's own will against others and their possible resistance. In this context, the possibility of enforcing is tied to a specific ability or essentiality—e.g. authority—of the one who—in the end still as a form of superordination and force—possesses power, so that in everyday language—also regarding its productive meaning of being able to have an effect and to create—in the end it is still bound to repression and violence. In this context, the result of powerful enforcing is the lasting (and not only singular) establishment of relationships of subjugation that in this way are also discussed as social inequality and always contain an economic meaning. Its proximity to forms of institutionalized rule is thus on the horizon. But how power is explained in everyday life, on what it is based, and in what way it refers to humans and their constitution remains disputed as controversial and superficial. However, it is suspicious that rather simple models—like e.g. 'power as an impulse' or the 'will for power'—dominate the discourse and are a burden for the explication of each anthropological assumption (see Gehlen, 1961).

Thus, it is hardly surprising that just that definition of power is again and again recapitulated and even estimated 'right' (Dahrendorf, 1963, p. 569) which seems to re-formulate these elements of an everyday meaning also theoretically and therefore gives a certain consecration to them. Thus, for about 80 years particularly Max Weber's definition of power may be considered a sociological core definition which not only has often been accepted, but which is also of extraordinary significance in terms of the history of doctrines and which meanwhile has lead to numerous 'plagiarisms' (see Hradil, 1980, p. 22; Hejl, 2001, p. 398): 'power means every chance of pushing through one's own will within a social relationship even against resistance, no matter what the basis of this chance is' (Weber, 1972, p. 28). However, worrying in terms of power theory is the fact that Weber's definition may be considered a conceptual prototype although he himself did not further pursue it: as 'all imaginable qualities of a human and all imaginable constellations' may 'enable' someone 'to enforce his will in a given situation' (ibid., pp. 28–29), the idea of power is 'sociologically amorphous' (ibid., p. 28) and due to its arbitrariness as well as instability and its abstract nature, which cannot be determined more closely, as well as its universality it is 'not a scientifically useful category' (ibid., p. 542). Immediately after having introduced power as a basic concept of sociology Weber drops it in favour of the concept of rule, which in his eyes is more precise. 'Rule is supposed to mean'—as Weber's new approach states more precisely—'the chance of finding obedience with determinable persons for an order of certain content' (ibid., p. 28), and it marks a social relationship of 'finding obedience for an order' (ibid., p. 29) which is both definitely understandable and determinable as well as institutionally reliable. Also his differentiation and analysis of different 'types of rule' (see Weber, 1972, pp. 122–176) provide evidence for the strange uncertainty of the concept of power as simple 'influence' (Weber, 1972, p. 122) and increases the tendency of discussing forms of rule and power mostly (only) in respect of aspects of legitimacy: 'The fact that this and not anything else was chosen as a starting point for a differentiation can only be justified by success. [...] The legitimacy of a rule—as early as it has certain connections to the legitimacy of property—has definitely not only 'ideal consequences' (ibid., p. 123). However, by emphasizing this Weber does not only restrict the problem of rule to the—legitimacy-bearing—relation of order and obedience by way of discipline (see Weber, 1972, p. 29 and p. 123). He also spoils for himself the possibility of a theoretical 'criticism of power', as he predominantly reflects the legitimacy problem of rule as a necessary social order which is based on agreement. Also Weber's methodological starting point to his way of understanding 'sociology of rule'—anchoring all that is social in the 'subjectively meaningful action of the individual' (see Weber, 1972, p. 1 and p. 6ff) and therefore being able to think of society only as 'socialization' (Weber, 1972, p. 21ff)—contributes to further conceptual restriction which decisively determined the course of subsequent power-theoretical discourses (see Breuer, 1991; Imbusch, 1998).

But if one contrasts this everyday interpretation and its scientific analogue in the form of Weber's sketch with conceptual-historic evidence, it is not merely possible to show that 'power' has always been discussed in more and other aspects, so that the modern interpretation becomes visible as a really problematic reduction. Much more, such a 'traceology of power' (Röttgers, 1990, p. 32) proves that 'power' without considering its (historic) multidimensionality can only be conceptualised in a reduced way and therefore needs far-reaching re-contextualizing. Thus, if we follow the conceptual-historic discussions, which do not only adjust 'power' in its relation to 'freedom' by distinguishing between justice and force (*potestas*) but unfold it most of all as a determination of the relation of possibility and reality (*potentia* or rather 'δύναμις') (see Röttgers, 1990; Ricken, 2003, pp. 48–53), it becomes obvious that 'power' evades any (normative) concrete determination. The effect is that inevitably every attempt at its juridical and causal objectification leads back to modal logic (and thus contingent theoretical) thoughts. Thus, with the aid of reaching back to Röttgers's account of conceptual historic evidence (see

Röttgers, 1990, pp. 491–504) some (changed) marks of the concept of power shall be named and confronted with the everyday concept.

First, power cannot be convincingly characterized as a substance or an effect of substances but must definitely be understood as a relation, as it names a relation which cannot sufficiently be explained by one aspect of its origin: neither innate nor acquired factors, neither wealth, property, or other privileges nor internally attributed abilities and skills give by themselves reason to power and thus cannot be understood to be its source. 'Thus, power is not anything which somebody "owns" but something he exercises: we have power only as power over others, without them the concept of power is senseless' (Paris, 1998, p. 7). For if power was 'something to possess, we would have it even if there were no others and even where (in isolation) there are no others' (Röttgers, 2002, p. 391). *Second*, power always marks a social relationship: it can neither be found at a centre nor can it simply be explained as being linear—e.g. as a simple influence—but it must be understood as a relation of forces, as a network of forces which are also competing and directed towards each other and thus as the fight between power and counter-power or resistance into which assumptions of causality and intentionality must be embedded. Logically seen, power is thus *third*, closely connected to the problem of possibility and reality. This aspect of necessity and impossibility marks—as two ways of not being able to be different in case of which one would just not speak of power—that difficult problem of 'other possibility' which means neither simple possibility nor simple factuality but which in the form of 'real possibility' as well as 'possible reality' can only be aimed at in a relational way: 'Power is to action as possibility to reality' (Röttgers, 1990, p. 412). Thus, it seems prudent to explain power on the basis of the concept of contingency as an 'other possibility' (see Ricken, 1999; 2003): on the one hand, power as a phenomenon of possibility refers to its non-necessity in each case, so that 'power is "made" and can [always] be made different from how it is' (Popitz, 1992, p. 15). On the other hand, a contingency-theoretical approach also suggests referring power to uncertainty, combining it with insecurity, and placing it in finiteness, so that in the end it can be understood as 'power over possibilities, i.e. power over power' (Röttgers, 1990, p. 494) which—under conditions of scarcity—shifts, restricts, and asymmetrically shapes each possibility of action of potential actors in order to produce 'security of order' and 'continuity' in the face of always possible insecurity, uncertainty, and vulnerability resulting from both. In this context it is *fourth*, decisive that power and freedom must not just be understood as merely contrasting, so that power and freedom might claim to be separate and contrary phenomena. Much more, it is about explaining both of them as aspects of a social context, referring to each other and being interwoven (but still clearly distinguishable). *Fifth*, power as a concept of possibility is inevitably connected to interpretation, so that 'symbolization [...]' is 'thus a necessary feature of power' (Röttgers, 1990, p. 493). Even practicing power by simply threatening with (supposedly) 'brute force' needs imagination and cannot be explained without symbolic acts of recognizing and accepting (see Bourdieu, 2001, p. 220). Changing 'from the level of trying physical power to that of sym-bolizations' (Röttgers, 1990, p. 497) is inevitable for the practice of power. Thus, modalizing, not realization is its dominant mode. The result is that power cannot simply be—intentionally—traced back to violence and cannot be considered its 'alleviation'. Much more, power and violence are structurally different—and what is worse: violence as the basis of power constellations—when it is actually necessary—makes power collapse, as it consumes itself by way of its realization and non-symbolically showing its means (see Röttgers, 1997, p. 130). Thus, power acts as a means of control in the space of possibility on the level of imagination, so that 'the ability of controlling the imaginations of being able to control future actions is probably already the most important part of the ability of controlling future actions' (Röttgers, 1990, p. 494). At the same time, this symbolic structure of power implies that power as power—if it wants to be effective—must both present itself and hide, so that by way of its representations and symbolizations it is always also constantly 'on the run' (Röttgers, 1990, p. 501). This, however, makes *sixth*, any attempt at trying to use power as a normative concept an absurdity. 'Power must be planned as a strictly non-normative concept; unmasking power as well as [general] criticism of power does not make much sense' (Röttgers, 1990, p. 412): not only as it was simply naïve to reject power as such, also not only as every criticism of power exposes itself to a performative dilemma by itself trying—by way of unmasking mechanisms of controlling possible actions of others—to control imagining being able to act (if in different ways) and by therefore being 'caught in the same trap where it tried to catch others' (Röttgers, 1990, p. 494). Much more, this is true because power seems to be ubiquitous, and no absolute or at least sufficiently generalizable criterion for distinguishing 'good' or 'evil' power can be found, by help of which one might convincingly escape the ambivalence of the 'double' aspect of power—separating others and alliance with others. Criticism of power—both theoretically and practically—demands its 'de-demonizing' (Paris, 1998, p. 7) and can (almost) only be done analytically.

All this, however, suggests one thing: power is not an object-theoretical concept by help of which 'something' could be named and represented but it must be understood as an observation-theoretical concept. Thus, it does not refer together with or separately from other aspects to something that could be identified as being really objective and independent of each approach but with power an aspect of all kinds of (social) action is marked which cannot be separated from interpretation and reflexivity. Thus, that which becomes visible as 'power' is absolutely dependent on how 'power' is thought of and also conceptually understood. But 'power' always allows us to recognize social relationships from the perspective of its determinedness by others. Regarding each of its 'possibility of being different' it is not merely a contrast to freedom but is interwoven with it, so that both can be consequently adjusted only as transcendental concepts (with eminently practical results) that in each case allow us to observe other aspects of sociality—both determinedness and non-determinedness.

2.

By the panorama as sketched above, the currently observable fashion of Foucault's power theorems can also be understood as expressing some theoretical dissatisfaction with traditional concepts of power which in most cases—despite emphasizing the relational nature of power—do not allow us in the end to interpret particular mechanisms of control and regulation as power strategies which try to employ processes of self-determination and which thus cannot simply be deciphered as repression tactics. Furthermore, their basic conviction—power 'extends the freedom of one person against another person by breaking his/her "no", by denying his/her freedom' (Sofsky & Paris, 1994, p. 9)—despite of all acceptance of both the determinedness and limitedness of humankind, nourishes the (illusionary but most effective) idea that power but not freedom is a social phenomenon which 'starts whenever humans meet' (ibid., p. 12). Symptomatic: 'One person's action ends with the other's resistance, with his/her undeceivable independence and freedom to do something else than demanded. Power proceeds against this' (ibid., p. 9).

However, just a brief look at recent power theory teaches us that the constantly re-formulated oppositionality and hierarchization of freedom and power is far from being convincing and fruitful. Simmel's surprisingly early suggestion (1908) of seeing power relationships by way of 'their correlation to freedom' (Simmel, 1992, p. 246) and of sketching them as complex 'relationships of superordination and subjugation' (ibid.), which—if it may sometimes be painful—cannot sufficiently be understood without taking into account the 'co-effectiveness of the subordinated subject' (ibid., p. 162), is directed against an obviously wide-spread 'popular way of expressing' (ibid., p. 161) where 'excluding any kind of [one's own] spontaneity within a relationship of subjugation' (ibid.) is put into mind, expressed by figures of 'force', of 'having no choice' or even of 'definite necessity' (ibid.). In this context Simmel's conclusions are pioneering: *first*, superordination and subjugation must be understood as 'complicated interaction' (ibid., p. 165) where there is neither 'absolute influencing' nor 'absolutely being influenced' (ibid.), so that on both sides activity and passivity are interwoven—resulting also in 'all leaders [...] being lead' (ibid., p. 164). But *second*, this close 'interaction' cannot only be referred to phenomena of superordination and subjugation but is also true for—analogously structured—processes of liberation, so that also 'liberation from subjugation' (ibid., p. 252) does not only aim at 'not being ruled' (ibid., p. 254) but in almost all cases can (and must) be explained as a new 'start of some rule' (ibid., p. 252). This correlation of power and freedom can *third*, be appropriately described only by the term 'government' (ibid., p. 163f), as it allows both thinking of one's own activity and accepting one's own way of life as being 'governed'. In this context, Simmel's adjustment of the problem does not only focus on subjectivity as a relationally 'situated existence' (Meyer-Drawe, 1984), which is only distorted by the dichotomy of 'being subjugated' and 'being subjugating', but he uses it also for an anthropologically dimensioned thought where 'subjugation' to others, 'superordination' as well as 'resistance and opposition' (see Simmel, 1992, p. 171) are combined in such a way as to make visible the 'two sides [...] of one behaviour of man which are completely integrated in themselves' (ibid.) and thus need not be read as always later restrictions of a supposedly original freedom.

Hannah Arendt's clear differentiation of 'power and violence' is vividly formulated: 'Violence can always destroy power; out of the barrel of a gun grows the most effective command, resulting in the most instant and perfect obedience. What never can grow out of it is power' (Arendt, 1970, p. 54). Thus, a second marker can be placed which follows Simmel's observations on the relational nature of power. It determines power as 'human ability' 'not only to act or to do something but to form an alliance with others and to act in agreement with them' (ibid., p. 45). Arendt's result—'it is never a single person who has power; it is possessed by a group and it is existent only as long as the group sticks together. If we say about someone that "he has the power", this means in reality that he was entitled by a certain number of men to act on their behalf' (ibid.)—aims less at the problem of normativity and consensuality as Habermas deduced from this (see Habermas, 1978) but much more at the question of the sociality and plurality of humankind which is connected to it (see Arendt, 1981). From this perspective, however, power does not only become clear as a 'figuration' (the term is that of Elias), which by an individual-theoretical sketch [x ↔ y] can only be made visible in a reduced way. Much more, Arendt also succeeds adding the problem of mutual determinedness and dependency [x(y) ↔ y(x)] (see Ricken, 2006, pp. 62–65) into the problem of power and making it understandable as an ambivalent 'double': being both integrating action and alliance and dividing action and a process of isolation. Its completion by systemic and structural-theoretical thoughts, which not only adjust each determinedness of one's own possibilities of action merely by way of action theory, is then simply logical and—by way of referring to the 'second face of power' (Bachrach & Barratz, 1962)—has led to a more modal-logical 're-conception of a theory of power' (Luhmann, 1969, p. 167). As it has been obvious for a long time —as Luhmann says—'that [...] probably the greatest power is exercised by way of communication which is not based on the possibilities of force' (ibid., p. 166)—it is necessary to release power from its reduction to 'enforcing' and 'restricting action' and to understand it—in an abstract way, as could be expected—as a structural-functional 'selection process' i.e. a 'selection of premises of behaviour for somebody else' (ibid., p. 168) by help of 'a certain constellation of alternatives' (ibid., p. 151) and thus to spell it out in a media sense as 'processing of contingency' (Luhmann, 1975, p. 118): as a 'chance of increasing the probability of improbable selection contexts' (Luhmann, 1975, p. 12) and thus of absorbing the (also existential) uncertainty which results from 'double contingency' (see Luhmann, 1975, p. 9; 2000, p. 36, p. 41ff).

Before this background of cursorily chosen power-theoretical stances it is now possible to understand Foucault's sometimes still heavily disputed thoughts on the problem of power as a consequent (if not definite) continuation and clear definition of earlier marks: *on the one hand*, his way of labelling power as 'conduct of conducts' (Foucault, 1982, p. 221)—particularly emphasizing the relational nature of power—allows concentrating and systematically adjusting the earlier modal-logical perspective, so that power marks 'action answering to action' (ibid., p. 220) which operates in a 'field of possibilities' (ibid., p. 221) and by way of goading, inspiring, making easier or more difficult, or by way of restricting tries to make 'possible action' 'more or less probable' (ibid.). As Foucault's explanation of 'the conducting activity' goes: 'to conduct in this sense means structuring the field of possible actions of others' (ibid.) without, however, ignoring each 'way of conducting' and 'way of obeying' of those who are 'conducted' in this way and without denying their 'freedom' (ibid.), no matter how it is determined. Unequivocally he notes: 'power is only exercised on "free subjects" and only in so far as they are "free". [...] Where the determinations are completed, no power-relationship exists' (ibid.). On the other hand, however, Foucault's genealogic works definitely illustrate the variety of historic power-formations and give evidence to their change from being a sovereign power which by way of standardization and repression mostly forbids and excludes, via disciplining and integrating power which by way of normalization regulates and includes, to being a bio- and pastoral power which under the condition of making life possible in a productive way tries to configure both conditions and self-technologies. (And indeed, in contrast to traditional readings of Foucault's reconstruction of historical power formations his typology of power may be read from a relational perspective using his term of 'conduct of conducts' (cf. Ricken, 2006, pp. 93–112) as a new point of view.) Foucault's historical perspective can be summarized as: 'the ancient right to *take* life or *let* live was replaced by a power to *foster* or *disallow* it to the point of death' (Foucault, 1990, p. 138), so that the thus merely indicated change of power formations can not only be understood as increasing backward movement and diminishing both direct and negatively operating power in favour of the different ways of a rather indirect and productive controlling, conditional, and structural power, which begin at a both physical and reflexive self-relation and aim at 'voluntary obedience'. Much more, this perspective on power enforces the dismissal of only negatively arguing models of power which in the end only interpret it either as 'repression' and 'forbidding authority' or as 'superiority of the relation' and which all too often reduce power to legal or economic figurations without being able to analyze the 'mechanism of power' (Foucault, 2000, p. 117); more exactly: 'if power was never anything but repressive, if it never said anything but no, do you really think one would be brought to obey it? What makes power effective, what makes it accepted, is simply the fact that it does not only weigh on us as a force which says no; it also traverses and produces things, it induces pleasures, forms knowledge, produces discourse' (Foucault, 2000, p. 120). Thus, it is only logically consistent that in Foucault power is precisely not '*exercised on*' (cf. Foucault, 1999, p. 39) precedent subjects but that they themselves are 'one of the first effects of power' so that the subject is 'not the opponent of power' but is itself a pure 'effect of power' (ibid.). Foucault's power analyses can thus be read as analyses of those mechanisms 'by which, in our culture, human beings are made subjects' (Foucault, 1982, p. 208): formation of subjectivity as well as 'submission of subjectivity' (ibid., p. 213) and through subjectivity.

   Foucault's power-theoretical approach is considered—even today—ambivalent: that which on the one hand is mostly perceived as a fruitful shift of perspectives is on the other hand often considered a particularly normative overexertion of the concept of power itself. Even if by re-adjusting the concept of power as that of 'conduct of conduct' one succeeds—thus is the frequent estimation (see Lemke, 1997, pp. 11–37)—with regaining the rich conceptual-historic heritage and with extending the analytical view towards currently changed formation mechanisms (cf. in particular Deleuze, 1993) by explaining power as a theorem of possibility, the enormous extension of the concept of power which is connected to this sometimes meets resolute objections. In this context it is less the way of setting the course which allows us to think of power as being decentralized, relational, and productive but, much more, the supposed omnipresence and normative ambivalence of power is still today a burden for the reception of Foucault-like power theorems and all that can be tied into the reproach of being 'metaphysics of power' (Breuer, 1987, p. 324). The nucleus of this criticism is the statement that adjusting power to be a 'universal key' (ibid.) for all social and spiritual phenomena must in the end lead to a 'relativist self-denial' (ibid.), as the empirical extension—symptomatic: 'the problem is that Foucault calls too many things "power"' (Fraser, 1994, p. 52)—inevitably results in normative overexertion. If everything is power, as the reproach says, maybe this or that kind of power can be analytically distinguished but it cannot be reasonably rejected. The underlying unmasking attitude in Foucault is said to be thus self-contradictory and to be fruitless in the end (cf. Honeth, 1991; 2003 and Kelly, 1994).

Although this frequently formulated objection—from Habermas (1985) to Taylor (1988) and Fraser (1994)—is catchy enough, it is also misleading: not only because those power-theoretical corrections as made by Foucault himself are constantly overlooked, so that mostly his subject-theoretical approach is perceived, but also because the nature and status of Foucault's concept of power are misunderstood by way of demanding objective and normatively clear ways of thinking to be able to keep to common concepts of criticism by way of reasonable self-determination. This, however, frequently leads to overlooking Foucault's statements that power first does not include everything (cf. Foucault, 1977) but is *in* everything and second 'that *that one kind of* power does not exist' (Foucault, 1982, p. 217), so that the almost transcendental adjustment of the concept of power as a 'screen for analysis' (Foucault, 1992, p. 33)—which is connected to this—is often misunderstood. But Foucault—as he himself says—is less interested in knowing what and why something is done but in the question of what one's own 'doing does' (cf. Dreyfus/ Rabinow, 1982, p. 187)—and how this could be observed. Thus, the often criticized ubiquity of power is less due to a disastrous (and inappropriate) totalizing of the concept of power (see Breuer, 1987, p. 331) but is rather due to its categorical shift towards a concept of observation, allowing us to comprehend how humans influence each other and try to structure their respective actions by way of acting. Thus, the exact adjustment of what Foucault calls power is important: 'in effect, what defines a relationship of power is that it is a mode of action which does not act directly and immediately on others. Instead it acts upon their actions' (Foucault, 1982, p. 220). As such 'an action upon action' (ibid.) power refers to 'existing actions' or to 'those which may arise in the present or the future' (ibid.), and in fact in a way that 'the "other" (the one over whom power is exercised) be thoroughly recognized and maintained to the very end as a person who acts' and thus 'a whole field of responses, reactions, results, and possible inventions may open up' (ibid.).

This, however, allows defining power more precisely in a double way: not only can it be outlined as a contrast to violence—'a relationship of violence [...] forces, it bends, it breaks on the wheel, it destroys, or it closes the door on all possibilities' (ibid., p. 220)—but also it can be referred to humankind's conditionality which must not be confused with conditioning (see Ricken, 1999, pp. 256–261). Thus, it is only logical that power and freedom are not in an antagonistic but in an agonistic relationship towards each other: not only that they are not mutually exclusive (as suggested by the logic of 'freedom disappears everywhere where power is exercised' (Foucault, 1982, p. 221)) but that they result from each other. 'Power is exercised only over free subjects, and only insofar as they are free. (...) Where the determining factors saturate the whole there is no relationship of power' (ibid., p. 221). After this, it is not a great step to understand 'freedom' itself as a 'kind of power' i.e. as 'conduct of conduct' (Foucault). Foucault's analyses of modern power strategies mark their central mechanism as that of individualizing and totalizing at the same time (cf. ibid., p. 212f) and impressively give evidence to their nature of 'governing by individualizing' (ibid., p. 212). Particularly this 'productive' adjustment of the concept of power which—apart from the rich typology of power—determines the reception of Foucault's theorems, as his estimation—'even though the struggle against the forms of subjection—against the submission of subjectivity—is becoming more and more important' (ibid., p. 213) can still today claim almost undisputed validity.

Foucault's power-theoretical re-adjustment may be convincing enough. Further explanations, however, are surprisingly superficial. Foucault's pointing out the fact 'that the balance of power is deeply rooted in the social nexus' (ibid., p. 222) puts an end to ideas of power being a structure 'above' society which could also be dissolved in favour of a 'society without a balance of power' (ibid., p. 222f), but still—particularly regarding the adjustment of the question of power towards being an answer—are not satisfying. For if one takes Foucault's remark—'living in a society means living in such a way as making action upon other actions possible' (ibid., p. 222)—seriously, not only the question of the power of power arises but also the problem that it must be possible to explain power by the example of and in relational 'inter-subjectivity' (see Meyer-Drawe, 1984). This, however, demands that we not stop at only generally influencing or even at frequently employing rather awkward constructions of a linear will of power or of striving for pushing through, but demands expressively investigating an interwoven way of conducting oneself and others beyond individual-theoretical approaches.

3.

If one follows the course as set out above—adjusting power towards being a concept of observation for social conditionality and productively referring it to each self-relationship—a significant systematic difficulty becomes apparent which is also a burden on Foucault's analyses: not only as power can neither be reduced to supposedly objective structures nor to only subjective intentions, so that every attempt at planning power without considering any kind of self-relationship must be considered power-theoretically 'naïve', but most of all as by this definitely non-linear conception subjectivity appears as a contradictory double and is on the one hand applied to power as a (prior) condition and on the other hand is discussed as a (resulting) effect and product of power. However, the attempt (and demand) of thinking both at the same time confronts with theoretical *aporias* which severely irritates the usual difference between 'inside' (freedom) and 'outside' (power) and so forces systematic re-structuring in order to understand subjectivity as a 'relational rationality'—as a kind of self-relationship and other-relationship which is dependent on others and results from them.

Now, a theory of Judith Butler's seems to be helpful, which she formed in the course of a subtle re-construction of the term '*assujettissement*', introduced by Foucault (see Foucault, 1976, p. 42) and meaning the simultaneous (and paradoxical) production and subjugating of subjectivity (cf. Butler, 1997, p. 2), titled 'Theories in Subjection' (cf. Butler, 1997 and 2003). Starting out from the impossibility of tracing power back to the subject nor of it being on the outside and opposite, Butler tries to connect the problem fields of power and subjectivity by help of a recognition-theoretically adjusted argument which allows us to relationally think into each other both 'being self' and 'being with others', so that subjectivity may appear both as not deceivable ('*subiectum*' as 'the basic object') and as not original ('*subiectum*' as subjected). Thus, she explains the paradoxical logic of subjectivation (see Butler, 2001, pp. 7ff) in two ways. On the one hand, Butler states that we can develop our 'attachment to ourselves' only through 'mediating norms which give us back a sense of what we are' (Butler, 2003, p. 62), for the subject is 'bound to seek recognition of its own existence in categories, terms, and names that are not of its own making' (Butler, 1997, p. 20)—with the effect that 'assuming terms of power that one has never made' (ibid., p. 21) appears to be nothing else but a 'mundane subjection on the basis of subject formation' (ibid.): 'within subjection the price of existence is subjugation' (ibid., p. 20). On the other hand, however, just that field which drops out of the (historically contingent and thus always particular) norm is the field where we must 'live without recognition' (Butler, 2003, p. 63) but which allows us to break through the imposed restriction and conformity without, however, being able to escape the superior norms of recognition. Butler's main conclusion—'only by persisting in alterity does one persist in one's "own" being' (Butler, 1997, p. 28)—reflects the peculiar paradoxical logic and calls for explanation: 'to be', Butler puts it pithily, we 'have to be recognizable' (Butler, 2003, p. 64). In addition, we must—at the same time—'put the norms into question through which recognition is granted to us', so that 'to be for oneself' always also means—by the 'call for new norms' of recognition—'to put at risk our own being' (ibid.), to detach ourselves from ourselves and to have to expose the painfully acquired self-identity again and again. It is this double movement of 'subjectivity' and 'going beyond' (cf. Rieger-Ladich, 2004) which labels Butler's subjectivity-theoretical concept of combining '*assujettissement*' (cf. Foucault, 1976, p. 42) and '*déassujettissement*' (cf. Foucault, 1992, p. 15). Her rejection, however, of the underlying connection of both with a 'very own', regardless of how it is understood, makes it not only understandable that the self can always constitute itself in a broken way but also makes clear that self-reference and self-revocation are dependent on each other: on the one hand, as perception by others cannot be changed into self-perception without breaks, so that the genesis of the self—if seen from the other's perspective—always shows 'cracks' which cannot be repaired and contains aspects of mutual (but unequal) strangeness; on the other hand, as the possibility of self-shifting and 'crossing over' (see Butler, 2003, p. 64) is not dependent on the condition of positive knowledge about oneself but to each revocation, as illustrated by biographical self-confession which—and rightly so—turns self-determination against heteronomy without being able, however, to connect it to verifiable self-knowledge.

Now, Butler's conclusion that our self is not only due to recognition by others but also to the fact that we are strangers to ourselves and to others is power-theoretically significant regarding several aspects: *at first*, as it identifies the fundamental reference to others as the probably central *place of power* and allows localizing it in the 'betweenness of humans'. For 'without appetite', as Butler states in her explanation, 'we would be free from coercion; but because we are right from the beginning at the mercy of what is outside ourselves and subjugates us to those conditions that shape our existence, we are in this respect irreversibly susceptible to exploitation' (ibid., p. 67). As every 'being oneself' is always dependent on and communicated by others, 'conducting one's own life' is always possible only under and in 'conducting conditions of others': 'the self forms itself, but it forms itself within a set of formative practices that are characterized as modes of subjectivations' (Butler, 2002, p. 19). *Second*, as by way of the recognition-theoretical combination of self-reference and reference to others she not only confirms the *structure of power* as 'conduct of conduct' (Foucault) but also she systematically gives reason to it and significantly enlarges it with regard to the question of phenomena. *Third*, because by her theory the—particularly current—*subject of power* can be explained more in detail, as 'subjugation' for the sake of recognition promises that which subjectivity cannot keep—'identity'. Butler's explanation of the readiness for subjugation is revealing: 'it is necessary to remember that the turn towards the law is not necessitated by the hailing [of recognition]; it is compelling, in a less logical sense, because it promises identity' (Butler, 1997, p. 108) It is precisely the inability—resulting from strict relationality—'to "be" in a self-identical sense' (ibid., p. 131) which constitutes our 'vulnerability' (ibid., p. 108) and our susceptibility to the 'lure of identity' (ibid., p. 130) and to the promises of completeness. In such a way, it also makes us—precisely in the name of supposedly achievable autonomy/independence—governable. Her mechanism—she 'makes us believe that this is about our "liberation"' (Foucault, 1977, p. 190)—is thus not only an 'irony of the dispositive' (ibid.), as Foucault provocatively formulated, but also a strategy which makes his statement of the 'submission of subjectivity' (Foucault, 1982, p. 213) more comprehensible. In so far as the 'own' can only be gained by way of the 'alien' and thus can never be completely possessed it tempts one to try to escape both from one's own withdrawnness and different nature regarding determination and assimilation—it may be in the form of subjugation and devaluation of others for the purpose of egocentric self-stabilization and self-enhancement, so that negating the other as somebody else supposedly allows one to minimize one's own dependency, determinedness, and vulnerability. Or it may also be in the form of subjugation to others for the purpose of secured recognition and self-avoidance, so that negating one's own self supposedly suspends it from being under pressure and being at risk. To formulate this pointedly: we can be governed not only because we are dependent on recognition by others but also as others and we ourselves are also always withdrawn, we want to govern. Butler's theory, however, *fourth* opens up a new perspective on reformulating criticism and resistance to the inappropriate alternative of self-determination and heteronomy and by way of withdrawnness and 'alienness' [*Fremdheit* or *Entzogenheit*— another translation of which might be 'strangeness' or 'dispossession'] to interpret it as a practical 'virtue of desubjugation' (cf. Butler, 2002). The latter's central mechanism of inevitable 'crossing over' results less from theoretical-generalizing arguments than from accepting one's own self-restriction by conformity (see Butler, 2003, p. 64): 'Maybe we really can speculate that the moment of resistance, of opposition arises precisely when we find ourselves restricted in our attachment. [...] The fact that the human passion of survival/self-preservation makes us susceptible and vulnerable to those who promise our bread also implies the possibility of revolt' (ibid., p. 64 and 67). Even if Butler's peculiarly 'existential' appearing reflections may at first seem to be strange in the context of Foucault's terminology (and seem to be incompatible), they allow us to state Foucault's approach on power more clearly: not only as they allow us to read his demand—'We have to promote new forms of subjectivity through the refusal of this kind of individuality which has been imposed on us for several centuries' (Foucault, 1982, p. 216)—as being genealogically reasoned and thus force us to contradict its 'aesthetic superficiality' towards superficial 'self-care' (see Schmid, 1991) but also it lets us understand 'power'—particularly if viewing it as the 'power of power'—as the 'processing of negativity' (cf. Ricken, 2005; cf. Heinrich, 1975; Rentsch, 2000): it may be because power as 'action power' threatens with 'negativity' and uses the latter strategically by means of threatening with violence and (finally) death resulting in vulnerability or it may be that power as 'conditional' or 'structural power' focuses 'negativity' both as need and dependency and thus tries to rule by help of incompleteness, withdrawnness and 'alienness' [*Fremdheit/Entzogenheit*]. But negativity is always considered a 'human stain' (as Phillip Roth has it) which—now turned against the human race as an objection—opens up enormous possibilities of interference and access only by changing the indissoluble (self- and other-) difference which forms humankind's nature (cf. Ricken, 1999 and 2006) into a fateful hierarchy where the supposedly achievable 'complete form'—particularly if thought of as being only regulative—makes perceiving negativity possible at first and both enforces its efficiency and makes it lasting.

Systematically seen, the thoughts on the 'power of power' as developed here now suggest a concluding, categorical readjustment: just as subjectivity must be thought of in a relational way, its widely common (and directed critically against 'one-dimensionality' (Marcuse)) double-dimensioned condition between givenness and posedness (see Habermas, 1973, p. 105) cannot be sufficient anymore. For this binary structure only allows us to distinguish between the given and the posed and localizes the specific feature of human subjectivity—as an ability of being able to behave (in a changed way) towards itself and therefore of being in need of at first producing itself—thus in a rather one-sided way on the 'task side'—with the effect that the opposition of self-determinedness and heteronomy, which has already been accepted to be problematic, is only reinforced and leads to latent devaluation of the given. If, however, subjectivity is understood as relational, i.e. as a 'relationship referring to itself' (Kierkegaard), besides givenness and posedness a third aspect occurs which results only from double relationality $[x(y) \leftrightarrow y(x)]$ and can be called withdrawnness or rather 'alienness' [*Fremdheit/Entzogenheit*]. Thus, it is subjectivity-theoretically necessary to make subjectivity understandable as three-dimensionality where givenness, posedness, and withdrawnness are interwoven as constitutional factors: in this case, subjectivity does not only mean not to be able to behave towards oneself and towards others in a 'complete' and transparent way (as one cannot succeed with completely bringing oneself away from oneself) but it means that one must behave towards this withdrawnness in oneself and from others, so that subjectivity might become clear as a 'difference' which just cannot be dissolved within 'identity' but is marked by ruptures, faults, and 'blind spots'. Thus, by withdrawnness a constitutive factor is named next to givenness and posedness, which must not be confused with alienation (from something familiar to one, belonging to one, native to one at birth, and from which one is subsequently alienated) and thus must be independently considered.

That which is subjectivity-theoretically logical as fundamental (and not only coincidental or 'artificially' invented) 'un-interpretability of the self' (see Gamm, 2000) is also power- and criticism-theoretically important and may only be indicated by help of a brief recourse to differentiations by Foucault: while sovereign power as 'conduct of conduct' can be read by way of the given (law) and the withdrawn (religion), which tries to minimize a state of posedness and—thus(!)—at first uses and strengthens it as a source of criticism so that the contradicting 'but for me' becomes an argument against a 'being in itself', pastoral power as 'conduct of conduct' aims at the posed which it tries to work on—if historically dimensioned in different ways—by rather putting the given into brackets. Bio-power (as bio-politics), however, could then be reconstructed as structuring the given by means of which the leeway of the posed shall be pre-structured and restricted. Two con-clusions shall be given as examples: first, the change from negative to positive power can be made understandable as systematically considering the state of being posed for the purpose of increasing and consolidating power which not only tries to generally consider each case of human stubbornness (see Foucault, 1977) but must thank the calculating observation for its existence that on the one hand all that which exists must in each case be made its own and that on the other hand it is also connected to (given) conditions (see Foucault, 1995). Secondly, however, criticism can be explained as in each case emphasizing one of the 'withheld' or even 'suppressed' factors: just as self-determination against (excluding it or wanting to determine it) heteronomy seems to be appropriate for criticism, the recourse to self-determination is mostly powerless if being posed has itself become the central field of power. In the face of the currently observed predominance of pastoral power constellations, which legitimate themselves by the 'for me' and by way of promising 'stable identities' try to install others as experts in my 'self-care' (see Bröckling *et al.*, 2004), it seems rather difficult to display aspects of 'withdrawnness' and 'brokenness' in such a way that they may become clear as each 'blind spot' of the actual 'regiment' instead insisting on self-determination and autonomy—without at the same time being able to at all claim validity as the substantial universalities and lasting criteria of criticism. (see Ricken, 2002).

By these few indications a categorical horizon may be sketched which—starting out from (three-dimensionally constituted) subjectivity—allows us to systematically formulate power as 'conduct of conduct' as well as to formulate criticism as 'practice of de-subjugation' in such a way that at the same time they may become clear in respect of their own nature and of (historic) variability and may be referred to each human self-interpretation. If this is convincing, a structural access will be gained in front of whose (three-dimensional) anthropological matrix each form of life, power, and criticism can be read (see Ricken, 2004a). Foucault's pointed rejection and rebuke saying that relationships of power are no 'relationships of reason' (see Foucault, 2000, p. 116)—if at first justified by being adjusted against intentionality—were then a problematic reduction withholding just that which constitutes power in the first place: that humans are not simply 'for themselves' or even only 'in themselves' but must lead their lives 'for themselves', but in the first place must lead them 'from others'—and because of this both can be governed and themselves want to govern.

Note

1. This article is a shortened translation of an earlier German text (cf. Ricken, 2004b). I want to thank the VS Verlag für Sozialwissenschaften for permitting the translation and printing, and especially Nicole Bulzer, Maarten Simons and Jan Masschelein for the translation. Most of the quotations in this article are from German editions and have been translated into English by the author.

References

Arendt, H. (1970) *Macht und Gewalt* (München, Piper).
Arendt, H. (1981/1958) *Vita activa—oder: Vom tätigen Leben* (München, Piper).
Bachrach, P. & Baratz, M. S. (1962) The Two Faces of Power, *American Political Science Review*, 56, pp. 947–952.
Bourdieu, P. (2000) *Pascalian Meditations* (Cambridge, Polity Press).
Breuer, S. (1987) Foucault's Theorie der Disziplinargesellschaft. Eine Zwischenbilanz, *Leviathan*, 15, pp. 319–337.
Breuer, S. (1991) *Max Webers Herrschaftssoziologie* (Frankfurt/Main, Campus).
Bröckling, U., Krasmann, S. & Lemke, T. (eds) (2004) *Glossar der Gegenwart* (Frankfurt/Main, Suhrkamp).
Burckhardt, J. (1949) *Weltgeschichtliche Betrachtungen (1868/1873). Historisch-kritische Gesamtausgabe*, R. von Stadelmann, ed. (Pfullingen, Neske).
Butler, J. (1997) *The Psychic Life of Power: Theories in subjection* (Stanford, CA, Stanford University Press).

Butler, J. (2002) What is Critique? An essay on Foucault's virtue, in: D. Ingram (ed.), *Political: Readings in Continental Philosophy* (Oxford, Basil Blackwell). [http://www.law.berkeley.edu/centers/kadish/what%20is%20critique%20J%20Butler.pdf]

Butler, J. (2003) Noch einmal: Körper und Macht, in: A. Honneth & M. Saar (ed.), *Michel Foucault. Zwischenbilanz einer Rezeption* (Frankfurt/Main, Suhrkamp), pp. 52–67.

Dahrendorf, R. (1963) Art. Macht und Herrschaft, soziologisch, *Religion in Geschichte und Gesellschaft*, 4, pp. 569–572.

Deleuze, G. (1993) Postskriptum: Die Kontrollgesellschaft, in: G. Deleuze, *Unterhandlungen* (Frankfurt/M. Suhrkamp), pp. 254–262.

Dreyfus, H. L. & P. Rabinow (1982) *Michel Foucault. Beyond Structuralism and Hermeneutics* (Chicago, IL, University of Chicago Press).

Foucault, M. (1971) *Die Ordnung der Dinge* (Frankfurt am Main, Suhrkamp).

Foucault, M. (1976) *Überwachen und Strafen. Die Geburt des Gefängnisses* (Frankfurt/Main, Suhrkamp).

Foucault, M. (1977) *Sexualität und Wahrheit, Bd. 1, Der Wille zum Wissen* (Frankfurt/Main, Suhrkamp).

Foucault, M. (1982) The Subject and Power, in: H. L. Dreyfus & P. Rabinow (1982), *Michel Foucault. Beyond structuralism and hermeneutics* (Chicago, IL, University of Chicago Press), pp. 208–226.

Foucault, M. (1992) *Was ist Kritik?* (Berlin, Merve).

Foucault, M. (1999) *In Verteidigung der Gesellschaft. Vorlesungen am Collège de France (1975–76)* (Frankfurt/Main, Suhrkamp).

Foucault, M. (2000) Truth and Power. An Interview in 1976 with Alessandro Fontana and Pasquale Pasquino, in: J. D. Faubion (ed.), *Michel Foucault: Power. Essential works of Foucault 1954–1984 (vol. III)* (New Press, The New York Press), pp. 111–133.

Fraser, N. (1994) Foucault über die moderne Macht: Empirische Einsichten und normative Unklarheiten, in: N. Fraser, *Widerspenstige Praktiken. Macht, Diskurs, Geschlecht* (Frankfurt/Main, Suhrkamp), pp. 31–55.

Gamm, G. (2000) Die Unausdeutbarkeit des Selbst, in: G. Gamm, *Nicht nichts. Studien zu einer Semantik des Unbestimmten* (Frankfurt/Main, Suhrkamp), pp. 207–227.

Gehlen, A. (1961) Art. Macht, in: von E. Beckerath *et al.* (eds), *Handwörterbuch der Sozialwissenschaften, Band 7* (Stuttgart, Fischer), pp. 77–81.

Habermas, J. (1973) Philosophische Anthropologie (ein Lexikonartikel), in: J. Habermas, *Kultur und Kritik. Verstreute Aufsätze* (Frankfurt/Main, Suhrkamp), pp. 89–111.

Habermas, J. (1978) Hannah Arendts Begriff der Macht, in: J. Habermas, *Politik, Kunst, Religion* (Stuttgart, Reclam), pp. 103–126.

Habermas, J. (1985) *The Philosophical Discourse of Modernity: Twelve lectures* (Cambridge, Polity Press/Basil Blackwell).

Hejl, P. M. (2001) Art. Macht, in: A. Nünning (ed.), *Metzler Lexikon Literatur- und Kulturtheorie* (Stuttgart, Metzler), pp. 398–399.

Honneth, A. (1991) *The Critique of Power: Reflected Stages in a Critical Social Theory* (Cambridge, MA, MIT Press).

Honneth, A. (2003) Foucault und die Humanwissenschaften. Zwischenbilanz einer Rezeption, in: A. Honneth & M. Saar (eds), *Michel Foucault. Zwischenbilanz einer Rezeption* (Frankfurt/Main, Suhrkamp), pp. 15–26.

Hradil, S. (1980) *Die Erforschung der Macht. Eine Übersicht über die empirische Ermittlung von Machtverteilungen durch die Sozialwissenschaften* (Stuttgart, Kohlhammer).

Imbusch, P. (ed.) (1998) *Macht und Herrschaft. Sozialwissenschaftliche Konzeptionen und Theorien* (Opladen, Westdeutscher Verlag).

Kelly, M. (ed.) (1994) *Critique and Power. Recasting the Foucault/Habermas debate* (Cambridge, MA, MIT Press).

Kierkegaard, S. (1992) *Die Krankheit zum Tode. Gesammelte Werke Abt. 24/25*, E. von Hirsch & H. Gerdes (eds), E. von Hirsch (trans.) (Gütersloh, Gütersloher Verlagshaus).

Lemke, T. (1997) *Kritik der politischen Vernunft. Foucaults Analyse der modernen Gouvernementalität* (Hamburg, Argument).

Luhmann, N. (1969) Klassische Theorie der Macht: Kritik ihrer Prämissen, *Zeitschrift für Politik*, 16, pp. 149–170.

Luhmann, N. (1975) *Macht* (Stuttgart, Enke).

Luhmann, N. (2000) *Die Politik der Gesellschaft* (Frankfurt/Main, Suhrkamp).

Meyer-Drawe, K. (1984) *Leiblichkeit und Sozialität. Phänomenologische Beiträge zu einer pädagogischen Theorie der Inter-Subjektivität* (München, Fink).

Paris, R. (1998) *Stachel und Speer. Machtstudien* (Frankfurt/Main, Suhrkamp).

Popitz, H. (1992) *Phänomene der Macht. Autorität—Herrschaft—Gewalt—Technik* (Tübingen, Mohr).

Rentsch, T. (2000) *Negativität und praktische Vernunft* (Frankfurt/Main, Suhrkamp).

Ricken, N. (1999) *Subjektivität und Kontingenz. Markierungen im pädagogischen Diskurs* (Würzburg, Königshausen & Neumann).

Ricken, N. (2002) Identitätsspiele und die Intransparenz der Macht. Anmerkungen zur Struktur menschlicher Selbstverhältnisse, in: J. Straub & J. Renn (eds), *Transitorische Identität. Der Prozesscharakter des modernen Selbst* (Frankfurt/Main and New York, Campus), pp. 318–359.

Ricken, N. (2004a) 'Menschen'. Zur Struktur anthropologischer Reflexionen als einer unverzichtbaren kulturwissenschaftlichen Dimension, in: F. Jaeger *et al.* (eds), *Sinn—Kultur—Wissenschaft. Eine interdisziplinäre Bestandsaufnahme, Band 1: Die Kultur in der Lebenspraxis. Zur Idee kulturwissenschaftlicher Grundbegriffe* (Stuttgart, Metzler), pp. 152–172 [Kap. 3.2].

Ricken, N. (2004b) Die Macht der Macht. Rückfragen an Michel Foucault, in: N. Ricken & M. Rieger-Ladich (eds), *Michel Foucault: Pädagogische Lektüren* (Wiesbaden, VS Verlag), pp. 119–143.

Ricken, Norbert (2005) 'Freude aus Verunsicherung ziehn—wer hat uns das denn beigebracht!' (Christa Wolf). Über den Zusammenhang von Negativität und Macht, in: D. Benner (ed.) (2005, in press), *Erziehung—Bildung—Negativität.* (49. Beiheft der Zeitschrift für Pädagogik) (Weinheim und Basel, Beltz).

Ricken, N. (2006) *Die Ordnung der Bildung. Beiträge zu einer Genealogie der Bildung* (Weisbaden, VS Verlag).

Ricken, N. & Rieger-Ladich, M. (eds) (2004) *Michel Foucault: Pädagogische Lektüren* (Wiesbaden, VS Verlag).

Röttgers, K. (1990) *Spuren der Macht. Begriffsgeschichte und Systematik* (Freiburg/München, Alber).

Röttgers, K. (2002) Die Macht, in: K. Röttgers, *Kategorien der Sozialphilosophie* (Magdeburg, Scriptum), pp. 387–405.

Schmid, W. (1991) *Auf der Suche nach einer neuen Lebenskunst. Die Frage nach dem Grund und die Neubegründung der Ethik bei Foucault* (Frankfurt/Main, Suhrkamp).

Schwartländer, J. (1973) Art. Macht, in: von H. Krings *et al.* (eds), *Handbuch philosophischer Grundbegriffe* (München, Kösel), pp. 868–877.

Simmel, G. (1992) *Soziologie. Untersuchungen über die Formen der Vergesellschaftung* (Frankfurt/Main, Suhrkamp).

Sofsky, W. & Paris, R. (1994) *Figurationen sozialer Macht. Autorität, Stellvertretung, Koalition* (Frankfurt/Main, Suhrkamp).

Taylor, C. (1985) *Philosophical Papers* (Cambridge, Cambridge University Press).

Weber, M. (1972) *Wirtschaft und Gesellschaft. Grundriß der verstehenden Soziologie* (Tübingen, Mohr).

Weinrich, H. (ed.) (1975) *Positionen der Negativität* (München, Fink).

10
Experience and the Limits of Governmentality[1]

Jan Masschelein

L'expérience est la mise en question (à l'épreuve),

dans la fièvre et l'angoisse, de ce qu'un homme sait du fait d'être.

Georges Bataille

As we know, Michel Foucault refused to understand critique in terms of an act of judging on the legitimacy or of a putting to the test by subjugation to the demands of reason. In his later work critique appears to be a practical refusal of a particular form of subjectivity, a kind of 'virtue' (Butler, 2002) being the *art* not to be governed in this way, '*l'art de n'être pas gouverné comme ça et à ce prix*' (Foucault, 1978, p. 38). Briefly stated, critique is about backing out of the call to relate to our selves and to others in a particular way. It is to free ourselves of certain conceptions about ourselves and our conduct. Critique is a 'project of desubjectivation' (Foucault, 2000a, p. 241) that is to be conceived of as a labour on and with oneself which aims at establishing 'new relationships with the subject at issue' (Foucault, 2000a, p. 242). This is what philosophy as critical activity and as ethos is about for Foucault: not so much to discover who we are, but to refuse what we are (Foucault, 2000b, p. 336).[2]

We can read this motive in the often-quoted passages with which Foucault, after a long silence, introduces the continuation and displacement of his *History of Sexuality*:

> As for what motivated me, it is quite simple; ... It was curiosity—the only kind of curiosity, in any case, that is worth acting upon with a degree of obstinacy: not the curiosity that seeks to assimilate what it is proper for one to know, but that which enables one to get free of oneself. (Foucault, 1985, p. 8)

The following elucidation by Foucault is particularly telling regarding the displacement he has in mind:

> There are times in life when the question of knowing if one can think differently than one thinks, and perceive differently than one sees, is absolutely necessary if one is to go on looking and reflecting at all. People will say, perhaps, that these games with oneself would be better left

backstage; or at best, that they might properly form part of those preliminary exercises that are forgotten once they have served their purpose. But, then, what is philosophy today—philosophical activity, I mean—if it is not the critical work that thought brings to bear on itself? In what does it consist, if not in the endeavour to know how and to what extent it might be possible to think differently, instead of legitimating what is already known? There is always something ludicrous in philosophical discourse when it tries, from the outside, to dictate to others, to tell them where their truth is and how to find it, or when it works up a case against them in the language of naïve positivity. But it is entitled to explore what might be changed, in its own thought, through the practice of a knowledge that is foreign to it. The 'essay'—which should be understood as the assay or test by which, in the game of truth, one undergoes changes, and not as the simplistic appropriation of others for the purpose of communication—is the living substance of philosophy, at least if we assume that philosophy is still what it was in times past, i.e. an '*ascesis*', askêsis, an exercise of oneself in the activity of thought'. (ibid., pp. 8–9)

And with regard to his own work Foucault continues: 'It was a philosophical exercise. The object was to learn to what extent the effort to think one's own history can free thought from what it silently thinks, and so enable it to think differently' (ibid., p. 9).

If we now connect both elements we could say that the work of 'critique' is: to pull oneself free of oneself and to dissolve or free thought from what it thinks in silence. This double dissolution takes place through the 'practice of a knowledge that is foreign to it', through an 'assay or test' in which—as Foucault explains at another occasion—'the critique of what we are is at one and the same time the historical analysis of the limits imposed on us and an experiment with the possibility of going beyond them [*de leur franchissement possible*]' (Foucault, 1997a, p. 319), so that—as Ricken states—critique is always a work at and on the limits (Ricken, 2000, p. 28). However, if philosophical activity as a 'work on the self', as self transformation is always experimental, then philosophical activity is also always related to an experience in which our subjectivity is at stake: a limit experience, which pulls the subject free of itself, which wrenches it from itself and prevents it from being the same (Foucault, 2000a, p. 242).

In this paper I will try to show how this activity could be described as an e-ducative practice. I use 'e-ducative' in the sense that Foucault himself indicated in one of his courses at the Collége de France, i.e. not in the sense of '*educare*' but of '*educere*': '*tendre la main, sortir de là, conduire hors de là*' (Foucault, 2001, p. 129). In this line an e-ducative practice is not (or not in the first place) about gaining knowledge or competence which resolves ignorance and incompetence but about '*une certaine action qui va être opérée sur l'individu, […] une sorte d'opération qui porte sur le mode être du sujet lui-même*' (ibid., p. 130). An e-ducative practice is a practice in which in a certain sense the subject is ruined or dies, a practice that involves acceptance of life up to death, up to annihilation. I explore this idea of 'de-subjectivation' as e-ducative practice starting from an example which Foucault himself gives of such a negative or critical practice: the writing (and reading) of experience books. Through this example I try to indicate that and how a certain subjectivity can be refused, that such a refusal is dangerous (and irreversible), that it is a public and uncomfortable undertaking and finally that this practice is not in need of pastoral care.

1. Experience Books as a Project of Desubjectivation

In a well known and revealing interview with Trombadori Foucault points to his own books as 'experience books' which he opposes to 'truth books' or 'demonstration books' (Foucault, 2000a, p. 246). An experience book is of course not a book on or about experiences (and certainly not about personal '*Erlebnisse*'). It is rather a book whose writing and reading is itself an experience: 'So it's a book that functions as an experience, for its writer and reader alike, much more than as an establishment of a historical truth' (ibid., p. 243). Experience is meant here in the fullest sense possible: 'An experience is something that one comes out of transformed' (ibid., p. 239). In line with what we heard earlier, we could say that writing (or reading) an experience book is thus a critical philosophical activity. In such a book, says Foucault, 'I am not concerned about communicating what I already thought or what I am thinking before I begin to write. Rather I am concerned ... that the book transforms me and transforms what I think ... I am an experimenter and not a theorist ... who constructs a general system, either deductive or analytical, ... I'm an experimenter in the sense that I write in order to change myself and in order not to think the same thing as before' (ibid., p. 240). This lines up with the writings of Georges Bataille, Friedrich Nietzsche, Maurice Blanchot and Pierre Klossowski, whose 'problem was not the construction of a system but the construction of a personal experience' (ibid., p. 241). This experience should, however, not be understood in the phenomenological sense.

> The phenomenologist's experience is basically a certain way of bringing a reflexive gaze to bear ... on the everyday in its transitory form, in order to grasp its meanings. For Nietzsche, Bataille, Blanchot, on the other hand, experience is trying to reach a certain point in life that is as close as possible to the 'inlivable', which can't be lived through. What is required is the maximum of intensity and the maximum of impossibility at the same time ... experience has the function of wrenching the subject from itself, of seeing to it that the subject is no longer itself, or that it is brought to its annihilation or its dissolution. This is a project of desubjectivation. The idea of a limit-experience ... is what was important to me ... and what explains ... my books ... , I've always conceived of them as direct experiences aimed at pulling myself free of myself, at preventing me from being the same'. (ibid., pp. 241–242)

In this sense experience books are means to get to an experience 'that permits a change, a transformation of the relationship we have with ourselves and with the world where, up to then, we had seen ourselves as being without problems—in short, a transformation of the relationship we have with our knowledge' (ibid., p. 244). This particular perspective on experience is according to Foucault the very heart of all he did. In this context the truth of what he was saying has been one of his central concerns. However, telling the truth is for Foucault not an epistemological question of establishing truth, but an ethical one that has to do with the relationship with ourselves and with the world. On the one hand, so he states, he is using the classical academic methods, but on the other hand he is only dealing with fiction ('there's no question of it being anything else but fiction' ibid., p. 242) since his problem is not to satisfy professional historians, philosophers, sociologists or educationalists:

> ... my problem is to construct myself, and to invite others to share an experience of what we are, not only our past but also our present, an experience of modernity in such a way that we might come out of it transformed. Which means that at the end of the book we would establish new relationships with the subject at issue: the I who wrote the book and those who have read it. ... For one to be able to have that experience through the book, what it says does need to be true in terms of academic, historically verifiable truth. It can't exactly be a novel. ... Now, the fact is, this experience is neither true nor false. An experience is always a fiction: it's something that one fabricates oneself, that doesn't exist before and will exist afterwards. That is the difficult relationship with truth, the way in which the latter is bound up with an experience that is not bound to it and, in some degree, destroys it'. (ibid., pp. 242–243)

In fact 'fiction' is here to be understood as the articulation of the failure (or destruction) of the actual government through exposing its games of truth and power. An articulation which itself constitutes a truth beyond truth so to speak, a truth which is in the future. As Foucault explains elsewhere, even if what he was saying (about the past) was not true, his writing has a truth in reality today. His hope is that his writings receive their truth once they have been written and not before (as if the book would just articulate what was known before or what can be said within a regime of truth): 'I hope that the truth of my books is in the future' ('*J'espère que la vérité de mes livres est dans l'avenir*') (Foucault, 1979b, p. 805, my translation).

Moreover, an experience book doesn't teach anything, it is not saving or delivering: 'I don't accept the word "teaching". A systematic book ... would convey lessons. My books don't exactly have that particular value. They are more like invitations or public gestures' (Foucault, 2000a, p. 245). But this characterization of his work is also based on the nature of the experience itself. 'An experience is something that one has completely alone but can fully have only to the extent that it escapes pure subjectivity and that others can also—I won't say repeat it exactly, but at least encounter it—and go through it themselves' (ibid., p. 245).

Now, at first sight it seems rather strange or even odd to refer to experience when trying to elucidate critique as a project of desubjectivation—although Gutting writes that experience is the best expression of Foucault's comprehensive theme (Gutting, 2002, p. 73). Indeed, one could not only state, as Gadamer did in 1960, that the notion of experience is 'one of the most obscure that we have' (Gadamer, 1986, p. 310), one could add that meanwhile every reference to 'experience' arouses a profound suspicion. It was the so-called post-structuralists, such as Jean-François Lyotard, Jacques Derrida and Louis Althusser who nourished this suspicion mainly with regard to the assumed self-evident character and value of experience and with regard to the claim of immediateness. And not only was Foucault himself labelled as a post-structuralist, but his work seemed to analyse precisely singular experiences (like that of madness or sexuality) as being part of or being produced by an apparatus or regime of knowledge and power. To rely, then, on the authority of what is called experience, and even vivid or pre-reflexive experience, seems to be not only naïve, but purely ideological and forgetful of either modern epistemology or critical history. In contrast, we find time and again the warning that 'experience' is constructed discursively, that it is always in itself an interpretation and that we therefore should avoid essentialising or objectifying this 'experience' (see Jay, 1998, p. 63; Scott, 1991, p. 777). Although most critics accept that it would be impossible to simply remove the word 'experience' from our vocabulary, they still maintain that it is discourse, language and power structures that build a matrix that produces 'experience' (and not the other way round). What is put under permanent critique is the experience that claims to be 'unified, holistic, coherent and present to itself'. Such claim appears in two forms. One which in the line of Dilthey's *Lebensphilosophie* relates experience to the immediacy of lived, prereflexive communication or meeting between the self and the world, and which Dilthey called: '*Erlebnis*'. And one which—connected to a certain German tradition of 'Bildung', like Buber and Benjamin—considered experience to refer to some cumulative wisdom, which is produced through time and through the interaction between self and world, so that it could only be projected at the end of a dialectical process. Both forms are rejected by the critics: the search for an authentic experience is but 'another version of a nostalgic yearning for a presence and an immediacy that never have existed and never will exist' (Jay, 1998, p. 64). In this context it is striking that Foucault, although he belongs to the circle of the critics we just mentioned, seems to value 'experience' in the passages cited earlier also in a totally different way as an unappropriated, expropriating and non-appropriatable experience. However, if we want to elucidate this we should be aware that Foucault avoids using 'experience' here as a concept referring to something (see Larrosa, 2004). As so often he resists the question: 'what is it?', 'what is experience?'. He does not attempt to answer the question 'which concept of experience' he is using. A concept always is an act of defining and confining, which brings reassurance and comfort. He rather tries to maintain 'experience' as a word, not as a concept. Concepts mean what they say, words also mean what they say but they mean also more and 'other' and therefore they remain uncomfortable. Moreover Foucault avoids to put 'experience' in the position of the 'soul' or of 'desire' or of 'the (un)consciousness' as something which we (should) have, should recognize that we have, should start to elaborate and make transparent (See Larrosa, 2004). Experience delivers no substance and no foundation (See also Flynn, 2005, pp. 2008–228).

According to Jay, this other way of thinking about experience, largely inspired by Bataille, Nietzsche, Blanchot and Klossowski, seems to offer us a way out of the sterile debate between those who stick to a naïve concept of immediate experience and those who simply reject the notion of experience as such. And following this line, I suggest that we could perhaps recover (negative) experience as a word to be part of critical educational thought in the actual 'learning society'. To indicate in what direction this could go, I want to comment on some of the passages I quoted earlier.

2. Writing Experience Books

(a) I start with the distinction between truth books and demonstration books on the one hand and experience books on the other. Writing a truth book means to write a book that informs, that puts forward a truth, communicates a truth, 'convey lessons'. It is a book that attempts to inform about something, to explain something, to prove or justify something. In this sense, writing a truth book implies a particular attitude, a particular ethos. It prescribes and requires an attitude in which one subjects or subjugates oneself to the demands of truth i.e. to the Logos of a particular regime of truth. And one addresses the reader in the name of this Logos, to which one claims to have access. One addresses the reader in the horizon or in the name of a tribunal or court (the tribunal of reason, of truth, of science, of humanity ...).[3] This means that in writing a truth book one takes in a certain way the position of a teacher, of a knowing or learned teacher ('*un maître savant*') as I would call it with reference to Rancière (see Rancière, 1986). That what is written from this position and attitude becomes a teaching (an explanation, proof, information, etc.) so that those who are addressed find themselves in the position of a learner (one who does not yet know, but could get knowledge exactly from the book). Truth books are books which are written by learned people, those who know or claim to know, (or who are in a certain way experienced) and are in fact bound up to an attitude which we could call, with Foucault, a pastoral attitude. This attitude implies that one puts oneself in the service of a regime, subjugates to its logos (for example 'communicative reason') and takes up demands and care in its name: without explanation no understanding, without proof and argument no truth. In this attitude one orients oneself in writing to a regime and a tribunal and addresses a reader who is known or familiar in the sense that this reader is supposed to subject herself to the same regime and the same tribunal. It is this subjection (or subjectivation) under a tribunal that allows the writer and the reader to be 'somebody', so that both get their position and subjectivity precisely in the horizon of this tribunal. And in the same time, as was indicated above, both find themselves also in a situation of teaching, where they obtain or take the position of learner or of teacher. These positions are positions in a pastoral-pedagogical regime of government that follows a certain logos and governs accordingly by installing an inequality between both, which can be defined and justified only with regard to the logos of that tribunal. The regime organises itself along distinctions as: knowing/not-knowing, adult/not-adult, enlightened/not-enlightened, human/

inhuman, mature/immature, etc. (see: Masschelein, 2004; Simons, 2004). To write a truth or demonstration book—to write as teacher—is to write from a particular position in a regime of truth and implies to define and justify the position of the reader as one who is in need of care, explanation, proof or emancipation, one who is in need of guidance of his or her conduct in the light of this regime. Such a writing is a comfortable writing, because it obtains (or loses) its authority from a code (or Law/Logos of the tribunal and the regime) and from subjecting to this code. Of course, one can write better or worse, one can have less or more knowledge, a worse or better argument but that doesn't affect or change fundamentally the pastoral position, i.e. to be a subject as and in subjecting to a regime.

As stated above, this applies also to the reader of a truth or demonstration book. This reader is not only taking up a certain position in a pastoral regime, she is equally taking up a particular attitude in which she considers what she reads as an expression of truth (of reason, science, humanity, ...), relates it to a certain tribunal and judges it accordingly (for example as more or less true, etc.). Just like the author herself such a reader does not put herself at stake. Following Blanchot such a reader could be characterized by 'her lack of modesty, her persistence to remain the same in front of what she reads, to be a (wo)man who can read in general' ('*son manque de modestie, son acharnement à vouloir continuer à être le même face à ce qu'il lit, à vouloir être un homme qui sait lire en général*') (Blanchot, 1955, p. 263).

So Foucault rejects very clearly this interpretation of his books. 'I don't accept the word "teaching". ... My books don't exactly have that particular value' (Foucault, 2000a, p. 245). His books are not truth books, but experience books. But what does that mean?

(b) First of all we should acknowledge that there are experience books which are in fact a kind of truth book or demonstration book (see Simons, 2004). These are books in which a personal experience is reported and/or the depth of one's soul is revealed. Such books are often demonstration books because they intend to justify one's own position by referring to (an) experience as well as wanting to introduce the other into a certain truth (and even bind them to that truth). Truth-readers consider such books as reports of the personal experiences of the author, which say something about the author and which therefore can only be understood and valued with regard to this author. Even when Foucault concedes that all the books he wrote were written directly out of a personal experience ('I haven't written a book that was not inspired, at least in part, by a direct personal experience' Foucault, 2000a, p. 244), this does not mean that they represent these experiences or transpose them into knowledge ('it's not at all a matter of transporting personal experiences into knowledge', ibid., p. 244). The experience books he wrote are not teachings but are written out from a totally different attitude, which is not the comfortable attitude of the teacher or the pastor. It is an attitude of ex-position, which allows to hear and see (i.e. to experience) something other and in this way enables us to liberate the gaze and the thoughts, so that the author (and the reader of these books) can see not only something other, but also can see and think differently and transform herself. Such writing is for Foucault a philosophical exercise, a form of 'askêsis' as we indicated in the beginning of this paper. It is a writing that is also a way of writing-one/the-self, of self writing (Foucault, 1997b). It is an operation that is performed on the way of being of the subject herself, an exercise in which the limits of subjectivity (and objectivity) are at stake. Writing means to expose oneself in order to allow for the possibility for 'seeing further', 'thinking further' or 'thinking otherwise' to occur.[4] To write (or read) an experience book means to put oneself to a test in confrontation with a knowledge that is foreign; it is an unprotected, exposed writing (or reading) insofar as it implies to abandon or renounce direction by religion, law or science, as also the dedication to realize one's deepest truth (see Dreyfus, 1990, p. 58). In this writing (and reading) one is not so much asking oneself whether it is false or true, but one exposes oneself to a foreign knowledge. One writes an experience book because one does not know what one is thinking or should think.

What is at stake is not to express what one thought before, but what is at stake is 'to lose ones face' i.e. in a certain sense one's subjectivity. This longing for anonymity has been expressed many times by Foucault. There is for example the quote of Beckett at the beginning of his famous conference on the author (Foucault, 1979c). And there is the equally famous passage in *The Archeology of Knowledge*: 'I am no doubt not the only one who writes in order to have no face. Do not ask who I am and do not ask me to remain the same: leave it to our bureaucrats and our police to see that our papers are in order. At least spare us their morality when we write' (Foucault, 1972, p. 17). This pursuing of the theme of 'having no face' is not to say that the subject of writing is not important, on the contrary. It relates precisely to the demand to withdraw subjectivity from the individualising action of the regime of power and truth. This regime confines what the subject can 'be', she draws the limits beyond which the subject no longer 'exists'. Writing experience books is an act of transformation of the subject at these limits.

On the one hand, this writing to lose one's face is a desubjectivating writing, in which one both undergoes (endures or experiences) and goes under, is dying. It is a writing in which the writer or/as teacher and the writing/teaching as well as the reader or/as learner go under, in which 'we' are exposed and are confronting each other as equals, not as an individual confronted with an individual, as the older generation confronted with the younger, but as a certain 'we' that shares this ex-position, this out-of-position. On a different occasion and related to another scene of teaching Foucault describes in a wonderful way how it is when one is losing ones face, when a regime of truth is put out of order or suspended, when the subject goes under, but remains at stake:

> The baffled master lowers his extended pointer, turns his back to the board, regards the uproarious students, and does not realize that they laugh so loudly because above the blackboard and his stammered denials, a vapor has just risen, little by little taking shape and now creating, precisely and without doubt, a pipe. 'A pipe, a pipe', cry the students, stamping away while the teacher, his voice sinking even lower, murmurs always with the same obstinacy though no one is listening, 'And yet it is not

a pipe'. He is not mistaken; because the pipe floating so obviously overhead (like the object the blackboard drawing refers to, and in whose name the text can justifiably say that the drawing is truly not a pipe) is itself merely a drawing. It is not a pipe. No more on the board than above it, the drawing of the pipe and the text presumed to name it find nowhere to meet and be superimposed, as the calligrapher so presumptuously had attempted to bring about.

So, on its bevelled and clearly rickety mounts, the easel has but to tilt, the frame to loosen, the painting to tumble down, the words to be scattered. The 'pipe' can 'break': The common place—banal work of art or everyday lesson—has disappeared. (Foucault, 1983c, pp. 30–31)

On the other hand, one makes through this writing and in this writing, in which one undergoes and goes under, also a 'personal' experience, which goes together with the engagement of the whole person. She implies the possibility that something other can be seen and thought, that an objectivity beyond a regime of truth can manifest and impose or inscribe itself. Or more precisely: what this writing makes visible is not something beyond the visible, something hidden behind the visible. This writing does not offer us a liberating or emancipating gaze, but liberates our gaze (eye). It offers the possibility to see how and what we see and shows us in this way a truth beyond the truth in a regime. In a certain sense one could say that it offers us the possibility to have a gaze on the world, without being captured by a regime.

(c) To write an experience book is an e-ducative practice that opens up the possibility to breathe new life into the words and to liberate the gaze. In this way it allows a certain truth-telling: 'I come to see, I come to hear'. '*Je viens de voir, je viens d'entendre*' (Foucault, 1971, p. 1106, my translation). If one takes the 'coming' here one understands also the movement or displacement which is involved. However, two things have to be added here. Firstly, to expose oneself or being-exposed does not point to a (universal) structure, but to a possibility. Secondly, it is necessary to perform a certain work or labour (askêsis), in order to be exposed, in order to be able to be attentive, in order to be able to experience something, to breathe new life in the words and to see differently or to see what is visible. Indeed, we should not forget that this practice involves a certain discipline, but not the (normalising) discipline related to the subjection under a tribunal, but related to certain exercises and actions that have to be performed. Experience books bring to the attention what is visible, but for what we had no eye. Even if this attention depends also on the way in which these books are written it is the attitude towards the book that is decisive. This attitude has to be worked at: she is a certain form of 'askêsis', although not a pastoral form. The 'askêsis' enables and produces a subject of experience, a subject that cares for the world and tries its assay. The liberating of the gaze makes demands for exercise and for acceptance of life up to death. E-ducative practices are practices of exposition. The subject of such practices, the subject of experience, with is not the subject of knowledge, can only be a paradoxical subject. It is not only paradoxical because it is active to become passive, or because it is subject and object (of experience) at the same time, so that de-subjectivivation and subjectivation (or forming of the subject) take place simultaneously. It is also paradoxical because it stays between two different logics: the logic of exposition (equality) and the logic of being subjected (inequality within a regime).

The e-ducative practice of writing is not preceded by the subjection under a regime or tribunal; this subjection is rather what is at stake in writing and not its starting point. Such a writing moves outside or at the limits of a certain regime of truth or government with its defined positions. It is itself ex-posed and leads us outside i.e. in the world as a public space, which is appropriated by no one and does not know any appropriate positions. It is a space for everyone and no one: no-man's land. This land has no entrance gate, we can not find it on any map. However, it requires a certain effort to be reached: a certain care for the self.

(d) The writing of an experience book is therefore to be considered as a practice in which one is caring for oneself and in which one is relating to oneself and to others (and to the world) in a particular way. That care involves neither a subjugation (under a tribunal) nor an introspection or investigation of one's soul, but rather requires an investigation of the world. An investigation in which one is present in such a way that, on the one hand, one is exposed and can go under, can lose oneself, and, on the other hand one is attentive in such a way that one can tell truth, a truth which does not require the subjection under a prescription or a norm/code, but nevertheless can have an effect for or in the reader. Foucault quotes in approval Blanchot's remark '*que la critique commence par l'attention, la présence et la générosité* [that critique starts with attention, presence and generosity]' (Foucault, 1979a, p. 762, my translation).

Being attentive means to engage in exercises which help to neutralise or eliminate the will to subject under a regime of truth and the energy with which the subject (as subject of knowledge) projects itself in the objects. This particular kind of attention and attentiveness implies and enables a being-present that puts the subject at stake and defers the expectation of a benefit (see also note 2). It involves a writing that relates to the reader in such a way that she is not put in a dependent, subjected position vis-à-vis of the writer. It involves writing a truth (a truth outside a regime of truth and therefore always only a fiction) as an exposition of one's own thinking and seeing, an exposition without name as a 'masked writing' of which Foucault says in a later interview: 'It's a way of addressing the potential reader, the only individual here who is of interest to me, more directly: "Since you don't know who I am, you will not be inclined to find out why I say what you read; just allow yourself to say, quite simply, it's true, it's false. I like it or I don't like it. Period"' (1997c, p. 323).[5] It is a writing which has effects—and Foucault recalls time and again that his writing had strange and particular effects (Foucault, 2000a, p. 243), but no effects benefiting the author. It is not so much writing in order to convince the reader, to direct her in a particular way, to make her accept a particular view or opinion; in this sense it is a generous writing, a writing without benefit for oneself. It is rather a writing which always puts 'me' and 'us' at stake simultaneously.

(e) When Foucault designates this writing and reading as a limit-experience, as a negative experience, then this has to do with it being a dangerous undertaking insofar as it is without warranty to come (at) home again. Or even stronger: an experience is something that transforms in an irreversible way. That is exactly why it is negative. But of course, we should prevent ourselves of dramatizing this limit-experiences[6]—it is no lyricism of transgression—while at the same time taking care that we do not render them harmless.

If one brings the different moments together, then it can probably be shown that writing (or reading) an experience book is an exercise of thought, which works in silence and consists in an attempt to hand over oneself with one's own hands, to make oneself into a question. Precisely because this writing implies an activity (and not just a passivity and surrendering) is Foucault able to call it a non-pastoral, non-Christian 'askêsis', an exercise and ethos which implies no obedience but acceptation (ac(t)-ceptation). Acceptation is not to accept the groundlessness or unfoundedness of our existence as structure of our being, but it is an acceptation that puts exactly the structure of our being (a subject) at stake. What can happen is not that we are enriched by an experience, that we have more experience and more knowledge, but that we are changed, that we have become someone else, that we relate differently to the world and that we can no longer value what was before. Experience therefore is not something that simply happens, but always something which happens to 'us'. We seem to live in a world in which an incredible number of things happen and also our lives seem to be full of all kinds of events, but very little seems to happen to 'us'. However, a limit-experience is precisely an experience that transforms us, which makes something in us to die. We can write dying and die writing, and cut every bond with the past. We can do something irreversible to ourselves, to our subjectivity. In this sense it is dangerous. Not because it would resist some concrete demands by the state (or by government in general), but because it questions the code in which such demands can be formulated and read; Because it questions the limits of the field of validity, of good and bad and, thus, runs the risk of immorality and trouble.

Closely related to this is Foucault's refusal to accept that there could be something which could count as a universal structure of human existence (which would be revealed by philosophy, anthropology, etc.) such as the 'groundlessness', the trauma of the other, the fate of the Daemon or even Experience as a substance to which we would be bound in an irreversible and essential way. It is exactly this view that fits or applies time and again to govern us and to justify the pastoral care of those who pretend to know about this presumed structure or substance and in this way can immunize themselves. Therefore, to state the possibility of limit experiences is to show that it is possible to detach oneself from being-governed, that liberation through de-subjectivation is possible. It is to maintain that experience is it owns authority while at the same time acknowledging that experience is no substance and not grounded on external criteria such as Reason, Science or even Theology. It is a paradoxical authority that always undermines her self (see Jay, 1998).

Or put differently: experience is meant by Foucault as a radical negative experience that is not to be rendered positive in an easy way. Therefore we can conceive of the experiment of transgression (in writing, reading, …) neither as a heroic search for Dionysian unity or for a reconciliation with one's inner Daemon nor as 'a singular exercise in aesthetic self-fashioning' (ibid., p. 74) or self stylisation. This would imply to emphasize experience as 'ex-post-facto-fiction' and as an element of a process of self formation and self realisation and to neglect the immediate experience which puts 'us' and thus the negative and the common at stake. It would make experience harmless. Like Bataille, Foucault recognizes that is impossible to *make* one's life into a 'work', into an aesthetically formed or built unity or identity. Life cannot be made. To make oneself into a question, or to put oneself in question means rather an exercise in exposing oneself, so that one can get lost. The care for the self is not a care for one's identity, but related to what Foucault meant by 'losing one's face'.

3. E-ducative Practice

So, an experience book does not offer teachings, does not convey lessons. It is a public gesture, an invitation to investigate one self. It is a gesture which attempts to introduce us into an experience (and not into the kingdom of truth or reason) and which tries to prevent us from remaining what we are. It is a book that does not aim at explaining or understanding how it really is and how we should read the present. To write and read an experience book means to expose ourselves as 'infants', as being without language, who receives language and has to be given a language, has to be given words. In e-ducative practices language is given and received (anew). But giving and receiving a language as words means that we don't know and cannot know what we give and what we receive: As the Argentinean poet Antonio Porchia so beautifully put this, 'What the words say does not remain. It is the words that remain, that endure, because the words remain the same, but what they say never remains the same' (Porchia, 1989, p. 111). This means also that these words, also the word experience itself, can lead us out, can lead us out of ourselves. That we must find out what the words are asking from us, what we owe them, what they say to us. The author as e-ducator gives words, shows something and 'makes' attentive. E-cudative practices offer no truth or only a truth in the future, they offer words as pure means, a medium through which something can happen to 'us'. In this context the e-ducator does not appear as a pastoral figure, who is speaking in the name of … (reason, salvation, …), but as a masked figure, no-one, (without face) who is speaking and writing in her own name or better: without a name. Her speaking and writing is not a means to an end. The listener or reader takes the book into an exercise of thought to transform herself. This exercise of thought is not like us playing with thoughts, but an exercise, in which thoughts put 'us' at stake.

As we have heard, Foucault understands experience mainly as a limit-experience that transgresses the limits of a coherent subjectivity as it functions within an actual governmental regime. Even if Foucault claims that his books are written out of a direct personal experience (with madness, with psychiatric institution, etc.), they aim in the first place at making new experiences possible. And if this is an exercise of changing oneself, it is an exercise that is no end itself. 'An experience is something that one has completely alone but can fully have only to the extent that it escapes pure subjectivity and that others can also—I won't say repeat it exactly, but at least encounter it—and go through it themselves' (Foucault, 2000a, p. 245). It must be clear from this that Foucault's notion of experience is indeed a paradoxical one and one which is difficult to delineate. Of course many questions listed by Martin Jay remain (see Jay, 1998, p. 78); but they appear in a different light. Can we avoid the transformation of a negative experience into a positive value? Does this negative experience have a value anyway? Does getting lost appear as positive? And is it possible to build or conceive institutions that would rest on this experience that is without clear authority and coherence? And is it possible to avoid that experience books become themselves truth books? At least it seems clear that experience cannot be reduced to discourse or to power structures, but that it has to be seen in some sense as what allows us to transgress the limits of a governmental regime. Transgression, then, is possible not through an heroic action or through an alternative aesthetic self-fashioning, but through taking the risk of an exposition, through experience. 'The limits of limit-experience have thus in some sense become equivalent to the very limits of critical theory today' (Jay, 1998, p. 78). However, in this way critique becomes the central issue of a pedagogy to come, a pedagogy to be invented, because such limit-experiences demand a form of attention, generosity and presence which are at stake in e-ducative practices. Such practices are uncomfortable practices that lead us into the world as expropriated or non-appropriated land, as no-mans-land and keep us there to the extent that they illuminate and disrupt our immunizing relations to our selves and to others.

Notes

1. This paper is a strongly reworked and elaborated version of a paper which was published in German under the title: '*Je viens de voir, je viens d'entendre*. Erfahrungen im Niemandsland' in: Ricken & Rieger-Ladich, 2004, pp. 95–115. Publication of translated parts of the paper was kindly authorised by the publisher: VS Verlag für Sozialwissenschaften.

2. I cannot pursue the issue of this refusal here in detail. Ewald comments that it makes no sense to ask: 'why should we change or transform ourselves? This is the question of the slave who is looking for subjection under a benefit. We should not change for, but against something' (Ewald, 1990, p. 93, my translation). And Butler argues that 'the will not to be governed in such a way' arises out of a crisis in which one lives. This 'will' must not to be considered as an original aspiration or as the affirmation of an original freedom although it is 'something like an original freedom'. Something like it, but not quite the same. It cannot be founded, only be found. (Butler, 2002; Foucault, 1978). There is indeed an ambiguity regarding the will as on the one hand this will, as the will to quality or the will to learn (to learn) for example, is the modern moral substance which constitutes the heart of the (self) government of the self (conceiving oneself as an individual with a certain will and accordingly bringing one's freedom into practice), where

on the other hand the will seems to indicate a kind of instance which allows for distancing oneself from this self government. This ambiguity regarding the will is not unrelated to the ambiguity of the word experience; See further.

3. See for example the very famous and telling first preface Kant wrote to his *Critique of Pure Reason* where this critique is called a tribunal and where the readers are addressed as judges of a court. Kant wants 'to institute a court of justice, by which reason may secure its rightful claims ... according to its own eternal and unchangeable laws' (Kant, 1997, p. 101) and writes: 'Here I expect from my reader the patience and impartiality of a judge ...' (ibid., p. 105).

4. As a philosophical exercise it requires an attitude in which one confronts what maybe could be called one's own infancy: the fact to not coincide with oneself as a subject in a pedagogical regime of government and truth, the fact that learner and teacher do not coincide with themselves (see also: Masschelein, 2005; Simons, 2004). Infancy could thus be regarded as the name for a potentiality that can never be resumed in an actuality; it would point to the limits of an actual regime of truth and government. In infancy as potentiality there is no inequality as is the case in the pedagogical regime, but there is a certain equality, an equality in the exposition. This infancy could also be related to Foucault's 'will not to be governed'. See note 2.

5. I changed the English translation in Foucault, 1997c since it is obviously wrong. In French we read: '*Puisque tu ne sais pas qui je suis, tu n'auras pas la tentation de chercher les raisons pour lesquelles je dis ce que je lis ...*' (Foucault, 1980, p. 925) which means exactly the contrary of the translation given in Foucault, 1997c: 'you will be more inclined to find out why I say what you read'.

6. Although Foucault calls Nietzsche an author of experience books in his sense: books in which 'we' and (our relations to) the present are at stake, he nevertheless warns us about Nietzsche over dramatising that present moment: '... *il faut avoir la modestie* [...] *ne se donnant pas la facilité un peu dramatique et théatrale d'affirmer que ce moment où nous sommes est, au creux de la nuit, celui de la perdition la plus grande, ou, au point du jour, celui, où le soleil triomphe, etc. Non, c'est un jour comme les autres, ou plutôt c'est un jour qui n'est jamais tout à fait comme les autres*' (Foucault, 1983b, p. 1267).

References

Bataille, G. (1954) *L'expérience intérieure*, in: *Œuvres Complètes. V.* (Paris, Gallimard), pp. 6–190.

Blanchot, M. (1955) *L'espace littéraire* (Paris, Gallimard).

Butler, J. (2002) Was ist Kritik? Ein Essay über Foucaults Tugend, *Deutsche Zeitschrift für Philosophie*, 50:2, pp. 249–265.

Dreyfus, H. L. & Rabinow, P. (1990) Was ist Mündigkeit? Habermas und Foucault über, Was ist Aufklärung?', in: E. Erdmann, R. Forst & A. Honneth (eds), *Ethos der Moderne. Foucaults Kritik der Aufklärung* (Frankfurt/Main & New York, Campus) pp. 55–69.

Ewald, F. (1990) Die Philosophie als Akt. Zum Begriff des philosophischen Akts, in: E. Erdmann, R. Forst & A. Honneth (eds), *Ethos der Moderne. Foucaults Kritik der Aufklärung* (Frankfurt/Main & New York, Campus) pp. 87–100.

Fimiani, M. (2002) Le véritable amour et le souci commun du monde, in: F. Gros (ed.), *Foucault. Le courage de la vérité* (Paris, PUF) pp. 87–130.

Flynn, T. R. (2005) *Sartre, Foucault and Historical Reason* (Chicago, IL, University of Chicago Press).

Foucault, M. (1971) Le discours de Toul, in: D. Defert, F. Ewald & J. Lagrange (eds), *Dits et écrits. I: 1954–1975* (Paris, Gallimard Quarto) pp. 1104–1106.

Foucault, M. (1972) *The Archeology of Knowledge* (New York, Pantheon Books).

Foucault, M. (1978) Qu'est-ce que la critique? *Bulletin de la Société Française de Philosophie*. pp. 35–63.

Foucault, M. (1979a) Michel Foucault et L'Iran, in: D. Defert, F. Ewald & J. Lagrange (eds), *Dits et écrits. II: 1977–1988* (Paris, Gallimard Quarto) p. 762.

Foucault, M. (1979b) Foucault étudie la raison d'état, in: D. Defert, F. Ewald & J. Lagrange (eds), *Dits et écrits. II: 1977–1988* (Paris, Gallimard Quarto) pp. 801–805. (English version: Foucault Examines Reason in Service of State Power, *Campus Report*, 1979:12, pp. 5–6).

Foucault, M. (1979c) What is an author?, in: J. V. Harari (ed.) *Textual Strategies* (Ithaca, NY, Cornell University Press) pp. 141–160.

Foucault, M. (1983) *This is Not a Pipe. With illustrations and letters by Rene Magritte* (Berkeley, CA, University of California Press).

Foucault, M. (1985) *The Use of Pleasure. The History of Sexuality. Vol. 2.* (New York, Pantheon).

Foucault, M. (1988) The Concern for Truth, in: M. Foucault, *Politics, Philosophy, Culture. Interviews and other writings 1977–1984*, L. D. Kritzman (ed.), A. Sheridan *et al.* (trans.) (London/New York, Routledge) pp. 255–270.

Foucault, M. (1997a) What is Enlightenment?, in: M. Foucault, Ethics, P. Rabinow (ed.), R. Hurley *et al.* (trans.) *Essential Works of Foucault, Vol. I.* (New York/London, Penguin) pp. 303–320.

Foucault, M. (1997b) Self Writing, in: M. Foucault, Ethics, P. Rabinow (ed.), R. Hurley *et al.* (trans.) *Essential Works of Foucault, Vol. I.* (New York/London, Penguin) pp. 207–222.

Foucault, M. (1997c) The Masked Philosopher, in: M. Foucault, Ethics, P. Rabinow (ed.), R. Hurley *et al.* (trans.) *Essential Works of Foucault, Vol. I.* (New York/London, Penguin) pp. 321–328.

Foucault, M. (2000a) Interview with Michel Foucault, in: M. Foucault, *Power*, J. D. Faubion (ed.), R. Hurley *et al.* (trans.) *Essential Works of Foucault, Vol. III* (New York/London, Penguin) pp. 239–297.

Foucault, M. (2000b) The Subject and Power, in: M. Foucault, *Power*, J. D. Faubion (ed.), R. Hurley *et al.* (trans.) *Essential Works of Foucault, Vol. III* (New York/London, Penguin) pp. 326–348.

Foucault, M. (2001) *L'Hermeneutique du sujet* (Paris, Gallimard).

Gadamer, H. G. (1960/1986) *Truth and Method* (New York, Continuum).

Gutting, G. (2002) Foucault's Philosophy of Experience, *Boundary 2*, 29:2, pp. 69–85.

Jay, M. (1998) *Cultural Semantics. Keywords of our time* (Amherst, MA, University of Massachusetts Press).

Kant, I. (1781/1997) *Critique of Pure Reason* (Cambridge, Cambridge University Press).

Larrosa, J. (2004) *Einige Notizen über die Erfahrung und ihre Sprachen* (unpublished manuscript).

Masschelein, J. (2005) L'élève et l'enfance: à propos du pédagogique, *Le Télémaque*, 27, pp. 89–94.

Porchia, A. (1989) *Voces* (Buenos Aires, Edicial).

Rancière, J. (1986) *Le maître ignorant* (Paris, Minuit).

Ricken, N. (2000) 'Aber hier, wie überhaupt, kommt es anders, als man glaubt'. Kontingenz als pädagogische Irritation, in: J. Masschelein, J. Ruhloff & A. Schäfer (eds) *Erziehungsphilosophie im Umbruch. Beiträge zur Neufassung des Erziehungsbegriffs* (Weinheim, Deutscher Studien Verlag) pp. 25–46.

Ricken, N. & Rieger Ladich, M. (2004) *Michel Foucault: Pädagogische Lekturen* (Wiesbaden, Verlag für Sozialwissenschaften).

Scott, J. W. (1991) The Evidence of Experience, *Critical Inquiry*, 17, pp. 773–797.

Simons, M. (2004) De school in de ban van het leven. Een cartografie van het moderne en actuele onderwijsdispositief (unpublished doctoral thesis, Leuven).

Index